"The secret of success is the constancy of purpose."

Benjamin Franklin

"Place integrity and honesty
above all else."

W9-CES-773

CACI Business Values

"People grow through experience if they meet life honestly and courageously. This is how character is built."

Eleanor Roosevelt

"The quality of a leader is reflected
in the standards they set for themselves."

Ray Kroc

"It's not hard to make decisions when you know what your values are."

Roy Disney

"Opportunity is missed by most people because it is dressed in overalls and looks like work."

Thomas Edison

CHARACTER

The Ultimate Success Factor

To Elizabeth Bussell —

Jack Jordan

June 26, 2014

CHARACTER

The Ultimate Success Factor

Dr. J. Phillip London

FORTIS

A NONFICTION IMPRINT FROM ADDUCENT
Adducent, Inc.
www.Adducent.Co

Titles Distributed In
North America
United Kingdom
Western Europe
South America
Australia

Character
The Ultimate Success Factor
By Dr. J. Phillip London

Cataloging-in-Publication data on file with the Library of Congress
Character: The Ultimate Success Factor

ISBN 9781937592394

Published in the United States of America by Fortis, an Adducent nonfiction imprint

Adducent, Inc.
Jacksonville, Florida
www.Adducent.Co

Also by the Author

Our Good Name; A Company's Fight to Defend Its Honor and Get the Truth Told About Abu Ghraib, Regnery Publishing, Washington, DC, 2008

Manufactured in the United States of America

10 9 8 7 6 5 4 3 2 1

DEDICATION

This book is dedicated to my parents, Jack and Evalyn London, who wanted me always to do my best. It is dedicated to my wife, Jennifer, who knows what the value of character is all about. I also dedicate this book to my children – to Phillip and his wife Jennifer, to Laura and her husband Jed, and to my sons Jackson, Jayson, and Jonathon – and to my grandchildren Evan, Andrew, Charlotte, Riley, James and Jasper – for whom I always want to be a good example.

I also gratefully dedicate this book to the many friends, colleagues, role models, mentors, and leaders from all walks of life that I have served with all of these years. They are many – and they are special.

"There is something even more valuable to civilization than wisdom, and that is character."

Henry Louis (H.L.) Mencken
1929

TABLE OF CONTENTS

FOREWORD
by Norman Augustine

As I sit at my desk wondering how to begin a preface to a book on a subject as profound and life-determining as "character," I reflect on the events of a few hours ago, when not one but two people in high positions, one an acquaintance of mine and the other a friend, were sadly disgraced for deeply hidden character flaws. Both were forced to resign from their positions, ironically on the same afternoon, one by the board of directors of a Fortune 100 company and the other to the President of the United States. Both had been highly respected individuals; one a high government official and the other just 56 days from assuming the role of CEO of a firm that had spent five years grooming him for the job. It took the board only about five minutes, upon hearing the facts, to send him on his way.

It is a shame that these two individuals had not read Jack London's book on character – and learned from it. The tragedy that each confronted could easily have been avoided. London's book is brilliantly researched, fascinating to read and filled not only with the philosophical basis for a life of character but also with numerous real-world – some very real-world – examples of doing the right thing...as well as, unfortunately, doing the wrong thing. In it he draws in part on situations he personally experienced while building the company he served into a highly profitable and equally highly regarded firm.

Were the two above-mentioned incidents simply anomalies that happened to be exposed on the same black Friday afternoon? I think not...unfortunately, they have too much company. In my own career I have had six other friends or acquaintances who were actually sentenced to jail. With the exception of one or possibly two of them, each were very decent individuals who made one humongous mistake – often not even for personal gain – and paid dearly for it. They had held high-level positions in government and were CEOs of major corporations – one was an enormously wealthy and successful young investment banker. All had enjoyed superb reputations and were widely admired for their accomplishments.

But *why?* How can one possibly explain, or even comprehend, such unexplainable behavior? How can one understand what is not understandable? I have puzzled a lot over those questions during my life, as obviously has Jack London.

Is the answer that, as Lord Acton said, "Power corrupts; absolute power corrupts absolutely?" Again, I think not. I have had plenty of friends with plenty of power who deservedly had impeccable reputations as well as plenty of power. The names of Omar Bradley, J.W. "Bill" Marriott, Jimmy Doolittle, James "Jim" Burke, George H.W. Bush, Warren Buffett, Sandra Day O'Connor, and many, many more come to mind.

Then perhaps the answer has to do with something called *character*...the subject of Jack London's book.

One of my best friends, Sandy McDonnell, the former CEO of McDonnell Douglas, who sadly died a few months ago, was one of those people with an impeccable reputation. We had known each other for many years – having gone to the same university, having both served as president of the Boy Scouts of America, and, as fate would have it, leading two major aerospace firms that were bitter competitors. We, together with our wives, often vacationed together, remaining close friends throughout, but never, never discussing business. When the firm for which I worked would defeat Sandy's firm in a competition for new business – which wasn't nearly often enough! – the first telephone call I would receive offering congratulations would invariably be from Sandy. After retiring he devoted his life to an organization he founded, the Character Education Partnership, devoted to teaching youth the supreme importance of character. In fact I once heard Warren Buffett say to his son that it takes a lifetime to build a reputation but you can lose it in one minute. As usual, Warren ...and Sandy ...had it right.

But sometimes it is not obvious what *is* the right thing to do. When traveling in Nepal a few years ago the group my wife and I were with frequently encountered locals who had built businesses out of capturing small wild birds, isolating them in tiny cages made of sticks, and charging tourists one dollar to give a bird its freedom. It seemed to be a booming business. One evening as we entered the hotel where we were all staying, one of my companions, to the admiration of everyone present, paid to have the *entire collection* of birds released. The next morning, it somehow became my duty to pay to release that day's collection of birds...but I refused...reasoning that if no one paid ransom the bird-napping business would come to the quick halt it deserved.

The question is, which of the two of us displayed more character? To this day I am really not certain of the answer.

But most cases are a lot more straightforward – contrast Johnson & Johnson's CEO Jim Burke's handling of the consequences of the Tylenol murders with Ken Lay's handling of Enron's affairs. The result has been that J&J is held in high esteem for Jim's courageous actions – while Enron had become synonymous with greed (a highly unfair judgment to the overwhelming majority of the firm's thousands of employees). Bo Callaway, a former Secretary of the Army and another person highly regarded for character, liked to say that "if rascals knew the value of honesty, they would be honest just because of their rascality!" Bo was a graduate of West Point...where Duty, Honor, Country are concepts that are revered.

But in contrast with the Enrons of the world there are plenty of positive examples. Consider the case of Brian Davis pursuing his first PGA tour championship in a sudden-death playoff with a million dollars in prize money on the line. During a backswing his club barely touched a weed growing in the area – apparently seen by no one... except, that is, for Davis. He promptly reported the incident to an official – and lost the tournament. That is what is meant by character.

Or the time when I was CEO of Martin Marietta and one of our divisions was competing for a substantial government fixed-price contract against one of our most demanding competitors. A few days before the bids were due, an envelope appeared in our company mail with a copy of the competitor's bid sheet, apparently sent by a disgruntled employee of the other firm. It was evident that the copy of the bid sheet was legitimate, and, worse yet, the bid price it displayed was slightly lower than the one we were planning to bid. Our employees promptly contacted the competitor and the government...and did not change our bid. Unfortunately, we lost the competition for the contract. I didn't even know about the situation until afterward – which suggested to me that our ethics program was working: our employees didn't have to ask permission of the CEO to do the right thing.

In fact, whenever I spoke to a group of employees at Martin Marietta or later at Lockheed Martin I always emphasized that our culture was based on three principles: to operate ethically; to take care of our customers; and to treat all people with respect. It seemed to work. If you do those three things the profits somehow take care of themselves.

A good test when contemplating taking an action is to ask if you would mind if your mother watched you doing it. (In my case, my mother lived to be 105 – so that pretty much kept me on the straight and narrow for much of my career!). For those not fortunate enough to have a mother who lives to be 105, Jack London's book should be required reading. That is true whether you are a high school student, a CEO, or anyone who will ever make a decision. Furthermore, the book is fascinating – at times even spellbinding – particularly if, as you read, you ask, "What would I have done in that situation?"

Which brings us back to the question, "Why?" "Why do intelligent people do dumb things?" The answer, I have concluded, is that they treasure some things more than they treasure their own knowledge that they are a person of character. In the end, it is not what others think about you that matters; it is what you know about you.

INTRODUCTION

"I am the master of my fate; I am the captain of my soul."
Growing up, I heard my father recite William Ernest Henley's
poem *Invictus* many times.[1] Written in his later years, the
powerful last two lines reflect the author's resolve as he looks
back on his life. Yet the one thing I've learned throughout my life
is that many people never learn this important lesson. There's
only one way to be the master of your fate or the captain of your
soul. It's owning who you are – it's owning your *character*.

Maybe I'm old-fashioned. In a time and in a city where
people judge others primarily by their titles, jobs, possessions,
and appearance, I prefer to judge a person by their *character*.
That's right – their *character*.

Where you work, who you know, and what you own may
give me some clues about you, but who you are at the core will
always be the most important thing for me.

Who am I? I go by the name Jack London.[2] While I am
neither the prolific author nor avid frontiersman that people
usually associate with the name, I've been on my own exciting
adventure.

My story started over seven decades ago as the son of a
retail shop owner in Oklahoma City, Oklahoma. It jumped to the
U.S. Naval Academy in Annapolis, Maryland in 1955 and since
then it has taken me to dozens of countries all around the world
and to nearly every continent. My first adventure started out in
1959 with a career in the U.S. Navy, but took a surprising turn
when I left active duty. In 1972, I joined a very small technology
company in Washington, DC called CACI. I was employee
number 35. Mastering the business over the next few years, I

---

[1] "Invictus" (Latin for "unconquered") is a poem by the English poet William Ernest
Henley (1849–1903). It was probably first published in 1875 in a book called *Book of
Verses*, where it was number four in several poems called *Life and Death (Echoes)*.
[2] My given name is J. Phillip London. The "J." doesn't stand for a specific name (it's
an initial only). It's for one of the 'J's' from my grandfather, J.J. London. The "Jack"
came along during my early days in the Navy. My father was also called "Jack" all of
his adult life, even though his given name was Harry.

became CACI's CEO in 1984 and, I think it's fair to say, built the company into an industry powerhouse during my 23 years at the helm. Today, the mid-Western shop owner's son is the Chairman of the Board of a $3.8 billion public corporation listed on the New York Stock Exchange, serving the information technology (IT) and national security market.

Over the 50-plus years since I first left Oklahoma, I've faced countless challenges and fought several major battles. I've also enjoyed a number of victories.

My family – my father and mother – had instilled good values and a work ethic in me and my brother as children. They also taught me self-reliance, the importance of taking care of yourself, and the value of independence. Being responsible for yourself and earning your way was a big deal around our home.[3]

However, the importance of *character* really came to light for me at the U.S. Naval Academy. The Academy describes its curriculum as a *moral education* for the ethical development of those who attend. Their *Honor Concept* (like an Honor Code at other universities) is based on "the moral values of respect for human dignity, respect for honesty and respect for the property of others."[4]

The emphasis on these values is essential, since the military is a team-oriented culture, where your actions can often be the difference between life and death – yours or someone else's. This moral education served me well as my 24 years of combined naval service unfolded and even more later as a business leader. During that time, the preeminent lesson for me was the significance of a person's character in shaping their success.

That lesson inspired me to write this book. I have incorporated the importance of character into CACI's culture and over the years I have written it into CACI management manuals.

---

[3] More than once I heard my father say "don't hold out your hand unless you have had it on the hoe." He meant that you shouldn't expect to get paid unless you've done the work. The story of *The Little Red Hen* was one we also heard often. It's a folk tale about how the rewards belong only to those who work for them.

[4] "About the Academy." http://www.usna.edu/Admissions/aboutusna.htm.

It also has been a reoccurring theme in my speeches. However, I became increasingly aware that outside my experience, the concept of character-based success was rarely discussed. Going through the shelves at well-known bookstores, I noted that there were many volumes about success, like "Top 10 Lessons to Get Ahead" or other such titles. Yet, I couldn't find one where *character* was at the heart of the book.

Again, these are lessons that I've learned throughout my life – in military service and in the CEO's chair, as a student and a teacher, as a child and a parent.

My family was mostly of English and Scotch-Irish ancestry. I was born and raised in Oklahoma City. Post-depression Oklahoma was not too dissimilar from John Steinbeck's *The Grapes of Wrath*. All of my grandparents had settled in the Oklahoma Territory well before statehood in 1907, and I had a great-grandfather who participated in the famous Oklahoma Land Rush on April 22, 1889.[5] He staked out his land claim near what is now the town of Yukon in Canadian County. (Even today in Oklahoma, these settlers are affectionately known as the *'89-ers*.) This was when the U.S. government opened up sections of Oklahoma to settlers for deeds of ownership. My mother would proudly say we came from "pioneers and dirt farmers," relishing in their independent spirit and self-sufficiency – and to differentiate us from the ranchers and cattle people. Her family had come from Illinois and Missouri. My father's people were pioneers who had come west from Arkansas and Tennessee. All of these families had come to America – or *the colonies* – in the 1600s and 1700s.

My childhood was book-ended by war. I remember sensing the anxiety of World War II even in kindergarten. As I got older and the war was underway, I can remember talking about Hitler and Mussolini with my friends on the school

---

[5] The April 22nd Land Rush was the first land run into the Unassigned Lands and included all or part of several counties across the Oklahoma Territory. Settlers could claim lots up to 160 acres and receive title once they lived on the land and improved it. I am a life member of the 1889ers Society of Oklahoma whose members are descendants of those who made that land rush.

3

ground. We also talked about Tojo, the Japanese dictator. We made paper airplanes and played air battles with them. Looking back, this may have foreshadowed my naval aviation days. My Dad would read the *Daily Oklahoman,* and I would look over his shoulder at the little black and white maps detailing the action and the war's progress. I had two close relatives, both officers, killed in combat during the war. My mother's brother, Gordon Leigh Phillips, had been a champion wrestler in high school and the first in her family to ever go to college.[6] We also lost my cousin, James Monroe "Maxey" Scott, Jr.[7] I had a number of other uncles and cousins that served, but all came back home alive. It was later in life that I learned that these other older men from my family had also served in combat in World War II.

Five years later, while I was in junior high school, the Korean War broke out. The prosperity and peace we felt in Oklahoma after the end of World War II was suddenly supplanted by the fear of communism, the Soviet threat and atomic bombs—a fear that would haunt our country for years to come.

In school, I was a good student and active in many sports and activities. I also held after school jobs, working in my uncle's bottling plant, as a car hop, and delivering newspapers – the *Daily Oklahoman* and the *Oklahoma City Times* (morning and afternoon papers widely subscribed to in the city). Even so, I always knew that I wanted to do more.

Despite the military influence early in my life, it wasn't until Christmas break of my junior year of high school that I began to think about the Navy. One of my high school friends had an older brother who returned home for the holidays during his third year at the U.S. Naval Academy in Annapolis, Maryland,

---

[6] A 2nd Lieutenant Infantry officer with the 83rd Division, Gordon was killed fighting SS Panzer units in Normandy in July 1944, just after the D-Day invasion. He had graduated from Oklahoma A&M only the year before. I was there at the train station when his remains were returned to Oklahoma in 1948.

[7] Maxey was killed in an air raid on his 17th mission over Germany in April 1944. He was a 2nd Lieutenant and bombardier flying B-17s with the 8th Air Force. He is buried in the American Cemetery in Cambridge, England. I visited his gravesite in 2006.

and told me all about his experiences there. The year before, my family had driven through Annapolis on an east coast vacation. Although impressed with the Academy as we drove through its grounds, hearing from my friend's brother about the Academy really got me thinking seriously about the Navy.

After some family discussions and research about the Naval Academy on my own part, I knew that's where I wanted to go. From then on, I pursued it with a passion. I stepped up my studies, prepped for the college boards, and contacted an Oklahoma senator and a congressman about securing a nomination. Since my family didn't have any college money for me, I also had to get a scholarship. I applied to Oklahoma University and Princeton University, and was, thankfully, accepted to both under the U.S. Navy Reserve Officer Training Corps (NROTC) program. After much correspondence and scoring well on the college boards, I made the cut for the Naval Academy with both Senator Robert Kerr and Congressman John Jarman.

Finally, I took Congressman Jarman's appointment and a few days after high school graduation, I made my way to Annapolis in June 1955. I was eager to get started there, but I couldn't believe how hot and steamy Annapolis was. It didn't help that in those days there was no air conditioning. But my excitement and youthful stamina got me through the long days of academic and naval classes, as well as the arduous physical and athletic regimen.

My four years at the Academy would be well-regimented and challenging. In those post-war days, it was a tough, rigorous and Spartan-like environment. You were also committed for the summers, which were spent on training cruises at sea. I got my first taste for world travel as a Midshipman, as we sailed the North Atlantic, Mediterranean and Caribbean.[8] These were exciting times for a kid from Oklahoma in the 1950s.

---

[8] My first cruise in the summer of 1956 began in Annapolis and went to Portsmouth, England and then to Copenhagen, Denmark. Our last stop was in the Caribbean and at the U.S. Naval Station at Guantanamo Bay, Cuba.

CHARACTER: The Ultimate Success Factor

The Naval Academy was a formative time of my life during a formative time for our country. The Academy's publicly stated mission consists of a rather long statement about developing capable officers, leaders for the future, for the Navy and the country. But in my time (1955-59) we knew the real mission was *to develop officers capable of achieving victory in combat at sea*. No mincing of words: We saw the Academy as a school to prepare us for warfare at sea. And we were proud of it.

The Academy's curriculum was based on the principles of integrity, dependability, and loyalty. Technical skills and knowledge had to be supported by the confidence that you were doing your fair share and performing to the best of your ability. This way, everyone could trust each other and work together as a team. It was also a place of culture and folklore, where you were surrounded by American history, early naval history – sea captains like John Paul Jones – and the rich heritage of America's naval heroes up to the present day.[9]

The Naval Academy changed everything; my life, my direction, and my view of the world. A young man from Oklahoma City was suddenly among military leaders and listening to people like the Secretary of the Navy tell us about their experiences and perspectives. During my first summer, and I'll never forget it, I had the good fortune to participate in a change of command ceremony at the Academy for the Chief of Naval Operations (CNO).[10] Despite the ceremony's extended weather delays and hours standing (and sweating) in rank, I got to see some of the Navy's great heroes. Several of these men

---

[9] One of the Continental Navy's first sea captains in 1776 was my distant relative, Captain Samuel Nicholson. He served throughout the American Revolution, took numerous prizes at seas, and was the first Captain of the USS *Constitution* ("Old Ironsides") in 1798. I have the honor of representing Captain Nicholson in the Massachusetts Society of the Cincinnati, where he was an Original Member in 1783.

[10] In August 1955, Admiral Arleigh "31 Knot" Burke relieved Admiral Robert B. Carney as CNO. Burke was a WWII naval hero in the Pacific War who got his nickname from his destroyer command days in the naval sea battles in the South Pacific. At the time, I was an 18 year old kid fresh from Oklahoma. The dignity and historic nature of that ceremony in Dahlgren Hall at the U.S. Naval Academy left an impression on me that I will never forget. I was proud to be there.

would become my role models. Going to the U.S. Naval Academy was by far the best professional career decision I ever made.

I graduated from the Academy in 1959 (class motto – *Rise 'n Shine with '59!*) with a Bachelor of Science degree in naval engineering. I spent 12 years on active duty as a regular officer (1959-1971) during the Cold War. I initially served as a naval aviator and carrier helicopter pilot with U.S. Navy "hunter-killer" task forces arrayed against the Soviet Union's strategic nuclear submarine threat.

My service included the Cuban Missile Crisis of 1962, as well as numerous other at-sea deployments. One honor was being with the airborne and "splash down" recovery team for Col. John Glenn's Mercury Program space flight on *Freedom 7* in the Caribbean on February 20, 1962 – also aboard the USS *Randolph* (CVS-15). I'll never forget that day. Glenn was our hero. America was in space for real!

In 1967, I earned a Master's degree in operations research at the U.S. Navy Postgraduate School in Monterey, California. Many of the lessons and viewpoints discussed in this book – the decision-making models and analytical perspectives, the concepts of commitment and intensity, and the pursuit of excellence with integrity – were all reinforced for me during my time at the Naval Postgraduate School. The school's overall orientation to national security sets it apart from other graduate schools. I gained much from my experience there and I am forever grateful.

In 1968, I transferred my officer designation to Aeronautical Engineering Duty Officer (AEDO). Later on, after my flying and sailing days, I served two years as Aide and Administrative Assistant to the Vice Chief of the Naval Material Command (1969-70) during the height of the Vietnam War. During the same time, on the GI Bill, I pursued a doctorate in business administration at George Washington University (GW), which I received "with distinction" in 1971. The pure business focus at GW was a significant career realignment for me. My previous degrees, not to mention work experience, were all involved with science, technology and engineering. This new world of management, economics, finance, business law and more, opened new horizons. It was during that time when I began to realize where my personal strengths and interests would likely evolve. In this way, GW provided me an important pathway to the future. Attending this fine institution was another important career decision I made in these early years.

For reasons discussed later in this book, I decided to leave active duty in 1971. Those years, 1969 through 1971, were a non-stop, 24/7 work program (day job and night job). I would always want to be part of the Navy, so I joined the U.S. Navy Reserve in 1971, retiring as a Captain in 1983. I served as commanding officer of aeronautical engineering units with the Naval Air Systems Command in Washington, DC in the early 1980s and enjoyed the professionalism of my reserve assignment and colleagues. I am very proud of my naval reserve affiliation and service.

During my life, from ages 17 to 34, I had imagined a Navy career, perhaps one day reaching the rank of admiral. Even when I left the Navy, I had no idea that my future, either as a profession or as a leader, would turn out to be so involved in the corporate world.

I am currently the Executive Chairman and Chairman of the Board of CACI International Inc, where I carry out my chairman duties with the board. Among other activities, I oversee strategic initiatives and act in a public relations capacity representing CACI to client organizations and the federal information technology industry.

CACI was founded in 1962 by two individuals: the late Herb Karr, a practical and visionary businessman; and Harry Markowitz, a computer programming genius. These entrepreneurs took an unsupported public domain software language that they helped create (while at the Rand Corporation) called *Simscript*, and realizing it presented a promising business opportunity, created a small two-person consulting company to train and support its users. In a short time, Herb and Harry went from doing business on a California park bench to launching a successful, but tiny venture in the nascent computer industry. By 1968, Harry Markowitz had left the company to pursue other ventures in finance and academia. Much later in 1990, Harry won the Nobel Prize for Economics.[11] In 1968, Herb stayed on as Chairman of the Board and after six years CACI's revenues had topped $1 million for the first time.

I joined CACI as a program manager in 1972 and advanced to a Vice President position by 1976. Over the years at CACI, we've watched the trends, and identified and pursued the most promising technologies and markets. In the 1970s, we pioneered easy-to-use database retrieval programs for the Commerce Department. We then applied this technology to projects for the Departments of Defense and Justice. Heads-up application, solution development and attention to client needs have enabled us to keep these organizations as valued clients and preeminent sources of business to this day.

I picked up on this "look ahead" way of business early on. I also had some solid grounding in strategic study, analysis, and planning while teaching elective courses as an instructor at the Naval Academy in 1967 and 1968.[12] One advanced course that I enjoyed teaching was Naval Strategy. In that setting, it was important to convey the distinction between *tactics* and *strategies*. So the curriculum I developed then reflected these differences in scope and scale – as well as objectives. While not a term frequently used in the business context, tactics deals with the "near-term" and the "close in"; the daily operational activities.   Strategy incorporates, among other things, environment or market positioning, including image projection,

---

[11] Harry Markowitz is a University of Chicago-educated American economist best known for his pioneering work in Modern Portfolio Theory. After leaving CACI in 1968, Markowitz joined Arbitrage Management where he helped create a hedge fund that represents the first known attempt at computerized arbitrage trading. Markowitz received the John von Neumann Theory Prize for operations research in 1989 and the Nobel Prize in Economic Sciences in 1990 while a professor of finance at Baruch College of the City University of New York. Markowitz is currently an adjunct professor of finance at the Rady School of Management at the University of California, San Diego (UCSD), the Chief Architect of investment advisory firm GuidedChoice, and serves on the advisory boards of several investment firms (2013).

[12] In 1971, the U.S. Naval Institute published *Naval Operations Analysis*. I worked at the time with my colleague, Lt. Cdr. Roger Garrett, to revise and publish this book for use in the NROTC curricula.

reputation and branding – concepts that apply to commercial business.

Building on legacy expertise and delivering quality client service became hallmarks of our CACI culture and reputation. These ideals served us well in the 1980s when we encountered a dramatic change in the federal landscape. As new contracting rules and regulations went into effect, we had to retool our business to succeed in a now formalized, but still rigorously competitive environment. We adapted, survived and, thanks to our business philosophies and culture, continued to succeed and grow.

The 1980s were also a time of major change for me. I was elected to CACI's Board of Directors in 1981. By 1982 I was an operating division president (managing the company's largest and most successful business unit), and managing CACI's extensive work in systems engineering, logistic sciences and advanced information systems. After some internal struggles in the executive suite when our President at the time got himself fired, I kept growing my business. During this time, CACI co-founder, Herb Karr stepped in temporarily as President, but he wanted desperately to get out of the company's daily operations. By that time though, I had built CACI's largest and most sophisticated operation, and it was growing very rapidly. It was hardly a surprise within the company when I was appointed CACI's President and CEO in 1984.

I was the first at CACI to carry the title of CEO (as well as President), and I was a full-time "hands-on" CEO. My first few years in the top job were dominated by CACI's operational turnaround in 1984-85 for both revenue and profit growth.[13] By then we had successfully adapted to the new and restrictive government contracting regulations. The biggest change was the Competition in Contracting Act of 1984. These years were full of horrific growing pains and real struggles, but our determination and perseverance paid off.

In the 1990s, CACI really took off, making the strategic change from a professional services firm to an information

---

[13] CACI's annual revenue in 1985 was $97.9 million.

technology (IT) solutions provider. It was truly a strategic repositioning and metamorphosis of our business model. We recognized that IT was shifting from individual software applications to networks and enterprise-wide projects. I was even one of the first in our industry sector to use the term "IT", setting aside the term ADP (automated data processing). Soon COTS (Commercial Off The Shelf) software and solutions became the wave of the future.

It was also clear it would soon be a "networked" world. We even used this term in our strategic positioning statement – ahead of many others. Our strategic vision directed the successful transformation of CACI into a more sharply focused information technology organization prepared for broader opportunities in the rapidly changing IT and network services markets. I dubbed this the "New Era" and it also led to CACI's rapid entrance into the information security and intelligence community arenas.

As a bold strategic move, we also started our mergers and acquisitions (M&A) program in the early 1990s, which by 2013 had led to over 59 successful acquisitions. That's quite a record since they have *all* worked out—some better than others, of course.

The next decade would also bring changes to CACI. After 21 years on the NASDAQ stock market, I switched our listing to the New York Stock Exchange in August 2002. That March, in another strategic move, CACI also tendered its first equity offering (a secondary offering) since the company's initial public offering in 1968.

Two separate, yet defining moments came in May 2004. In a $415 million, three-way deal, CACI purchased the Defense and Intelligence Group and related assets of American Management Systems, Inc. The acquisition with over 1650 employees positioned CACI as one of the nation's largest, focused IT providers serving the defense and intelligence community markets.

At the very same time, CACI was thrust into the Abu Ghraib scandal when an employee was wrongly alleged to have been involved in the abuses. The company eventually would be vindicated, but it was a substantial battle to get the facts out and fight the lies being told about CACI and its employees at the time. Then three years later in 2007, after 23 years as CEO, I handed off the baton to Paul Cofoni, who was our CEO for five years until he stepped down in 2012. Ken Asbury became our CEO in 2013.

In my four decades with the company, CACI has grown from a tiny professional services consulting firm to become an industry pacesetter in IT and communications solutions across markets in North America and Western Europe. Today, CACI fields a force of 15,000 people across more than 120 offices worldwide. We are a Fortune 1000 company and we are listed on the New York Stock Exchange as 'CACI'. I believe our performance and reputation has been outstanding. I believe we are rightfully proud of what we have been able to achieve.

In this book, I pass along ideas designed to help create a standard for how to go about doing things right – in business, in your career, and in your life. In doing so, I hope you will find these ideas both valuable and interesting.

There is a proverb that says, "May you live in interesting times." Thankfully, I have had the fortune to live through some of history's most fascinating times over my 76 year adventure thus far. I have known the cycles of depression and prosperity, as well as war and peace, times of atomic bombs and the Peace Corps, and times of the first phones and iPhones. It's been a good trip, and I am still on it. I have lived through a time of technology explosion; of television and of men on the moon, of computers and of the Internet. I've been military and civilian, ensign and executive, follower and leader, child and parent (and grandparent), and a husband, among many other roles. I've been around the world several times. I've traveled to over sixty countries and to all the inhabited continents. I've celebrated America's history and its veterans in my volunteer work, and I've enjoyed watching my children and family grow. I look forward to the even more interesting times that are sure to follow. As for personal beliefs, I am certainly a "God-fearing" soul. My life priorities are formed around faith, family and country. My wife and my family are everything to me – the joys of my life. I treasure my heritage in this great land. Our founding documents – the Declaration of Independence, the Constitution, and the Bill of Rights – to me are treasures of priceless value, to be guarded and preserved always.

How I have chosen to live and tried to live in these interesting and challenging times is written about in this book. The message is also conveyed in these favorite words of mine from George Washington (June 20, 1788): "The opinion of honest men, friends to freedom and well-wishers to mankind, where ever they may happen to be born or reside, is the only kind of reputation a wise man could ever desire."

I trust that you would agree.

J. Phillip "Jack" London
August 2013

CHAPTER 1

FACING THE FACTS

"Things may come to those who wait, but only the things left by those who hustle."
Abraham Lincoln

Who you are and what you become is up to you. If you don't like who you are, or what you have become, it's your fault. If you do feel good about it, then it's also to your credit. It may even mean you have had to overcome enormous barriers—physical, economic, social or cultural.

Throughout your life, you make choices about what you believe in, how you will act, and what you want to do. The results of those choices are the life you lead. It's the careers you create, the interests you pursue, and the relationships you cultivate. Clearly, some situations happen that are beyond your control, and there are elements, like *luck*, for which you can't account. Some might even prefer the term *fate*. But good or bad, you have arrived at the place where you are today.

It's easy to accept credit when things go right. And it's easier still to lay blame elsewhere when things go wrong. But the hardest thing for many of us is to accept complete responsibility for ourselves. I realize no one gets it right every time. I also know that nobody's perfect, but you can learn from your mistakes and change your thinking or behavior. I also know that not every situation works in your favor, but you can choose how to react – devise a solution – and proceed. The point is **you can't deny your responsibility for your life** – who you are and what you have become. The capacity to accept this responsibility is reflected in your character.

WHAT IS CHARACTER?

Character is a complex aggregate of mental and ethical traits that form the nature of a person. These combinations of traits are unique to each person and distinguish each one of us from everyone else. Character also reflects who we are inside and out. On the inside, character is morality; the principles in which you believe and on which you base your actions. On the outside, your reputation is what your character is judged to be.

A person's character is a complex aggregate of moral and ethical qualities. This is *not* the same thing as personality. While personality can represent a person's character, it is not a complete representation of it. And while someone's personality can be relatively consistent (e.g. optimistic, shy, easygoing), character is truly a work in progress. Eleanor Roosevelt said, **"People grow through experience if they meet life honestly and courageously. This is how character is built."**

I also believe that a person's character is formed through the sum and total of a person's choices throughout their life. How would you judge the character of a person who chooses not to accept (denies) responsibility for their circumstances? Is this someone you would seek out or want to be associated with?

Can you honestly say that you take accountability for your choices and own your decisions? The 2006 movie *The Pursuit of Happiness* (based on the book by Chris Gardner), depicts Gardner's personal struggle as a homeless single father trying to start a career as a stockbroker. Gardner, who had a turbulent childhood, spent several years in the U.S. Navy in the 1970s, where he became a skilled clinical researcher in surgical techniques. Gardner originally considered a medical career, but a chance encounter while living in San Francisco changed his life. On his way to work one day, Gardner asked a man in a new red Ferrari what he did for a living. The man was a stockbroker and soon helped Gardner meet branch managers of brokerage firms. Gardner was accepted into a training program at E.F. Hutton, but never started because on his first day he discovered that his hiring manager had been fired.

Having quit his previous job and left destitute through other personal problems, Gardner had to start from scratch. In 1982, he became a top trainee at Dean Witter Reynolds and was later recruited by Bear Stearns. Still rebuilding his life, Gardner faced another challenge when a former girlfriend left him with sole custody of their infant son.

Unable to stay at a boarding house because it didn't allow children, yet gainfully employed, Gardner and his son were secretly homeless until enough money could be saved for a rental home. Eventually, a church allowed Gardner and his son to stay at their shelter for homeless women. By 1987, Gardner started his own brokerage firm and today is the CEO of Gardner Rich LLC. He is also a motivational speaker and philanthropist.

Gardner's success could be summed up in something his mother used to say to him as a child: "You can only depend on yourself. The cavalry ain't coming." The driving message in Gardner's books and speeches is that **you have to take personal responsibility for your life**.

> *"There's something empowering about accepting responsibility. When you admit you drove there, you realize you can drive out of there"*
>
> Chris Gardner

Gardner realized this lesson at one of the worst points in his life. "At my lowest, living in a public transit bathroom station with a 14-month-old baby tied on my back, one of the things I had to ask myself was, 'How did I get there?' I had something to do with the circumstances and conditions that were now my life."

Gardner adds, "Before you can progress, you have to say how did I get here? I had something to do with it. A lot of people don't want to hear that, wanting to believe it wasn't my fault. It may not have been your fault, but it's certainly your responsibility."[14]

---

[14] Seth Eisenberg, "Condoleezza Rice's Journey and Advice for Our Own," *FatherhoodChannel.com,* October 17, 2010, http://fatherhoodchannel.com/2010/10/17/condoleezza-rices-inspiring-journey-and-advice-for-our-own-017/.

WHY CHARACTER IS THE MAIN DRIVER OF SUCCESS

Character is the primary driver of success because it means that you – and you alone – are responsible for what you do and what happens to you. And by choosing to do the right thing, instead of simply anything, you will learn how to define and gain success and live with yourself.

It's hard for many people to accept that they are solely responsible for creating their future and deciding how successful they will be. I believe that our society has many more people today than ever before who have this paternalistic view.[15] But the realization, that you alone are responsible, is a big advantage. There are few guarantees in life beyond the proverbial death and taxes, but **your character will absolutely determine the kind of life that you will live**. This is what I believe—and that is what this book is all about!

Character-driven success is recognizing and optimizing your choices. My concept of *character-driven success* is rather simple. You are the key to achieving the desired outcomes for your life. In every challenge, success or failure, and everything in between, there is one common denominator – you. It's the only constant, and it's the only thing over which you truly have control. You are the one who decides how to conduct yourself, treat others, and handle situations. It's also how you recognize your shortcomings and learn from your mistakes and make the necessary changes! It is reflected in your priorities, decisions, and actions. Your character, your beliefs and your value system are what differentiate you from everyone else. In turn, your character plays a key role in determining how you are treated.

What do I mean by *success* in character-driven success? It is the knowledge that you have acted with honesty and integrity, and performed to the best of your ability (given it your very best). It's also having an appreciation for all the people who helped you get there.

---

[15] There are those who would argue that our government's social policies have made our society more paternalistic, making people more dependent and less self-reliant.

It is not necessarily the attainment of wealth, position, rank, or power, although these things may come with achievement. And let's be clear, the accumulation of wealth is not a bad thing. But what value does success have when it's gained by unethical or unlawful means, for dubious purposes, or at great moral cost?

I believe the desire or ambition to achieve success is commendable. Even so, *how you go about it* is important. How you define and pursue your ambitions and goals reflects your character.[16]

> *"Try not to become a man of success, but rather a man of value"*
>
> Albert Einstein

I focus on the concept of character-driven success for two simple reasons. The first is to reassert the idea of *self-accountability*. I offer plenty of evidence to show how important this is. Interestingly enough, the academic community studies personal accountability from a scientific perspective. Since I'm interested in this topic, I pay attention to what's being said about personal accountability in life.

I reflected upon two articles on this subject that crossed my desk recently.[17] One article from a psychology journal found

---

[16] I like Aesop's Fable about the goose that laid golden eggs because it goes straight to the point. It's the familiar story about a country man who discovered he had a goose that laid eggs of pure gold, but was overcome by greed and killed the goose to get it all at once. I've frequently seen this type of individual along the way in my career, always lusting for the "big hit."

Then there are Pyrrhic victories. The phrase, attributed to the Greek historian Plutarch, refers to a victory that is offset by staggering losses. It dramatizes the fact that achieving some goals is simply not worth the cost.

In Oscar Wilde's *Portrait of Dorian Gray,* the eponymous character preserves his handsome looks with a painted portrait that ages in his place, reflecting his debauchery as disfigurements in the portrait. Despite a change of heart, the portrait continues to get uglier. Gray tries to destroy the painting with a knife, but is found aged and dead from a stab wound to the heart, while the portrait has returned to its original handsome form. The lesson here is certainly about character: The only person who wins when you sell your soul to the Devil is the Devil!

[17] Roy F. Baumeister, Kathleen D. Vohs, and Dianne M. Tice, "The Strength Model of Self-Control," *Current Directions in Psychological Science,* Vol. 16, No.6, 2007, pgs.351-355. Ben Sherwood, "Lessons in Survival, The science that explains why

that self-control was a key to success in life. It seems that like any physical muscle, self-control can wear out with use, but it can also be improved with practice. This fits well with how I observe the world around me and how people can improve themselves. The other article from a news magazine summarized findings on why elite military forces are so good in crises and survival. Apart from physical reasons, training that focused on managing stressful situations was a big factor. So, not only do we have the ability to deal with tough situations, we can even learn to be better at it. That we are responsible for our own destiny may seem obvious. Many of the principles noted here may even seem obvious, but it's the obvious that is often overlooked.

Many books focus on developing skills, maneuvering through situations and other success-oriented how-to's. But no amount of learning will create true success if your character is in question. You create (or change) your outlook, your credibility, and your momentum by taking the *road less traveled* or *paving your own way.*

HOW CHARACTER DRIVES SUCCESS

I explain character-driven success in five sections. The first section of this book is titled **Keystone: Character.** In architecture, the *keystone* is a wedge-shaped piece at the summit of an arch that holds the other pieces in place. *Keystone* also refers to the part that other things depend on for support. Like the keystone that is the fundamental piece of an arch, your character is the fundamental part of your success. While some parts of your character are inherent, such as patience or drive, most parts are your choice and within your control. For example, what do you do when you get too much change at a store? How do you treat other people? And what can you learn from other people's character? Of course, people with questionable or bad character may become successful, but the success they achieve is either fleeting or objectionable. I'm not interested in

---

elite military forces bounce back faster than the rest of us," *Newsweek,* February 14, 2009, http://www.newsweek.com/2009/02/13/lessons-in-survival.html.

compromised success. After all, how long will an arch with a faulty keystone last?

The second section of this book is called **Blueprint: Vision**. Any substantial structure requires a blueprint, a detailed plan of how a building or piece of equipment is designed. Some folks may have written 5, 10, 20-year life plans, but that's not what I mean. Character-based success may start with knowing who you are and what you stand for, but you have to take it further. What do you want to do? Where do you want to go? How will you design your life? Life is full of ideas and opportunities. Some are obvious, others require insight. Vision is the strategic part; setting out the big picture plan. This section talks about using judgment, dealing with change and the unexpected, and identifying unique opportunities to be different and great. Remember, vision creates direction and momentum, but character is the blueprint that guides how you follow that direction.

The third section is called **Structure: Action**. Just as there is no building without construction, there is no success without effort. Wishful thinking isn't enough. You have to build your life and create your success one step at a time. Sometimes, taking that first step is the hardest. Others struggle with decisiveness, self-expression, or taking the lead. No one will come to your door with a job offer, a proposal, or a check (I haven't seen any of those sweepstakes commercials in a long time). You have to put yourself out there and own it; easy or hard, quick or long; good or bad. Remember, without a solid character, your structure – your success – won't stand for long or even get built at all.

The fourth section is called **Appraise: Resolve**. The only thing in life that has its own momentum is time. Everything else needs a push to keep going. Many people might see this ongoing effort as a burden. However, it's actually a blessing. Every so often we need, or are forced, to stop and assess things. Sometimes, it's assessing a risk. Other times, it's assessing whether to go any further. All building projects are appraised for their worth. The same goes for success. Is this worth it? You have to answer this question all the time on the road to success. And each time you do it is a test of character. The will to succeed isn't just the determination to get things right. It's also the courage to do what's right. And this resolve enables you to be successful in life, over and over again.

The fifth and final section, called **Build: Momentum,** brings all of the lessons together. Unlike construction projects that end up as brick and mortar buildings, success has no final product. The most important lesson here is that we are constantly building ourselves and our future, because we are all a work in progress. We should never stop trying to be more and do better. This is success in its most genuine and most realistic form.

Once you acknowledge this – facing the facts – then you're ready to better understand what success is all about. Success is not simply an achievement marked by milestones. It's a state of mind. We have to learn how to take advantage of this mindset. It's long-term and flexible, and sometimes an unexpected road.

In the end, our best intentions and efforts may or may not work out. Sometimes, it's a matter of recognizing and acknowledging what's not working. At other times, it's figuring out what we think will work in the future. Again, these decisions are your responsibility. They are up to you.

This book is intended to pass along some of the lessons and principles behind character-driven success that I have learned in my 50-plus years in the military and in business, as well as throughout my life.[18] In some ways, I've been laying the foundation for this book all my life. One of the main reasons I was drawn to the Naval Academy and military service was its emphasis on character, including the personal, organizational,

---

[18] My interest in character-driven success also comes from Freemasonry. In the 1700s, the Freemasons evolved from a building trades guild into a brotherhood for building a man's character and values. George Washington and Ben Franklin were both Masons. Freemasons also included other developers and signers of both the Declaration of Independence and the United States Constitution. It's easy to see that some of the ideas and values of Freemasonry are found in these documents. Today, as an international society of fraternal friendship, Freemasons focus on personal development, intellectual discourse, and charitable work. I am proud to be one.

and national aspects. In all of my years as a CACI executive, I've given numerous speeches and written many papers and documents on ethics, business culture, and leadership. Every aspect of CACI's success has been based on our character; how we conduct ourselves and our business.

Throughout this book, I draw upon my own experiences as well as those of others I have known. For example, I have learned over the last decade the importance of setting high expectations and what a powerful tool it is. At CACI, Paul Cofoni, our CEO from 2007 until 2012, had as his slogan: *Be the Very Best.*[19] If you genuinely ask your team to be their best and repeatedly stress its importance, they will rise to the occasion. Likewise, if you were to set that same expectation for yourself – and not wait for others to do it – imagine what you could accomplish!

As a history buff, I include some examples and anecdotes that illustrate these principles and prove that these principles are timeless. Let's take setting expectations. One of the best examples of this principle is the British Admiral, Lord Nelson. During the Napoleonic Wars with France just as the famous Battle of Trafalgar (October 21, 1805), off the coast of Spain was about to commence, Admiral Horatio Nelson sent a flag signal from his flagship to all of his ships that said "England expects that every man will do his duty."[20] This statement made on that remarkable day over 200 years ago has become part of the positive psyche of the English people.

Although Lord Nelson was fatally wounded that fateful day, the British defeated a much stronger and larger combined French and Spanish fleet that represented Napoleon Bonaparte's interests in European maritime domination. Nelson's victory is

---

[19] Paul Cofoni became CACI's CEO on July 1, 2007 when I became Executive Chairman after 23 years in the CEO position.

[20] The full text of Nelson's note written in his cabin before joining *Victory's* signal lieutenant, John Pasco, reads: "Mr. Pasco, I wish to say to the fleet 'England confides that every man will do his duty'. You must be quick, for I have one more signal to make, which is for close action." Nelson's full name and title was Horatio Nelson, 1st Viscount Nelson, 1st Duke of Bronte. His military rank was Vice Admiral of the White.

memorialized at the magnificent Trafalgar square, the large plaza in central London dedicated to that triumphant day.

In this book, I've included quotes from historic figures, business leaders, and other well-known figures from popular culture. There are several reasons why I like to do this. First, they are succinct, memorable, and familiar. Second, it demonstrates that these principles derive from and are applicable across the board. And as I review my travel journals, I find that these principles apply in many other cultures, too. On some level, people are people the world over.

A couple of years ago, I gave a speech at an event for small businesses in government contracting. It had been decades since CACI was considered small. Nevertheless, the event organizers thought attendees would benefit from my experiences. At the beginning I talked about the value of small businesses in our industry, and how they are important partners to larger firms like CACI. But the focus of the speech was about the importance of a strong, ethical culture and putting it in place from the beginning of the company. I said: "No company or organization can thrive, no small business can grow into a big business, without first knowing who you are. If I have learned one thing in my nearly four decades of government contracting, it is this: Without a solid, ethical, accountable corporate culture, you will not succeed (continue to grow *and* be respected)."

Later, many people thanked me for talking about culture. Several of the small business leaders were in the process of shaping their cultures as the core of their growth. In every organization, *character drives success*. As the famous hotel chain entrepreneur, J.W. Marriott, once said, "Success is a combination of many things, but a good character is the foundation of the kind of success that will bring you real happiness."

Life today is complicated. Much happens that is beyond one's control and expectations. Yet there's one common denominator throughout – you. So knowing who is responsible for your success and what success is really about, after all, is up to you. It's all about *facing the facts*.

24

KEYSTONE: Character

The foundation for any worthy development, progress or success is character – *your character*. Character is a statement about your moral and ethical qualities – what you believe in, what you stand for, and what you expect of yourself and others. How you act on these qualities is your statement of character. Character will determine how far you will go and if you succeed or fail.

The good news is that your character is completely within your control. You have a choice when it comes to how you think, how you act, and how you interact with others. Along the way, there are people you can look to who can help you make these choices. They are sometimes called role models or mentors. However, you and you alone are accountable for what will happen.

What is your character?

CHAPTER 2

INTEGRITY IS NON-NEGOTIABLE

"The time is always right to do what is right"
Martin Luther King, Jr.

What is *integrity*? The word comes from the Latin *integritatem* meaning *the adherence to moral and ethical principles or codes*.

Since this definition doesn't fully capture the meaning, let's look at the people who created the word – the Romans.

Is it honesty? There's a carving of a man-like face in a 6th century church in Rome called the *Bocca della Verita* or the *Mouth of Truth*. It was believed that if someone told a lie while their hand was in the mouth of this large sculpture, it would be bitten off. I've seen the Bocca della Verita several times when I've visited Rome and put my hand in its mouth. I'm pleased to say I still have my hand!

Is it accountability? According to legend, when the ancient Romans constructed a large gateway arch, they would make the architect stand under it while the wooden construction supports were removed. They thought it was one way to ensure that the arch wouldn't fall.

Is it loyalty? For Ancient Romans, loyalty – or *fides* – was a prized virtue, which held together families, as well as the social order through their client system. Yet loyalty was also a political tool, ensuring the support of powerful families who controlled the Roman political and commercial landscape, and the longevity of those families' power through their supporters. Loyalty otherwise was far more provincial, binding slaves to masters, soldiers to specific units or military leaders, and people to local governments throughout the Empire.

We've come a long way since Ancient Rome. Honesty, accountability and loyalty add to the meaning of integrity; however, when it comes to defining *integrity*, one meaning still prevails – **doing the right thing.**

We often hear that integrity is about doing the right thing *even when no one is looking*. That last part is very important. Too many people do the *wrong* thing because they think they're only guilty if caught: employees embezzling funds, politicians accepting bribes, celebrities doing drugs, spouses committing adultery, or students cheating on exams. Even if no one discovers the indiscretion, one lapse in judgment can easily snowball into many more. A 2009 study by the Josephson Institute of Ethics at UCLA found that "cheaters in high school are far more likely as adults to lie to their spouses, customers and employers and to cheat on expense reports and insurance claims."[21] If you have to hide your mistakes – it's one monumental mistake!

Integrity also means refusing to engage in behavior that evades responsibility. If a cashier gave you more change than you were owed, would you keep it? If you saw an associate cheating, would you report it? Many people would say *no* because they don't snitch. How about an office mate watching a movie on a computer or a DVD player during work hours? Perhaps you don't want to get involved. What if your neighbor's child got scared when asked about the repeated bruises on his arm or face? Would you keep your suspicions to yourself?

What if you discovered that a product your company made could kill its users? Johns Manville, the company behind asbestos, knew as early as the mid-1930s about its adverse health effects. Yet, there were no warning labels on its packaging until 1964. Company executives hid the damning information and went as far as having company doctors lie to asbestos workers, telling them their health was fine.[22] The decision is yours, but who else does your indifference or silence effect?

---

[21] "Josephson Institute of Ethics Releases Study on High School Character and Adult Conduct, Character Study Reveals Predictors of Lying and Cheating," October 29, 2009, http://josephsoninstitute.org/surveys/index.html.

[22] By 1982, over 17,000 lawsuits had been filed against Johns Manville. That

We are all familiar with the cliché that *no one is perfect.* It's even illustrated in the bible verse, "He that is without sin among you, let him first cast a stone" The key is not fooling ourselves by rationalizing our bad decisions or by being tricked into doing something we know isn't right. And having good intentions isn't sufficient. Integrity comes down to choices and actions. It's not just about *knowing* what's right or wrong – it's about *deciding what the right or wrong thing to do is in any given situation and doing it consistently.* These choices mean knowing what you stand for – and everyone else knowing it too. Your character is always being put to the test, and failure is not an option.

INDIVIDUAL INTEGRITY

Individual integrity has more to do with personal success than anything else. It determines your credibility and establishes your limits. It sets expectations of what you will and won't do, and what you will and won't accept. This, in turn, determines how people will treat you.

Integrity is one of my primary criteria in hiring people at CACI. Just as I would not want to buy a product from a company I don't trust, customers and colleagues do not want to work with people they don't trust. I want to work with people who can be relied upon for quality performance and the good judgment to do the right thing.

In terms of personal success, integrity is shown by whom you choose to surround yourself. You are defined and judged by the company you keep. So keep good company!

The importance of the company you keep was a lesson drilled into me at the Naval Academy. In fact, ethics is part of the Academy's academic curriculum.[23] There were high standards set

---

year, the company filed for Chapter 11 bankruptcy protection. Since then, the company has reinvented itself as the Manville Corporation and has been noted for its commitment to ethics and preventing a similar situation from reoccurring.

[23] Midshipmen at the Naval Academy today have four required courses in their curriculum on leadership, ethics and the law. The Academy's Stockdale Ethics Center offers resources and programs to empower ethics in decision-making, including

across the board, but none more important than the standards for teamwork. In an organization with so many moving parts and arrayed responsibilities, it was vital that you knew your job and trusted that your teammates also knew their job and what they were doing.

One of the most complex operations in the Navy is that of aircraft carrier operations at sea. These "runways at sea" can only work successfully with a fully coordinated, operational team. There are many people involved in flight operations. For example, Shooters are naval aviators who are responsible for launching aircraft. Also on the flight deck are Handlers who are responsible for the planes' movements about the flight deck before launching and after landing. From Primary Flight Control on the top bridge, the Air Boss takes overall responsibility for controlling takeoffs and landings, monitoring nearby aircraft, and overseeing planes on the flight deck. Meanwhile, other ship's staff monitors weather conditions, operate radar systems, maintain equipment, and keep the deck clear of debris (among many other responsibilities). The whole team works under inherently hazardous, highly technical, and time-sensitive conditions.

> "Alike for the nation and the individual, the one indispensable requisite is character – character that does and dares as well as endures, character that is active in the performance of virtue no less than firm in the refusal to do aught that is vicious or degraded."
>
> Theodore Roosevelt

When a carrier is in full swing, aircraft are taking off and landing quickly in an area of about three and a half football fields. One wrong move and someone can get sucked into a jet engine, blasted into the ocean, or crash an aircraft. When working under such dangerous and risky conditions, you must do your very best. Yet it's just as important to know that everyone

---

conferences, research, and simulations that address personal conduct and ethical dilemmas. At the invitation of the Superintendant, I gave an after dinner talk on ethics to some midshipmen at the Academy several years ago.

else on the ship is doing the same.[24] There is no room for error. It's a "zero defects" environment. And that's why personal responsibility and integrity are important, especially in the context of teamwork.

This idea of integrity as a team is also prevalent in the U.S. Marine Corps. As part of its tradition since 1775, "Never Leave a Marine Behind" is the motto that's instilled in boot camp. It means in combat, marines never leave a wounded comrade behind. Some men have even been killed while retrieving their comrades' bodies, knowing that the dead Marine would have tried to do the same for them. This principle is based in part on preventing a wounded Marine from falling into enemy hands. It creates a bond of trust between Marines that lets them know they can always rely on one another.

Such standards of behavior are both ancient and universal. The legendary ancient Japanese samurai warriors adhered to *bushido,* a unique code of conduct that emphasized virtues such as loyalty, honor, obedience, duty, filial piety, and self-sacrifice. In antiquity, the militaristic Spartan culture of Greece encouraged discipline and physical toughness, and emphasized the preeminence of the Spartan state. These codes and cultures thrived in their time because they were needed and they set very high standards. Expectations about performance and duty were supreme. They still are!

Most of us will never face the life and death situations faced by the men and women of our military forces. Nor will we live in rigid cultures like those of the Samurai or Spartans. But these examples still hold true.

---

[24] I had to do my part as well. In 1961, I had to pilot a helicopter rescue mission. During carrier training exercises, a Marine pilot trainee took off at the wrong angle on the carrier deck and crashed his plane over the side of the ship. My crew and I plucked the wet young pilot out of the water. He was lucky to get out of his rapidly sinking plane. You can easily understand that teamwork is critical in life and death situations. At the day's end that young pilot thought we were really great!

ORGANIZATIONAL INTEGRITY

The quality and character of the people you surround yourself with reflect what you stand for, and, hence, play a big role in your success. It is also why you should choose wisely the organization for which you work. Pick your friends and colleagues carefully.

There are many ways to identify an organization's culture and values – its character – in advance, before you go to work for them. Go to the organization's website and learn what is said about the *values* and *culture* (if nothing is said, you might eliminate the organization from further consideration). How do they compare against other companies? What do current and former employees say on discussion boards? How did they treat you in the interview? What was your gut feeling when you visited their office? As PricewaterhouseCoopers CEO Sam DiPiazza once said, "It has become dramatically clear that the foundation of corporate integrity is personal integrity." I would add that if your impression from the people with whom you have interacted is less than stellar, then this may not be the place for you.

In the early 1980s, I read the best-selling book *In Search of Excellence* by Tom Peters and Robert Waterman. It was a superb collection of lessons learned and best practices of top companies. One example about first impressions that particularly struck a chord with me was in the chapter on customer relationships. I read about an incident that hit close to home. It seemed that a person who worked at the Pentagon in the Office of the Chief of Naval Operations spoke about the difference between one employee who excelled at understanding the client and others who were not so good at it. The narrator said, "I was always distressed that they [civilian mid-level managers] were so demotivated towards work, but so animated in general. A lot of them were selling real estate or running other small businesses on the side."

That last part struck me. When I had been in the Naval Reserve, I had a similar experience. While I was on an active duty training assignment chasing down aviation ground support equipment back orders for Reserve aircraft squadrons, several colleagues around me in that Navy office were working on personal business projects during Navy business hours – including real estate sales! Perhaps, as a Navy man, I was extra-sensitive to this flagrant lack of integrity.

The example from *In Search of Excellence* showed me that others had also noticed the problem, and it left a bad impression. This one example tends to tarnish the reputation of the thousands of conscientious, hard-working and competent professionals in the Department of the Navy.

Successful cultures are based on ethics and accountability.[25] A company's culture tells you *what* to do and *how* to do it. It tells you *how* to behave and *how* to perform. It shows you *what* your organization represents and *how* to represent your organization. It tells you *what* challenges to take on, *how* to tackle these challenges and *how* to react in the face of adversity. It tells you *what* success you seek and *how* to lead your teams to achieve their best, for your company and for your clients.

I can proudly say that CACI is a perfect example. Integrity is the cornerstone of CACI's culture. At CACI, integrity, honesty, fairness and respect are given the same importance as quality client service, shareholder value, and career opportunities. Our values are institutionalized in our culture documents, like our *Culture* and *Mission Statements, Credo,* and *Operational Philosophy.* They are codified in our corporate policies. Part of CACI's culture is a long-standing ethics and compliance program. CACI was one of the first information technology (IT) contractors to establish standards of ethics and business conduct. CACI's ethics and compliance program was firmly in place many years ago, and 10 years before government contractors were required to do so. Our ethics and values program has been publicly documented and available since the mid-1980s when I became CEO and wrote them down. While no one person and no individual company is perfect in every way, I can proudly say these standards are our objectives and what we expect of everyone.

---

[25] In speaking here of "culture," the concept is also applicable to any organization, be it commercial, government, military, sports, etc.

CHARACTER: The Ultimate Success Factor

Integrity is the one characteristic that is tested every day. That's why it is so important to know what you stand for, and to associate yourself with people in your personal and professional lives that stand for the same thing. Each one of us is confronted every day with simple and not so simple choices that affect not only our well-being, but that of others.

"The buck stops here"

Harry S. Truman's desk sign

Think about the last thing you ate today. From the farmers who produced the ingredients to the manufacturers who processed and packaged the food, many people were responsible for ensuring the quality and safety of the product. What would happen if someone along that chain compromised their integrity? What if someone knowingly allowed products contaminated with salmonella to get shipped to stores? What if someone chose not to do the right thing? Of course, it would be a disaster. In our society and our culture, we rely on each other every day – all day long.

When something does go wrong, manufacturers or producers are expected to alert consumers. What if pharmaceutical companies delayed alerting users about the potentially severe side effects resulting from the use of certain medications? In the first four months of 2012, there were 128 recalls, market withdrawals, and safety alerts issued by the U.S. Food and Drug Administration.[26] The products recalled ranged from frozen foods to dietary supplements. Food and drugs are familiar examples, but what about commercial airplane safety, maintenance and reliability? Personal integrity or the lack of it, in these fields can mean life or death.

The most famous case of integrity and public safety was probably the Tylenol crisis. In 1982, Johnson & Johnson faced a public relations and product tampering crisis when seven people in Chicago died after having ingested Extra-Strength Tylenol capsules, which were later determined to have been laced with

---

[26] U.S. Food and Drug Administration 2012 Recalls, Market Withdrawals & Safety Alerts, http://www.fda.gov/Safety/Recalls/ArchiveRecalls/2012/default.htm.

cyanide by an unknown source. The deaths made national news and caused a massive, nationwide panic. While Johnson & Johnson may not have caused the deaths, they assumed the responsibility for maintaining public safety. The poisonings also made it necessary for Tylenol maker Johnson & Johnson to launch a PR program to safeguard the integrity of both their product and their corporation.

The company's approach, led by then CEO James E. Burke, was rooted in a corporate commitment to its customers' health and well-being, which Johnson & Johnson put before profit and financial concerns in dealing with its crisis.

Johnson & Johnson immediately instituted a nation-wide recall and halted all advertisement for the product. The recall amounted to about 31 million bottles being withdrawn from the market and a loss of more than $100 million (1982 dollars) for the company. Johnson & Johnson soon followed with tamper resistant packaging, a switch to caplets, and an intensive marketing campaign to restore confidence in the Tylenol name. Today, Tylenol remains a household name and Johnson & Johnson's handling of the crisis is considered to be a premier example of corporate integrity. This episode also created the Federal Drug Administration's current requirements for safety packaging, like tamper-resistant bottles, of all such consumer goods. Today, virtually all packaged products have some kind of tamper-resistant covers.

CACI'S INTEGRITY IS TESTED – ABU GHRAIB

I know first-hand the importance of personal and organizational integrity in action. In April 2004, CACI was thrust into the international spotlight when an *illegally leaked* U.S. Army report by Major General Antonio M. Taguba, given to *New Yorker* magazine's Seymour Hersh, cast "suspicion" on one of our employees for being "either directly or indirectly responsible" for the mistreatment of detainees at Abu Ghraib prison. At the same time, pictures from the dismal and overcrowded prison depicting the abuses by a fringe group of U.S. soldiers were shown on national television by CBS' *60*

Minutes II. Overnight, the scandal tarnished anyone associated with Abu Ghraib – whether responsible for the abuses or not – including us.

What ensued was a salacious *feeding frenzy* rarely experienced by any company. The hungry media and other opportunists twisted the unsupported allegations of torture and abuse into a guilty verdict without regard for the facts or the truth. Their reports created a damning public perception of CACI and made CACI a target for misplaced anger and politically-driven criticism.

The Abu Ghraib scandal put who we were, what we stood for, and everything CACI had accomplished at risk. Our responsibility was to protect and sustain the livelihoods of our then 10,000 employees, the investments of our shareholders, and most importantly, the vital work we performed for our valued military and government clients. I am pleased and proud to say that our well-defined culture was our guide in doing so.

The first of CACI's *Ten Business Values* is to "Place integrity and honesty above all else." So, we quickly acknowledged the allegations, but we would not speculate or comment on anything that wasn't first proven to be fact. We also made it clear that we would not condone or tolerate illegal or inappropriate behavior by any employee engaged in any CACI business – period! If evidence from the investigations showed that someone had broken the law, we would respond accordingly to *do the right thing*.

> *"The opinion of honest men, friends to freedom and well-wishers to mankind, where ever they may happen to be born or reside, is the only kind of reputation a wise man could ever desire."*
>
> George Washington

Inspired by Johnson & Johnson's handling of the Tylenol crisis, we developed a hypercrisis management strategy that addressed the various crisis challenges and those affected by it.[27]

---

[27] Dr. Jennifer Burkhart, a consultant to CACI at the time, pointed to the Tylenol crisis as a model for dealing with company crises. Drawing on her background in

We established two-way communications with our clients, our employees and our investors about what was happening. Getting the facts and setting the record straight was paramount. We launched an aggressive response campaign to push back against the errors and misinformation in the media. CACI was included in nine probing government investigations in all and we cooperated fully to the best of our ability at every turn because we weren't going to hide anything – no matter what. We wanted the truth to come out.

In the end, the government investigations, supported by sworn Congressional testimony and other official records, found no validity to the accusations against CACI.[28] The Abu Ghraib scandal was the biggest challenge CACI had ever faced, but our long-standing culture and ethos provided the moral compass that guided us through it.

As CEO during the time of CACI's biggest crisis, it never occurred to me to do anything other than the *right thing*. Why would I want to jeopardize our employees' livelihoods, shareholders' investments, and our clients' work, as well as ruin my personal reputation all at once? I wonder where companies like WorldCom and Enron would be now, if they understood the importance of integrity? Where were their cultures, values, and ethical frameworks? How important were these values to Lehman Brothers, Countrywide, or any of the other failed companies of the 2000-2010 decade? Did they ever consider the thousands of employees, vendors, customers, investors, or even their own families, when they made their awful decisions?

Most companies are good citizens and have a genuine interest in operating ethically, obeying laws, serving their

---

psychology and marketing, Dr. Burkhart crafted the conceptual framework for CACI's hypercrisis management strategy.

[28] Not one current or former CACI employee was ever charged by the U.S. government with any wrongdoing. Furthermore, CACI was never even implicated as a contributor during the courts-martial of the Army soldiers who were found guilty of committing the abuses.

We were also confronted with major litigation assaults from civil suits filed by individuals claiming to be detainees. One of these suits was appealed to the U.S. Supreme Court, but the court refused to hear the case.

customers honestly and taking care of their employees (the backbone of their operations). Not every company is Enron or a WorldCom! Unfortunately the few bad apples and their damaging headlines tarnish the vast majority of honest and ethical companies out there.

The consequences of systemic failures of integrity can damage individuals and organizations alike. On a larger scale, institutional corruption undermines competition, good governance, sustainable development, and democratic process. In fact, the long-term viability of our federal republic, here in America, is based upon the integrity of its leadership; the legislative, judicial and executive branches.[29]

It's true that standards can be set and violations can be addressed. However, it's also true that no rule or law can force or prevent dishonest people from dishonest behavior. You can't regulate integrity.[30] Crooks will continue to find ways to break the law because that's what crooks do!

One aspect of integrity that has been greatly lacking is *dignity* – the dignity that always accompanies the people and organizations that possess integrity. Dignity is not about ego – it's about conducting oneself, not just appropriately, but with

---

[29] One must also remember that there is an important difference between what is legal and what is moral or right. Consider that slavery was legal in the United States for over 200 years, but it was neither moral nor right. Adolph Hitler, one of mankind's most immoral villains, rode the rise of ultra-nationalism and economic recovery to wrangle power over the legislative and executive branches of Germany – predominantly through legal, bureaucratic means. Integrity is essential in preventing systematic exploitation of the law to advance immoral agendas.

[30] Laws and regulations can only define and punish illegal activities; they cannot prevent unethical behavior. Reacting to public outrage or political opportunity, lawmakers, it seems, have an unfortunate tendency towards over-zealous legislation to deal with such problems. Too often, regulation exceeds what's necessary. Individuals and organizations that did not create the problem also get penalized along with – and sometimes instead of – the violators. The bad apples should be prosecuted appropriately under statutes, but not to the detriment of the entire group. In the view of many, the Sarbanes-Oxley Act of 2002 was a prime example of such excessive regulation.

self-respect and an appreciation for your responsibilities. In a way, it's integrity in action.

Politics is a perfect example. Living and working in Washington, DC for several decades, I have had a front-row seat to the deterioration of dignity and decorum in our political system. Of course, misconduct – personal, professional, or political – is nothing new. Scandals have touched everyone from ancient emperors to our politicians of today. The quality of conduct by many of our elected officials today, however, is most disappointing. From foul language to belligerence, to entitlement abuse and greed, immaturity and selfishness is unfortunately more near the norm these days. Sadly, we have come to expect misconduct in politics as well as from others in the public arena. Scandals no longer shock or surprise us. And apologies come across as orchestrated and insincere. Which too often, they are!

You can never earn respect and admiration, or lead, without a certain level of dignity. Dignified behavior tends to bring out the best in people. It's inspirational and motivational. People will follow tyrants, but only to collect the spoils or save their own hides. Dignified leadership has always proven to be the most effective and enduring. Dignity also creates a mutual respect that enables people to work together effectively. You may disagree with a co-worker or fellow board member in a meeting, but you can discuss and resolve the differences without attacking each other. You can even respectfully agree to disagree and not bad mouth each other afterwards.

Boards of Directors are a good example of dignity in action. I have been on the Board at CACI for three decades and as Chairman for the last two. I have also been on the boards of many other organizations of varying size and purpose. I can safely say that boards that function the best have a high sense of decorum. The members respect each other and treat each other appropriately. These directors don't have to like each other. However, members of well-functioning boards simply do not stoop to name-calling, pettiness, or any other disruptive behavior. Collaborative and productive boards also don't permit members to indulge in behind-the-back character assassinations. Accusers are required to address those they accuse face-to-face, as in any honor court. The company thrives when the board supports the company. The directors may not necessarily agree with everything the management team does, but it supports them in achieving their goals. For me, the best boards are conscientious as well as competent, and the best also operate with dignity.[31]

Architects may no longer have to stand under their structures to prove their integrity and our hands may be safe from lie-detecting sculptures, but the importance of integrity never wanes. Integrity is invaluable. The lack of it is patently detrimental. People mostly do what they want to do. You may not be able to control their actions, but you can *always* decide how you conduct yourself. So the next time you are faced with a moral dilemma and may be leaning toward not doing the right thing, remind yourself that *integrity is non-negotiable.*

---

[31] Boards that operate with dignity also attract directors of the highest caliber. For example, I doubt that people like former Chairmen of the Joint Chiefs of Staff, Admiral Thomas H. Moorer, USN (Ret.) and General Hugh Shelton, USA (Ret.), would have served on CACI's Board if our integrity had ever been in question. Adm. Moorer served from 1987 to 1993. Gen. Shelton served on CACI's board in 2006 and 2007.

CHAPTER 3

ATTITUDE IS MORE IMPORTANT THAN YOU THINK

"Attitude is a little thing that makes a big difference."
Winston Churchill

First impressions are made in seconds and you never get a second chance to make a good first impression. I learned this pearl of wisdom years ago and have never forgotten it. This is true for individuals and for organizations.

What would you think if the CEO picked you up at the airport for your interview with the company? That's what happened to one executive candidate. Flying into Omaha to interview for the top job of Helzberg Diamond Shops, Beryl Raff was surprised to find Warren Buffett, the CEO of Helzberg's parent company Berkshire Hathaway, waiting for her in his gold Cadillac at the airport. After their meeting at the office, Buffett took Raff to his country club for lunch and then a tour of the town. Buffett then promptly offered Raff the job, which she accepted a few days later. Raff noted that Buffett's ease, charm and attentiveness made him someone for whom she wanted to work. Buffett knew that to hire a top notch candidate, he needed to make that good first impression.

First impressions are made every day. You're introduced to two people at a party. One greets you with a smile and the other with indifference. With which one do you keep talking? At which store would you keep shopping? The one where the employees understand the products and give their full attention to customers? Or the store where employees can't answer your questions or can't even be found on the sales floor? During a job interview, two candidates have similar credentials. One candidate seems enthusiastic and friendly. The other candidate comes across as overconfident and presumptuous. Which candidate would you hire? The one with the better attitude!

Attitude is a characteristic we use to judge if and how we relate to someone. The impact of someone's attitude is obvious. Yet, the attitude most often overlooked is our own because we tend to associate attitude with *other* people. We have a hard time accepting our flaws and the fact that we may be the cause of our own problems. Your attitude is reflected in how you are thought of and treated. It's easy to say you don't like someone because of their attitude. Yet, someone may be saying the same thing about you.

In dictionaries, *attitude* is typically defined as a person's perspective and disposition towards things as well as a way of saying and doing things. Your attitude influences your behavior – in fact, it's reflected in *everything* that you do. Again, the good news is that you have complete control over your attitude. You can both *choose* your attitude and *change* your attitude.

ATTITUDE EQUALS MOTIVATION PLUS EXECUTION

As it relates to leadership, attitude can be simplified into two factors: motivation and execution.

MOTIVATION

The first part of attitude is motivation. Motivation drives behavior. It is why you do what you do and what you do it for.

CARING

Ask yourself: *What do you care about?* Do you care about art? In 1508 Michelangelo may have reluctantly accepted Pope Julius II's commission to paint the Sistine Chapel. Yet once the Pope agreed to Michelangelo's more complicated design, the artist spent the next *four years* painting over 5,000 square feet of frescos on that famous ceiling. All who see this masterpiece today marvel at its breathtaking beauty and complexity.[32] Thankfully, Michelangelo had a change of heart and attitude!

What's your attitude about helping people? In the post World War II era, polio was considered the most frightening public health problem in the United States. In 1947, a young medical researcher, Jonas Salk, accepted an appointment to the University of Pittsburgh School of Medicine. The following year, he started on a project to determine the different types of polio viruses. Using the project as an opportunity to develop a vaccine against polio, Salk and his team devoted the next seven years to this goal. His family even volunteered to be the first to test the new vaccine. In 1955, Salk's new vaccine was declared a success after 18 months of field trials. Because of Salk's dedication, a crippling illness that once infected tens of thousands every year has been virtually eradicated. His attitude and motivation reflected his desire to help people.

"Have a positive attitude and spread it around, never let yourself be a victim, and for goodness sake – have fun."

Jack Welch

Not everyone is destined to create an artistic masterpiece or cure a disease. Most people likely care more about family, security and personal welfare than altruistic goals. Yet the lesson is still the same: You won't succeed at anything in life if you don't care about it – in a big way.

Think about your work. Most of us spend more time at work in a single day than we do with family or even sleeping. How much do you care about your work? Do you work for pocket money, to pay the bills, or to simply keep your job? Or do you believe that what you do has a purpose or benefit? Believing in what you're doing is valuable. A steady paycheck is strong enough motivation to go to work. Imagine how your motivation

---

[32] I have been to the Sistine Chapel in the Vatican in Rome, Italy on three different occasions over the years. It is one of the most famous works of art in the entire world and always breathtaking to see.

would change if you felt your work was very important and enduring!

The Perdue brand of poultry products is a household name in much of America today because the family behind it had the right attitude. Perdue was founded along Maryland's Eastern Shore in 1920 by Arthur Perdue as a "backyard table-egg business."[33] Arthur, who established the company's values of quality, integrity, trust and teamwork, was active in the business up until his death in 1977 at age 91. Arthur's son, Frank, became the company's third full-time employee in 1939 and took over the top spot in 1950. Noted for his 18-hour days, Frank Perdue's business strategy and investments vertically integrated the company and helped make Perdue an industry leader. He also became famous as one of the first corporate executives to be featured in their company's television commercials. The tag line, "It takes a tough man to make a tender chicken," represented the family's commitment to quality. In 1983, grandson and son Jim Perdue left a career in marine biology and joined Perdue as an entry-level management trainee. After working in numerous departments in the organization, Jim assumed both the chairman and spokesman positions in 1991. In fact, "Jim works in a cubicle, but walks the halls of his 46 plants and labs. He's involved in everything, right down to the recipes."[34] That work ethic and attitude has taken Perdue from the backyard to a $4.6 billion operation with 22,000 employees.

Perhaps your job isn't your passion. That doesn't mean that you don't care about why or how you do your job. Since 2010, a reality television series has followed top executives of several corporations as they worked undercover within their own organizations. Larry O'Donnell, president and COO of Waste Management, a leading sanitation and recycling company, joined unsuspecting employees in their daily duties, including vacuuming out portable toilets. Even though the employees did

---

[33] Perdue Corporate History, http://www.perdue.com/company/history/generations.html.
[34] Denise Koch, "WJZ Talks to Chicken Man Jim Perdue," May 14, 2008, http://wjz.com/specialreports/chicken.jim.perdue.2722936.html.

not work under the most pleasant of circumstances, O'Donnell was astonished at their work ethic. The employee who cleaned the toilets showed significant pride and a positive attitude in his work. O'Donnell also spent the day with two other employees, who performed their duties without complaint despite suffering from major health problems. It's safe to say sanitation wasn't the passion of these employees, but they were prime examples that caring about how you do what you do is just as important.

I was lucky to learn this lesson early. During my childhood in Oklahoma, I remember listening to my mother's stories about our ancestors. With great pride, she said they had come across the country in covered wagons and were "pioneers and farmers". My grandparents and great-grandparents, originally from Illinois and Missouri, had settled in central Oklahoma before statehood. My great-grandfather, James Wesley Phillips, participated in the historic Oklahoma Land Rush on April 22, 1889. My mother spoke with pride about their sturdy independence and self-reliance. Looking back, it was a lesson that became integrated as part of my work ethic and values. As a teenager, working in my uncle's small bottling factory, my motivation was to prove myself enough to keep my job, but more importantly, to make him proud of me. Then I discovered that doing a good job also led to promotions and raises. I was motivated to achieve more and make more money, so I cared about my performance. My self-confidence, as well as my skills and knowledge, grew along the way. I learned that while my immediate task, my project, or my job may not be the thing I cared about most, I found motivation by connecting it to something I did care about. This notion of *connectivity*, putting things in perspective and looking for the inherent value and growth, has always served me well.

Caring has real value. In academic literature, *psychic income* is typically defined as intangible benefits above and beyond the utilitarian or monetary value derived from an activity. One example is the status afforded by the purchase of luxury goods.

Jonas Salk's polio vaccine could have been a huge cash cow, but Salk likened patenting his vaccine to patenting the sun. His motive had been to develop a safe and effective vaccine as quickly as possible. And what did Salk want in return? "I feel that the greatest reward for doing is the opportunity to do more."[35]

Psychic income is part of any compensation package. In fact, it may be the most important part in many cases. The military is a prime example. One does not enter the military with visions of economic largess. Although the military does (in a sense) provide full-time employment and job security, income is determined by pre-set pay scales that are unlikely to produce millionaires.[36] Servicemen and women who embark on a life-long military career do so for many other reasons; service to their country, travel, education and training, family tradition, or just seeking other opportunities. Now, that's not to say that post-military careers can't be profitable, but economic wealth is not a factor before retirement. There are also many other career fields where money isn't a primary motivator. Employees at non-profit organizations can sometimes earn more in similar positions in the private sector, but their organization's mission is seen as more important. The teaching profession is also one where meaning often outweighs income. The clergy is another example where mission supersedes salary. Some in religious service take vows of poverty. For many people, caring is worth more than earning.

Attitude is also a vital part of deciding with whom I want to work. At CACI, I wrote three management manuals aimed at giving our leadership team some well-proven lessons and advice on business, from the importance of corporate culture to business development. One manual is dedicated to recruiting

---

[35] After the polio vaccine, Salk founded the Salk Institute for Biological Studies in La Jolla, California in 1960. It is consistently rated as one of the country's top centers for medical and scientific research. In the 1980s Salk's research focused on finding an AIDS vaccine. I drove by the Salk Institute many times while visiting CACI's nearby Torre Pines' office. As a youngster who grew up during the days when polio was a summertime horror around public swimming pools, Salk was a savior to my generation.

[36] During the Revolutionary War, Continental Army soldiers earned low and inconsistent wages. Their deaths often left their families destitute. My ancestor, John Burnett, 10th Virginia Regiment of Foot, died while in Washington's army at Valley Forge. His wife, Mary, had to be given food rations by her generous neighbors in Amherst County, Virginia.

and hiring. In that manual, I listed my **four recruiting criteria**: **Attitude, Integrity, Commitment, and Expertise**. [37]

Attitude intentionally comes first. Employees who have a good, positive, and consistent attitude with their colleagues, supervisors, and customers are employees with whom people want to work. Employees with a bad or inconsistent attitude either will be difficult to work with, or will cause problems for their colleagues. In either case, our employees need to get along so we do a good job for our clients. A good attitude is critical – mandatory – for success.

Next in the sequence comes *integrity*. Just as we would not want to buy a product from a company we don't trust, customers and colleagues do not want to work with people they can't trust. At CACI, we want to work with people who can be relied upon to follow the rules, deliver a quality performance and have the good judgment to do the right thing. Integrity is a "must-have" requirement.

In turn, the third criterion is *commitment*. It's a fact that candidates who are not fully committed to their position and the company's goals will not fully and enthusiastically support the progress of the organization. Of course, this includes full commitment to the clients' programs and projects as well. We need people who know how to make a commitment and stand by it. Some people may see CACI as a brief stop on their career path. Or maybe their vision of themselves doesn't fit with the direction the company is going. If this is the case, go no further. Working with CACI is not an experiment.

Finally, after ascertaining that a candidate has the right *attitude, integrity*, and *commitment*, I then look at the candidate's *expertise*. It comes last because domain expertise is only a part of the equation. If the most renowned experts have an attitude problem that makes them difficult to work with, or if they are not reliable, or if they are not fully committed to the project or the company, then they won't fit and will harm your organization. When I have to decide between two candidates who

---

[37] The title of that CACI management manual is *How to Hire Heroes the CACI Way.*

have similar domain expertise, I choose the one with the better *attitude, integrity*, and *commitment* every time!

In his bestselling book, *Good to Great,* Jim Collins wrote that it was not just people, but *the right people*, who are a company's most important asset. Identifying the *right people* depends more on character traits than technical attributes. A study at Harvard University found that when a candidate is hired, 85 percent of the time it is because of their attitude. Only 15 percent of the time is it because of their technical expertise. Remember: You don't get a second chance to make a good first impression, whether you are the interviewer or the interviewee!

This belief about attitude was cemented for me as a result of one of my own management experiences. A number of years ago, we had an executive at CACI who was brought in for a senior-level position. He came to us with a good resume, and things worked well at first. However, over time a darker side emerged. It was almost like Dr. Jekyll and Mr. Hyde. His good work was slowly undone by a serious attitude problem. Too often, he was rude, ridiculing and harassing people, particularly in meetings. Stories surfaced about verbally abusive behavior in one-on-one situations. It became clear that this executive had a hidden agenda and seemed to favor underhanded and behind-the-back dealings. Sneaky, haughty behavior isn't appreciated or rewarded in our company. His bad attitude would soon catch up with him.

As it turned out, the executive had put together a letter pressing for my dismissal, which he wanted other managers to sign. He apparently intended to then present the letter to the Board of Directors and stake his claim on the CEO job. One Sunday afternoon, a colleague called me at home to tell me about the letter. At first, I thought it was a joke. After checking into it, I then called one of our senior directors who wasn't aware of the situation either. This board member then put together an unannounced investigation and soon disclosed that the plot was true. Later, a Board meeting was called and the executive was fired by the board – on the spot.

This situation reminded me of Niccolo Machiavelli's book, *The Prince.* Machiavelli warned that if you want to take down the prince, the first attempt has to be successful. Otherwise, your goose is cooked. More importantly, this executive's attitude showed he only cared for himself and obviously didn't care how he behaved toward others. Fortunately, we did care.

Bad attitudes come in many forms (sneakiness is just one type). These behaviors run the gamut from professional athletes who use performance enhancing drugs illegally to corrupt public officials. They're often in plain sight.

For example, in 2011 there were at least 473 reported cases of major embezzlement in the U.S.[38] These embezzlers were typically individuals in accounting and finance positions who stole, on average, $15,189 a month from their employers. In the year's worst case, a 71-year old Oklahoma man, along with the help of at least two accomplices, swindled $70 million from some 13,000 trust accounts he controlled for customers at several cemeteries he owned in Michigan and Tennessee. Indicted in 2007, the man was sentenced in 2011 to 20 years in prison and ordered to pay $48,670,000 in restitution. How do such people live with themselves? Also where were all of the auditors and management supervisors?

I have also learned to avoid arrogant types or "big shots." I find it virtually impossible to work with someone whose head or ego is so big that they can't get through the door without Vaseline! No matter how much they may have accomplished (or think they have), their egotistical attitude and self-centered behavior are not justified. They tend to overrate – exaggerate – their abilities yet typically under-perform or fail to meet expectations. They over-promise and under-deliver, yet expect constant accolades. People don't like being around them. Any power or influence they have is usually temporary. You don't have to be the one to burst their bubble, but you should stay out of the way because it will splatter!

---

[38] 2010 Marquet Report on Embezzlement, http://www.marquetinternational.com/pdf/the_2011_marquet_report_on_embezzlement.pdf.

AMBITION

If motivation is one part *caring*, then the other part is *ambition* or desire to achieve. For some, ambition has a negative connotation. You may recall Gordon Gecko's famous line in the 1987 movie *Wall Street* – "Greed is good." The need to achieve is actually considered inherent to human nature. According to Abraham Maslow's hierarchy of needs, a psychological theory of motivation, people are motivated by unsatisfied needs.[39] According to Maslow's theory, physiological, safety, and social needs, categorized as deficiency needs, must be satisfied first. But at the highest level of the hierarchy are self-actualization needs. Maslow referred to these as *growth needs*. Unlike deficiency needs that stem from a lack of something, growth needs stem from a desire to fulfill our greatest potential.

Maslow studied the biographies of several well-known historical figures while developing his theory. He believed that Albert Einstein, Eleanor Roosevelt, Abraham Lincoln and Frederick Douglass were prime examples of self-actualized people.

Achievement can be defined in terms of wealth, power, or fame. Likewise, it can be defined in terms of social welfare and individual fulfillment. For example, you may care about your career, but what do you want to achieve or accomplish in life? Is it a certain job title? A specific job location? Enough money to retire? Maybe public acclaim or recognition? Ambition, however, may or may not be defined by specific goals. The point is the same in any case; having and achieving a desired outcome.

I need to make an important distinction here between *mission people* (being goal-oriented in motivation) and *political people* (being self-centered in motivation). I think these two types are easily identifiable. The difference isn't always black and

---

[39] Maslow presented his theory in his 1943 paper, *A Theory of Human Motivation,* and later developed it further in his 1954 book, *Motivation and Personality.* Maslow was a psychologist and professor at Brooklyn College and Brandeis University. I first learned about Maslow while studying for my doctorate at George Washington University in the late 1960s.

white, of course, but the behavior patterns are fairly easy to recognize even in the gray.

Mission-oriented people are driven to achieve goals, the mission, be it broad or limited in nature or scope. They are also driven by the accomplishments achieved along the way. In a group setting, they may have their own interests, but they do not typically pursue them in place of the group's mission objectives – which come first.

"Outstanding people have one thing in common: an absolute sense of mission."

Zig Ziglar

Politically-oriented people also want to achieve goals, but only as long as they get something out of it for themselves. They are in it primarily for what they can get for themselves. They also like to take credit for what others do, and to lay blame elsewhere when they make a mistake or when their work doesn't pan out. This is the hallmark of the true political type. For example, a project can fail to meet all of its mission objectives, but politically-motivated individuals will mostly (perhaps only) care about what they achieved or got out of it for themselves. They will also try to prioritize their own interests ahead of everything else in group settings.

Ambition exists in both types of people, but the politically-motivated are not the kind of people I want in our company or on any team that I am on. And at this point in my life, it doesn't take me long to tell the difference between *mission-oriented* and *politically-oriented* people.

As a case in point: CACI has been serving the U.S. Navy's ordnance community on various jobs since 1968. Ordnance logistics have come a long way, evolving in scope and complexity. Further, our Navy ordnance clients and organizations have changed several times over the years. In this dynamic environment, our drive to understand and fulfill our customers' missions has been key to CACI's work on these projects over the years.

CACI's mission-oriented drive manifests itself through sustained innovation and commitment. Sustained innovation is the ability to identify and implement improvements consistently and continuingly, managed over time. CACI went from early innovations in ordnance information systems in the 1970s to becoming a leader in real-time logistics systems for the Navy today.

Staying at the forefront of technological and process advancements has certainly helped CACI serve its clients well over the years. However, nothing has helped more than CACI's commitment to the mission – the dedication and desire of our employees to achieve more for our clients all the way along.

CACI's Ordnance Information Systems teams were never afraid to take on any ideas the government wanted to try. One Navy project manager, in particular, used to proudly point out how CACI always responded positively to doing whatever he needed done on the job. This reputation is part of what has gotten us this far! It is our "can do" attitude and our willingness to see a difficult job through to a successful conclusion.

That "can do" attitude has been the mainstay of our Navy ordnance project team. It starts with the hiring process. Candidates are evaluated, not just for their technical skills, but also for their attitude and commitment. That enthusiasm shows in their work. Employees say the drive to innovate is contagious. Team members have a zest for the work and enjoy creative input from different people on their team. Another reason for our employees' drive and longevity is their commitment to the war fighter. These shared values have also sustained our employee base on our Ordnance Information Systems contracts, which enjoy remarkably low turnover rates. Not only does CACI retain knowledge and experience, our Navy clients develop business relationships with people they can trust to get the job done right.

Achievement doesn't come without concentrated effort. Ambition creates focus and action. Identifying desired outcomes helps you define targets, set priorities, and allocate resources. It reduces the waste of time, money, and energy. Ambition also makes goals seem more tangible and achievable. Even if you only have a general idea of what you want to achieve, you'll be more likely to try to do it – if you are naturally ambitious.

This is how people seem, at times, to be capable of *doing the impossible*. High ambition early in life is often the mechanism that stimulates great achievement in particular fields. This is true in music, science, mathematics, and great conquests. The early life achievements of Alexander the Great, Wolfgang Amadeus Mozart, Albert Einstein and Napoleon Bonaparte are excellent examples. More contemporary examples include technology giants like Bill Gates, the late Steve Jobs, and Michael Dell. Gates and Jobs were in their early twenties when they each co-founded Microsoft and Apple, respectively. When Dell (of Dell Inc.) was 27, he became the youngest CEO ever to have his company ranked in the Fortune 500.

That attitude influences behavior is a given. Understanding that your attitude is a choice gives you an advantage in whatever you want to achieve. Just ask yourself two simple questions: what do you care about and what do you want to achieve? It's the most direct way of finding out what motivates you.

Of course, you have to first decide on what you want. Yet there's an enormous difference between thinking and talking about something and actually making it happen. Motivation may get you started, but what counts is how you finish.

EXECUTION

The second part of attitude, therefore, is execution. Obviously, you must think through in detail the sequence of actions required to achieve your goals. It's the difference between failure and success. Execution is more than an action plan.

You are guided by the steps to reach your goal. But what actually compels you to take each and every step is your attitude. Specifically, I find two characteristics that are needed to achieve goals: *persistence* and *commitment*.

PERSISTENCE

Some people have a hard time taking action. Instead, they fall into familiar pitfalls, such as incessantly preparing for action or, similarly, never deciding exactly what their goals are going to be. Both of these pitfalls can be fatal. *Persistence is the part of your attitude that reflects an emotional need to get things done.* It's the "fire in your belly" that makes you march relentlessly through the detailed steps and actions necessary to reach your goal. It's avoiding that trap of endless preparation – forever "getting ready." It's refusing to fail. These are the hallmarks of winners.

Did you know the staple of American breakfasts everywhere, Cheerios, almost didn't happen? In 1941, Lester Borchardt, Vice President and Director of Research at General Mills, and his team were trying to invent a machine that created puffed cereal. After spending a considerable amount of time and money without success, Borchardt's boss told them to quit. But Borchardt was confident that they had a good idea. So he – unimaginably – ignored his boss and continued working on the machine. Two months later they were successful and Cheerios was born.[40]

History is full of wonderful stories about persistence and perseverance. At the 1815 Battle of Waterloo in Belgium, an Anglo-Allied army led by the Duke of Wellington in conjunction with Prussian forces under Gebhard von Blücher's command, defeated Napoleon Bonaparte and the Imperial French army. Waterloo marked the end of Napoleon's rule as Emperor of France hence the saying "meeting your Waterloo." All this, despite the fact that Blücher had brought his Prussian army through a long and arduous march across a muddy countryside to the battlefield. There, Blücher's forces delivered a crushing blow to finish the allied victory over Napoleon. Blücher's force was not even expected to reach the field that day.

What always impressed me, and I'm still impressed, was that Blücher was 72 years old at the time of Waterloo, more than twice the age of the troops he was leading.[41]

---

[40] Borchardt worked at General Mills for more than 35 years. According to his daughter, Borchardt ate Cheerios just about every morning of his life until he died at the ripe old age of 99.

[41] Although I never really admired Napoleon, his perseverance and commitment can't be denied. Napoleon's ambition took a young Corsican artilleryman in 1785 and led him to proclaim himself the Emperor of France in 1804. In 2005, I visited the Waterloo battlefield and later I travelled down the Rhine River from Cologne. Along

Now turn back to the year 1869, when Major John Wesley Powell was leading the first recorded expedition down the Colorado River through the Grand Canyon.[42] Along the way, the explorers lost one of their boats and most of their supplies and faced life-threatening rapids. Then three crew members decided to abandon the river and try climbing out of the canyon. Powell wished them well but was determined to go on. After running two more rapids, the expedition reached safe water and completed the journey. The climbers, however, were never found. Persistence has been a driving force in people throughout our history.[43]

Persistence, however, should not be confused with *stubbornness*. Not every plan works and not every goal is attainable. Stubbornness is trying to force the unworkable to work. The word *crazy* comes to mind. As the saying goes, insanity is doing the same thing over and over again and expecting a different result.[44]

In 1972, Bill Gates and Paul Allen started their first company. It was called Traf-o-Data and focused on automated

---

the way, I made a planned stop at Pfalzgraf, at the village of Kaub on the island in the Rhine where Field Marshall Blucher took his 10,000-man force across the river en route to Waterloo in Belgium.

[42] Powell was also the founder and first president of the Cosmos Club of Washington, DC, established in 1878 and dedicated to the advancement of its members in science, literature, and art. Many members of Washington, DC's scientific community met there regularly, and it was the birthplace of kindred organizations such as the National Geographic Society in 1888. I have been a member of the Cosmos Club since 1996.

[43] Over forty years ago, my mother gave me a framed copy of a quotation from Calvin Coolidge, our 30th President, as a birthday gift. It says: "Nothing in the world can take the place of Persistence. Talent will not; nothing is more common than unsuccessful men with talent. Genius will not; unrewarded genius is almost a proverb. Education will not; the world is full of educated derelicts. Persistence and determination alone are omnipotent. The slogan 'Press On' has solved and always will solve the problems of the human race." I've kept it hanging in my office for years and it has always been an inspiration to me. My parents had lots of good advice for me about values and character.

[44] This quotation has been attributed to several people. Among the most popular are Albert Einstein and Benjamin Franklin. It has also been called a Chinese proverb. Another documented citation claims its author as Rita Mae Brown, an American writer, in her 1983 book *Sudden Death.*

car-counting machines. The start-up had minor success, but suffered from hardware challenges and Gates' absence while attending Harvard University, among other things. In 1975, Gates and Allen had given up on Traf-o-Data and handed over the company to a friend who had been helping them with their hardware problems. By 1979, Traf-o-Data ceased operations. Gates and Allen's first business had failed. Giving up on Traf-o-Data, however, gave them the experience and opportunity to start another company called Microsoft.

What's the lesson here? How about the fact that flexibility and the ability to change can be the difference between persistence and futility, success and failure?

COMMITMENT

Execution also means *commitment. Commitment reflects an obligation or intent to see things through to their completion.* On the individual's part, it's dedication. By others, it's the perception of being dependable and reliable.

History is also full of examples of people who exemplify commitment. Rome wasn't built in a day – and neither were the pyramids in Cairo, the stone statues on Easter Island off the coast of South America, or the stone monuments at Stonehenge in England.[45] These were no simple undertakings.

Commitment is more than applying effort and dedicating resources – it is also about committing yourself. For example, in 1776, the signers of the Declaration of Independence pledged to each other their lives, their fortunes, and their sacred honor. They knew exactly what this pledge meant. If independence could not be won, they would be tried and executed as traitors. And indeed, by the end of the Revolutionary War, many of the signers were either dead or had lost everything they had. Some lost their lives, others lost their fortunes. But their sacred honor

---

[45] I have been to the pyramids outside Cairo and stayed at the nearby Menahouse Hotel. I have also been out to Stonehenge, west of London, several times, but I have not yet made it to Easter Island, home of the "long-ears!"

remained steadfast, and America became a free nation. Now that's the ultimate example of commitment.

Alfred Krupp, one of the early leaders of the famous German steel and munitions dynasty, was well-known for his relentless commitment.[46] Krupp built the company by sheer determination. In fact, he was obsessed with building it. Throughout his life Alfred's mission was the continued long-term survival of the company. His vision was for the Krupp *concern* to progress as a dynastic enterprise. He championed the company's horizontal and vertical expansion, especially into steel production, which then led to stainless steel products, cast steel cannons, and iron tires. Krupp also spent much of his time travelling on both sales and R&D trips. He also insisted on bootstrapping (building the company from within), as well as implementing corporate welfare programs to ensure employee loyalty and productivity.

A notorious insomniac, Krupp wrote constantly, including letters, memos, and notes – the congratulatory type as well as the scathing kind – to employees. After all of the employees had gone home and the lights were turned out, Krupp would walk through his factory, inspecting operations and even picking up litter off the floor. For Alfred, leading the company was more than a birth right, it was his raison d'être. Alfred Krupp was the epitome of the *Konzern Herr*. In building an enterprise of any major consequence, the mindset of the Konzern Herr is exactly what it takes. And I have never forgotten this.

---

[46] The legendary Krupp commitment was especially interesting to me after reading William Manchester's *The Arms of Krupp,* the family history. Although all companies have leaders, the Krupps' had the *Konzern Herr.* Manchester defined the term as the owner of the Krupp concern, but it really meant more. It implied a personal obligation to both the day-to-day operations and the long-term sustained viability of the enterprise. I have always had a kindred feeling toward the *Konzern Herr.*

Alfred (1812-1887) is also known for creating the Krupp family estate, Villa Hugel, in Essen, Germany where I once made a visit. When going through it, I thought a lot about the *Konzern Herr* and what made him tick. I could almost feel his presence. The contents of the estate are now gone, but the mansion still houses the corporate and family archives.

Individual commitment to achieving goals is a necessity for accomplishing those goals. In team-based environments, commitment is also essential to achieving common goals. This means many things; doing your share, not letting your colleagues down, and being loyal. At CACI, our operations motto "Quality Client Service and Best Value" (QCS/BV) expresses our commitment to our clients. While we have served some of our clients for more than 25 years, commitment is more than longevity. It's our unrelenting, unwavering commitment to our clients that demonstrates how we do business. It's in our genes; it's in our culture. It's simply part of how we do business.

In the wake of September 11th, a CACI team providing litigation support to the Executive Office of U.S. Attorneys worked around the clock to help prosecute a terrorist-related case. They had to scan over a million pages of evidence for the U.S. Attorneys and the FBI. What was most impressive was that everyone in the group – from document analysts and paralegals to vice presidents, senior vice presidents, and an executive vice president – worked in shifts to get the job done, and done on time.

Persistence and commitment are the traits needed to maintain and sustain action. That's why motivation without execution amounts to nothing.

When it comes to achievement and success, especially when it's about something of consequence and real significance, there is nothing more important than attitude. The belief in one's self and belief in the possibility of making it all happen is extraordinary in its power. And it's also a quality that separates people; the leaders from the followers, as they say. You can take two people with the same IQ, education, and experience, and for some reason, perhaps something in the DNA, one person will have a greater will to prevail, to succeed, and to achieve. These people will find a way to get it done. They'll overcome obstacles and criticism. These are the ones who refuse to fail. They insist on success.

Unfortunately, however, many people would rather play the victim or find excuses. Others hide behind pessimism or can't overcome low self-confidence or low self-esteem. Just remember, those who can't, will have to get out of the way of those who can.

There is an important caveat here. The right attitude put into action can lead to many significant accomplishments. Having this quality is necessary, but not sufficient. Sometimes our optimism leads us to bite off more than we can chew. You have to know the difference between a challenge and what may be too difficult for you at the time.

An observation Herb Karr, one of CACI's founders, first made when he worked in a large research department at the Rand Corporation illustrates this point. There were about 50 professionals in the department, who mostly ranged from very bright to brilliant. Yet somehow, nearly all of these talented people were working on problems that were many times more difficult than they could ever solve. Consequently, their output was nearly zero and almost worthless. On the other hand, if each had undertaken a problem that was within reach, the department's output could have been enormous and useful!

Then there's the example of the Alamo. At the Battle of the Alamo in February and March of 1836, Mexican troops launched a 13-day siege on the Alamo Mission near San Antonio. In what was called the *Texas Revolution*, settlers had driven all Mexican troops out of Mexican Texas. But the Mexican leaders were not going to give up so easily. Approximately 1,500 Mexican troops engaged less than 200 Texas settlers over a fateful two-week period. During that time, Alamo co-commanders James Bowie and William B. Travis and their forces fought off minor skirmishes and two larger attacks. But the third Mexican offensive, a huge effort, was successful. All but two of the Texan defenders were killed, including the famous frontiersman Davy Crockett. Their defiant attitude and courage was not enough to overcome the overwhelming odds. Simply put, in the end, there were just too many Mexicans.[47]

---

[47] The defeat sparked a panic that caused the Texas army of settlers and the new Republic of Texas' government to flee. However, the battle inspired many Texans and other American adventurers to seek revenge. Their battle cry was "Remember the Alamo." In April 1836, the *Texians,* as they were called, defeated the Mexican Army

CHARACTER: The Ultimate Success Factor

In many cases, achieving success is simply a case of mind over matter. You can push through obstacles and overcome challenges. On the other hand, sometimes what you have in mind doesn't matter! The obstacles and challenges are too great, as the tragic Alamo example clearly shows. But even when the right attitude isn't enough to achieve a particular goal, it will still help you become successful over the long haul.

Attitude influences why and how you do what you do. Motivation drives behavior and comes from what's important to us and what we want to achieve. Execution is based on persistence and commitment, and shows our determination to achieve. Most importantly, we have the ability to choose and change our attitude along the way. Our attitudes have a direct effect on how much we are able to do, achieve, and grow. Likewise, our attitudes also influence how others see and treat us. It's amazing how much depends simply on how we think, how we conduct ourselves, and how we act toward others.

There may be more to it than simply a smile and a 'can-do' spirit (although it doesn't hurt), but *attitude is more important than you think.*

---

at the Battle of San Jacinto, ending the revolution. I have visited the Alamo several times, always coming away with the same horrible feeling of being trapped and overwhelmed in that small building

CHAPTER 4

IT'S NOT ALL ABOUT YOU

"No man is an island."
John Donne

For thousands of years, people have looked up and seen an ever-changing sky. The sun, moon, and stars stirred in constant and, sometimes, predictable motion, while the earth stood still. Or so they thought. In the early 16th century, Nicolaus Copernicus, the father of modern astronomy, offered proof that the sun, and not the earth, was the center of our universe.

Copernicus had help. He referenced the findings of ancient Greek astronomers and other scholars from antiquity in his work. Copernicus' theories would be corroborated by Galileo Galilei and Johannes Kepler a century later (with earlier observations by Tycho Brahe).[48]

---

[48] Several ancient Greek astronomers believed that the earth was not stationary, but did not propose the sun as the center of the universe. Galileo's drastic improvements to the newly invented telescope confirmed Copernicus' astronomical observations. Kepler's laws of planetary motion include the finding that the orbit of every planet is an ellipse with the Sun as the focus. The planets' elliptical velocities are proportional to the paths they sweep from the sun.

Kepler's work was based on Tycho Brahe's discoveries. Tycho Brahe was a 16th century Danish astronomer whose last assistant was Kepler. Brahe revolutionized astronomical instrumentation by creating and calibrating instruments, and regularly checking their accuracy. Brahe is also known for the revolutionary process of observing celestial bodies throughout their orbits, by which he was able to identify previously unknown orbital anomalies. Brahe's observations and extensive recordings allowed Kepler to discover that planets had elliptical orbits.

For several decades I have been fascinated by the work of these remarkable men, visiting their homes, work places and final resting places; Copernicus (Warsaw, Poland), Galileo (Florence, Italy) and Brahe (Prague, Czech Republic). Perhaps one day I will visit Kepler's in Regensburg, Germany. Interestingly, Brahe lost the bridge of his nose in a duel with a fellow Danish nobleman while at university in Germany

Without the contributions of those other scientists, how far would have Copernicus' ideas gone?

Because of Copernicus and the others, we know now that the sun doesn't revolve around the earth. With the exception of most kids (and a few grown-ups), we also know that the sun is the only thing the earth revolves around. So why would we think that success is only about ourselves?

Goals, and the means to achieve them, are often egocentric. We can become self-absorbed in the process. It's easy, because the things we can do and control are given the most attention. That success is a solitary endeavor is, however, a myth.

What about individual successes? Consider the sailor who circumnavigates the globe solo, nonstop and unassisted. While they might have been alone on the boat, these 'solo' sailors are supported by a team. The support team will have prepped the sailor and the boat for the trip. They will have plotted the course with the latest navigation tools and will follow the weather for any changes. Directions on how to fix broken equipment are a satellite phone call away.[49]

What about other solo feats? Amelia Earhart was known for her many solo aviation feats and records. But did you know her biggest feat was someone else's idea? Charles Lindbergh's solo flight across the Atlantic in 1927 had made him an American hero and made aviation of popular interest. Amy Phipps Guest, daughter of industrialist Henry Phipps, became interested in being the first woman to fly (or be flown) across the Atlantic. Phipps soon concluded that the trip was too perilous to take herself, but offered to sponsor a project where another, more qualified woman would take the trip. In April 1928, Earhart got a

---

and Brahe wore a prosthetic to hide the damage. The prosthetic was believed to have been silver and gold, but some evidence suggests Brahe also had one made of copper.

[49] Canadian-American writer and adventurer Joshua Slocum is recorded as the first person to have single-handedly circumnavigated the globe. Leaving Boston on April 24, 1895, Slocum took over three years to complete his journey. Not only did Slocum not have modern equipment, he also chose to navigate without a chronometer, relying on dead reckoning instead. Slocum wrote about his voyage in *Sailing Alone Around the World* in 1899.

phone call asking if she would like to fly the Atlantic. Most of the journey would be instrument flying, for which Earhart had no training. So she joined two male pilots as a passenger, also keeping the flight log. In June 1928, Earhart became the first woman to be flown across the Atlantic. In an interview after the flight, Earhart is reported to have said that maybe one day she would try it alone. That day came four years later. In May 1932, with help from her technical advisor (Bernt Balchen), Earhart completed the solo flight across the Atlantic.[50]

Competitive athletes are supported by a crew of coaches, trainers, equipment and medical staff. A Tennessee woman swimming the 981-mile length of the Ohio River in 2010 for women's education causes was assisted by kayakers. A British comic actor who ran the equivalent of 42 marathons in 51 days in 2009 even had a "modest support team, consisting of his tour manager, a sports therapist and an ice-cream van, which dispenses free ice-creams as he goes."[51]

Then there are those successes that would have never happened alone. Who once said, "There is no *I* in team but there is in *win*." That would be basketball legend Michael Jordan. Jordan may have started by himself, shooting hoops as a kid, but he would have never developed into a successful player without a team.

Even legends have to learn this lesson. Jordan's coach at North Carolina, the legendary Dean Smith, once chastised the freshman saying, "Michael, if you can't pass, you can't play." Coach Smith's emphasis on passing the ball was spot on. In 2007, a Brigham Young University study found that the best

---

[50] Earhart disappeared in July 1937 during the last phase of an around the world flight. She is believed to have been lost near Howland Island. It was there that my good friend, RADM Richard Blackburn Black, USNR (Ret.) had been stationed as a young researcher with the job of tracking and contacting Earhart on her leg to the Hawaiian Islands. Black told me about the ill-fated search and rescue efforts he had participated in at the time. I met and knew Black in the 1980s. He died in 1992.

[51] Patrick Barkham, "After 1,100 miles and 52 days, Eddie Izzard has finishing line in sight," *The Guardian*, September 14, 2009, http://www.guardian.co.uk/culture /2009/sep/15/eddie-izzard-charity-run.

predictor of success in the National Basketball Association during a season was the number of assists. Basically, passing the basketball to set up a score was more important for winning than scoring attempts.

We can take two lessons from this. First, while individual skill and effort are important, *teamwork is often a more important factor in winning.* Second, *you don't have to be the star to be a winner.* Success is rarely ever a purely solo achievement. Even the proverbial "self-made man" had help along the way. From asking for advice to picking a business partner, or from working on teams to leading them, your colleagues are an empowering and influential element that greatly increases your chance of success.

PEOPLE ARE AN *ASSET*

It all starts with how you view people. We've all heard the saying, "it's not what you know, but who you know." Certainly, a good network of contacts is always useful. So is having the support of friends, family and associates. The real question is do you view people as an "Asset" or an "asset?" You read that correctly. It's the same word, but has different meanings. People can be *Assets* because of the relationships you form with them. You may share an affinity or a mutual experience, even the same goal. Yet the connection is multi-dimensional, possibly even long-term. (I like to call them *Assets* with a capital A because A also stands for *allies*, which these people are.) Or people can be viewed as "assets"; as circumstantial resources to be used for specific purposes. (I'll put this definition in quotes to denote its dubious nature.) The former is always the better definition. The latter is ingratiating. The difference, however, is not always clear. Sometimes we don't realize which way we're being treated. Other times, intentionally or unintentionally, how we treat others isn't so sincere. And that's not good.

DISTINGUISHING BETWEEN ASSETS

How can we tell the difference? There are several distinctions in how we view and treat people.

The first distinction is *purpose.* Some people are out for themselves, and others are out to achieve something. For example, let's say a benefactor is persuaded to make a sizable donation to a cause or charity. Does the person or the group that solicited the donation express appreciation? Do they follow up with their supporter with news on how their money is being used and what it has helped to accomplish? Or do they simply pat themselves on the back for scoring a big gift and mark their calendar to call the contributor again next year? Relationships have varying durations, closeness, and expectations. However, no one likes to feel like they are being used and then discarded.

The second distinction is *competitiveness.* Competition can be very healthy; a great motivator and incentivizer. What is the motive – is it to outdo your peers or to do the job well? For example, consider a company that operates in a consumer-driven market. To encourage their sales and marketing team, a company holds a contest with extra rewards going to the top sales performers. The goal is to create distinction for their company and their products in the market. What happens, though, when an employee pressures customers or makes promises that are difficult for the company to keep simply because they want to beat out their colleagues? This is destructive competition. It's counterproductive and harms the organization. The person that tries to prove they're better than everyone else frequently comes out looking like a chump instead of a champ.

The third distinction is *integrity.* We're all familiar with the clichés here. "It isn't what you do, but the way that you do it" and "The ends never justify the means." We know that goals can be achieved in many ways. Dishonesty and manipulation may even get you there quicker, and with even better results, but at what cost? No one likes to be associated with a *user*. In fact, it will alienate people who can genuinely help you. Worse yet, it can turn against you and make your goals even harder to achieve. There's nothing that justifies mistreating people.

CHARACTER: The Ultimate Success Factor

Leona Helmsley was already a successful real estate broker when she married multi-millionaire real estate investor Harry Helmsley in 1972. The couple went on to build a multi-billion dollar empire, including the Tudor City apartment complex, the Empire State Building, and several famous hotels in New York City, including the Helmsley Palace. Helmsley had a reputation for being a petulant, rude, and tyrannical boss. Her well-publicized and outrageous behavior earned her the nickname "the Queen of Mean." After her only child, a son, died in 1982, Leona evicted his widow and sued her son's estate. The Helmsleys' hostility and greed caught up with them in 1989 when Leona was convicted of federal tax evasion and other crimes. She served 19 months in prison and two more under house arrest. The Helmsleys' last years were spent in isolation. When Harry died in 1997, Leona's friends reportedly could be counted on one hand. She was estranged from her grandchildren and reportedly left two out of her will completely. In 2007, Leona Helmsley died one of America's wealthiest women, but alone and best remembered for her ruthlessness and humiliating behavior.[52] She's a classic case that proves it's not just *what* you achieve, but *how* you achieve it.

The last distinction is the *outcome*. At the end of an effort, do you feel a sense of pride and accomplishment or was it an opportunity for self-aggrandizement? I used to see this distinction on resumes all the time. A candidate boasts of having boosted sales a significant amount or having written a considerably large or important technical document or software package. I know that it is quite unlikely they did all these great things alone, but they sure want you to think that! This type of behavior happens everywhere and all the time.

---

[52] After prison, Helmsley pursued more charitable endeavors, giving $5 million to help families of New York firefighters after 9/11 and $25 million to New York's Presbyterian Hospital for medical research. Helmsley also left most of her $4 billion estate to the Leona M. and Harry B. Helmsley Charitable Trust. Helmsley was later found mentally unfit when drafting the will and the two omitted grandchildren received sizable amounts from her estate. In the 1980s, I stayed several times at the Helmsley Palace on Madison Ave. while on business in New York.

Take a group project, for example. A charity event raises substantial money for a cause. Organizing the event itself was a considerable effort. At the end, one volunteer boasts that they raised more money, did an endless list of tasks, and made so many sacrifices to make the event a success. Even if their claims were true (they're usually not), who would want to work with this person again? Not all contributions to a group effort will be the same. If self-promotion is more important than the outcome, people will think twice about giving you any "help" the next time.

> "He who wishes to secure the good of others has already secured his own."
>
> Confucius

The idea here of people as an *Asset* is not about how to manipulate people to your advantage. Nor is it about winning friends or influencing people. It is about inclusion and realizing that you are not on your own and that great things almost always have to be achieved with the support of other people.

INCLUDING YOUR *ASSETS*

You can genuinely include people in your path to success in three ways.

The first way is *investment*. We invest time, energy, and consideration into our relationships. Likewise, others invest in you. Of course, people flow in and out of our lives, but that doesn't mean you shouldn't treat others as a long-term commitment. How do you feel when you're treated with a "what can you do for me" or "what have you done for me lately" attitude? You don't feel very good and aren't likely to reciprocate any good will. Interesting, isn't it? The *Golden Rule* always applies.

The second way is *participation*. There's nothing less fruitful than a life lived on one's own and only for oneself. Not only is giving your time and energy to others a gratifying experience, it puts you in touch with other people who have the same values and interests as you. It allows you to cultivate experiences and relationships. There's a reason why they say "the more you give, the more you get!"

The third way is *appreciation*. Just about every person is struggling to find a purpose and path for themselves. Appreciation starts with gratitude for what you have and the opportunities you are given. It also includes admiration for the efforts and successes (and even failures) of the people around you. That's why I'm a big believer in role models. Many people have accomplished great things. I appreciate not just what they've done, but *how* they've done it and what it teaches us.

In my younger days, I was fortunate to have worked with some of the great Navy heroes of World War II. These fine men may have gained a lot of recognition for their military achievements, but it was their values and treatment of others that I remember most. Such role models offer great lessons in how to approach and live life. I hope you have had several quality role models in your life. It's a great experience!

Speaking of role models, let's go back to Michael Jordan. The Chicago Bulls won three consecutive NBA championships in 1991, 1992 and 1993. They were the first team since the Boston Celtics in the 1960s to achieve a "three-peat." In each championship, Jordan won the NBA Finals MVP and the scoring title. In the first two, he won the regular season MVP.

Yet there were 11 other players on the team; 14 if you include the extra players for practice and injury. There were also about 10 coaches and trainers and upwards of 100 staff in the front office. Let's not forget the thousands of fans who supported the team during the 110 games in the regular and post seasons. Jordan may have been the star, but he didn't do it alone. Many people helped and they all were winners.

EMPOWERMENT THROUGH *ASSETS*

Understanding the roles and values of others in your life is essential. So how do you translate this into action? How can it empower you?

EMPATHY

The first step towards empowerment is to know what empathy is all about. As I see it, empathy is the key to all successful relationships, be it family, friendships, teammates, colleagues, employees, leaders, etc. You should always have an awareness, acknowledgement and respect for other people's values, experiences, and opinions. Empathy, however, is an action of understanding. In the simplest terms, it's putting yourself in another person's shoes and seeing things through their eyes. Now empathy isn't necessarily first-hand knowledge of a person's feelings or experiences. Nor does it require sharing the same values or desired outcomes. That's just not always possible or even necessary. What it does mean is being aware of and considering other people's perceptions, motivations, and needs. By helping us connect with our people *Assets* on a personal and meaningful level, empathy can create motivation and opportunity for empowerment.

For example, why do people sometimes agree to be mentors? A big reason is empathy. People have often told me that they mentor others because they personally relate to their mentee and want to help them the way they had been (or wanted to have been) helped when they were in that position. Mentees, on the other hand, look for help in perceiving their challenges and opportunities with the support of people who have already been in similar situations.

Empathy is essential for building trust and establishing a rapport with others. It's a process which requires diligence and thoughtfulness. Through empathy, we also get a better grasp of situations, make better decisions, and improve problem-solving. These are the foundations for empowerment.

Officials in Massachusetts were able to reduce costs associated with the abuse of homeless shelter privileges through empathy. The policy had been to give hotel vouchers to people arriving after the homeless shelters had reached capacity for the night. While the reasoning behind this policy was honorable, the costs for the program skyrocketed. After further investigation, officials realized that people who genuinely wanted shelter were the first to arrive. Those who arrived later often waited for the shelter to fill up so they could get a free hotel room as an overflow condition. So without notice, the policy was changed. Once the shelter had reached capacity, the hotel vouchers would be offered to those who had arrived first at the shelter. This switch weeded out the fraudulent abusers and opened beds for those who actually needed a place to stay. By changing their perspectives to that of the shelters' users – empathy – they were able to resolve several problems.

That's why empathy is an action – you have to try to identify with the other person's interests. That means moving beyond ourselves. On the flip side, empathy also means learning how people perceive us. We will often have to expose ourselves and allow others to be empathetic to us, too. Empathy is essential to seeing people as *Assets* and not as an "asset" to you.

AS AN INDIVIDUAL

Individually, empowerment is about developing your network. You are empowering yourself by connecting with others. Networking is a well-known method for job searches, but it's just as important in other parts of our lives. Alumni networks are a great example. Once thought useful simply for professional networking, university affiliations have become multi-dimensional. Alumni chapters help people moving to a new town and looking for new housing. Alumni chapters also participate in intramural sports and philanthropies, such as softball leagues and food kitchens. Social networking tools have also increased the ability to cultivate interests and relationships. Universities have online communities that allow alumni to connect with each other, for example. Others, like Facebook and LinkedIn, enable people to reconnect with old friends and colleagues, as well as meet new ones. They can also help you get involved in things that interest you. The point of networking is to meet new people, develop relationships and create opportunities with people like you. Do you need to hire someone? Do you want to get a group together to put on an event? The question is, how can you get the best people to work with you and your team? Whether it's for personal or professional reasons, **recruiting is the one thing you must do well to succeed**. Start close to home. Outstanding people that you know personally are your best sources of superstars. Remember, like attracts like.

Never be afraid to engage the best people you can find. Whenever you can, avoid enlisting subordinates. Whatever the business and no matter how clever you may be, if you hire (or draft) sub-par or mediocre people, your destiny will be to fail. On the other hand, if you surround yourself with talented, high-powered people, they'll see to it that you succeed no matter how much of a mess you may make. Your team can also make your life a whole lot easier. At CACI, for example, we look for team players - not individuals who aspire to be the proverbial "one-man band."

Getting the best people is the first part. The second part is getting the right fit; placing the *right people* in the *right job*. Knowing how to put a team together means the difference between success and failure. Herb Karr, CACI's co-founder, said that the trick is figuring out who the *monkeys* are and who the *ducks* are so you don't end up having the monkeys trying to swim in the pond and the ducks trying to swing in the trees.

For example, at CACI I've learned that many technical talents (excellent performers) can be uncomfortable in group settings and prefer a more private environment. Frequently, these fine people simply do not possess the people skills necessary for project management, especially managing other highly talented, technical people. And typically, they don't want to do it either. Technical brilliance is always valuable and always needed throughout the company, and often it's key to our ability to sell lots of good business. However, it's simply a fact that not everyone can be successful in leading these high tech teams. So getting the right people to do the jobs they are really good at doing is critical for success – for everyone's success!

Also, as you put things together, be sure to help everyone assimilate into their new team. In today's market, we don't even have a prayer of being a big winner without lots of synergy and collaboration. That takes a true culture of teamwork, a culture that can pull together resources, concentrate them on opportunities and projects, and orchestrate their application for the most productive results. In this way, remarkably, CACI has become far more than simply the sum of its parts.

One great example of achieving success through teamwork was CACI's Abu Ghraib crisis team. When CACI was implicated in the infamous Abu Ghraib scandal in 2004, I pulled together a small team of high-level CACI executives and employees who were supported by outside help. I looked to CACI veterans and senior pros, like Jody Brown and Ron Schneider. Jody directed the PR and communications front while Ron was our project details and action man on the operational side. Their 24/7 support and commitment are to their everlasting credit.

Also integral to the crisis team were Dr. Jennifer Burkhart and Z. Selin Hur, who provided strategic support and produced over 300 targeted media response letters. Jennifer and Selin maintained a database of brief responses to numerous reoccurring errors and misleading statements in the media. Using a template letter, Jennifer and Selin customized and sent response letters in a timely and efficient manner. This effort made a big impact on setting the record straight!

Greg Bradford, President of CACI's United Kingdom operations which provides marketing solutions and information systems, handled the fallout from CACI's only Abu Ghraib-related business loss; a local government agency which pulled a £90,000 contract. The bigger problem, however, was when a Member of Parliament (MP) wanted the Ministry of Health to suspend their contracts with CACI during the investigations, stating that British taxpayers would not want to support a company accused of torture. With some $1 million in contracts at stake, Greg met with the MP, explained the facts and CACI's efforts, and convinced the MP to drop his demands.[53]

I was also lucky to have Lillian Brannon, my Executive Administrator of 25 years, working behind the scenes. I could always count on her and had total confidence that she would

---

[53] Greg was also instrumental in fighting off corporate raiders in CACI's proxy fight in 1999. He proved his mettle then and I knew he would rise to the occasion the next time CACI faced a challenge.

provide all of the administrative backup and support I needed. From administrative duties to communications and more, I knew that every detail of both the crisis team and the CEO's office would be handled with the greatest of dignity and professionalism.

From outside the company, I turned to longtime legal counsel, Bill Koegel. Ever the quintessential litigator, Bill's determination to prevail in courtroom battles was unmatched. In several litigation situations, I had seen Bill's ability to manage hundreds of details, as well as his thoroughness in preparation and investigation. Most importantly, I knew Bill shared my focus on integrity. He would get to the facts and truth – whether it would be good news or bad.

In the end, it was the tireless contributions of these and many other people that got CACI through its biggest challenge. It was a challenge that no single person could have ever surmounted on their own. Sure, it was my persistence and determination to get the truth out and I led the charge. However, it took many dedicated people to set the distorted record straight. Talk about empowerment! This is how we did it to preserve our good name.

AS A LEADER

Sometimes you work with people one-on-one. Other times, you work together as a group. And at certain times, you are the leader. As a corporate leader for three decades, I've learned that *people are the most important factor*. They are the critical, precious resource because they make *all* the difference. Some leaders give this fact a lot of lip service. They say that people are important and then they behave otherwise. As a leader, you want to empower your organization, your people, and you want to make sure they know it.

A good leader knows that any organization doesn't go far without lots of good people accomplishing lots of good things day after day. They're the ones who create, sell and manage every aspect of your business. So it's surprising how many leaders don't make an effort to recognize or reward their people beyond a paycheck.

Good performers do good work because they take pride in their work. This can't be taught or even bought! Taking pride in what you do is an inherent personality trait. For this reason, we're always looking to recruit capable, conscientious people who come to CACI with this behavioral trait already hard-wired in their make-up. Retaining these people is the next step. This means telling them that they are appreciated, but it also means a financial reward. Herb Karr and I used to say ("kidding on the square"), that we needed to make sure our people knew they were important by "putting our appreciation on the tray."[54]

> "Treat people as adults. Treat them as partners; treat them with dignity; treat them with respect. Treat them – not capital spending and automation – as the primary source of productivity gains."
>
> Tom Peters & Robert Waterman
> *In Search of Excellence*

This means *you have to keep your part of the bargain.* Pay attention to people who make things happen. Make sure you let them know that you appreciate what they do and back up recognition with money. Without it, even the most public appreciation falls flat. Ignoring this part of your responsibility may not kill your operation in the short run. However, I guarantee you that you won't get big results if you don't take time to reward superior performance. In the long run, you'll see an exodus of good people looking for an employer who does appreciate and reward their efforts.

The leader's job is to create an environment of empowerment where good performers are rewarded for pride of accomplishment, for going the extra mile, and for achieving superior results. That's because people respond to challenges,

---

[54] The phrase "kidding on the square" means that you're joking, but at the same time meaning it seriously. Herb and I had both been car hops in our youth, working at root beer stands and nighttime burger and fries drive-ins. We liked to have people thank us and tell us we had done a good job. We would sometimes joke with the customers about getting a tip – "kidding on the square." However, we knew they *really* meant it when they put one big tip on the service tray.

value, praise and appreciation. Leadership isn't about being on top – it's about empowerment.[55]

As a leader, you also have to know how to deal with people who disappoint. It often comes as a surprise to new managers (and to other employees) that poor performers need to be fired. In many organizations, terminating ineffective people isn't customary. Instead, they're pushed to the side so the productive people can work around them.

Termination is not a step to take lightly. We work to give our employees every chance to excel and grow professionally. But sometimes, people just don't perform. Or the employee and the job aren't a good match in the first place. As a leader, you have to recognize this and take action. You won't be able to empower your team if you have poor performers that aren't addressed. Don't put up with poor performance, or others around you will soon be describing your efforts as poor performance as well. Of course, you should make every attempt to turn around the poor performance. If this fails, however, it's better for everyone to have poor performers leave.[56] Unfortunately, many leaders fail in this important role, either because they lack the nerve to act or they lack the people skills to deal with problem employees. Most poor performers know why they're in the hot seat. They may even be relieved to move on to something that is a better fit for them. Of course, some people won't see termination coming. In this case, be honest and professional. Put yourself in their shoes. The circumstances that led to the firing may be infuriating, but taking your anger out on someone will only make the situation worse. It's also totally unacceptable.

Whether working alone, as part of a team, or at the top, there is nothing you do, or want to do, that won't involve

---

[55] If you're still not sure what is meant by the term "empowerment," I suggest you take time to learn what it means. It's *the most important thing* a leader does in dealing with their people.

[56] Poor performers make more than their share of mistakes, which you have to clean up. Poor performers waste your customers' money and the company's money in the process. They are also distracting and counterproductive. Moreover, your good performers don't want them around and can lose motivation if you don't act. Your top people want to be on the "A" Team! And this is where you want them to be too!

someone else. You'll need to ask for help and to help others along the way. Sometimes it's for your personal success. Sometimes it's for a greater goal. Knowing people are an *Asset* and not an "asset" is essential to success. As Mark Twain once put it, "Really great people make you feel that you, too, can become great." That's because *it's not all about you.*

CHAPTER 5

DO AS I SAY AND AS I DO

"Few things are harder to put up with than the annoyance of a good example."

Mark Twain

The Most Admired People of the 20th Century, according to a Gallup/CNN/*USAToday* Poll, included many familiar names, such as Helen Keller (#5), Pope John Paul II (#8), and Henry Ford (#16). Who inspired these historical figures?

For many of them, family members were great influences. Mother Teresa's (#1) was her mother, a devout Catholic who took her children into town to bring food, clothes and money to the poor. John F. Kennedy's (#3) older brother Joe, who helped and protected a shy young Jack, was an early role model. Nelson Mandela's (#14) father and regent (guardian after his father's death) both insisted on furthering Mandela's education, redirecting him from a likely life as a mine worker. Mandela's ideas about African identity and race relations were also strongly shaped by several figures during his studies. During World War II, British Prime Minister Winston Churchill (#10) was such an admirer of the U.S. Marine Corps' courage and valor, that he memorized and sang all three verses of the Marine Corps Hymn to guests from other nations. Martin Luther King Jr. (#2) and Albert Einstein (#4) were great admirers of Mohandas Gandhi (#13).

What about the 21st century? According to the 2010 Junior Achievement Teens and Entrepreneurship survey *Harry Potter* author J.K. Rowling, media giant Oprah Winfrey, and skateboarding legend Tony Hawk are among the most admired by young entrepreneurs for being successful in multiple fields and making a difference in people's lives.[57] Who did these role models look up to?

Writing a book series that yielded a movie and merchandising empire took J.K. Rowling from living on welfare to billionaire status within five years. Rowling's real-life hero is Robert F. Kennedy. Some of Oprah Winfrey's well-known role models include poet Maya Angelou and music icon Tina Turner. However, it was the childhood memory of a group of nuns who brought her family food and gifts one penniless Christmas that inspired her charitable work. Tony Hawk is known as a skate boarding pioneer and for his success in business and philanthropy. In addition to other pioneering skateboarders, American motorcycle daredevil, Evel Knievel, was one of Hawk's influences.

What lesson can we take from these examples? **Even the most admired people looked up to someone else on their path to success.** Most things in life don't come with instructions, but life often comes with examples. Whether it is how to do something, use something or be something, there is usually someone you know (or have heard of, or read about, or even studied) who has tried it before – or something similar to it. People that have been successful and have figured out how to get things done successfully, things of importance and value, are good to know and emulate. They're called role models.

Role models are people whose behaviors are examples to be followed. Typically, role models are associated with children who aspire to be like someone special when they grow up. I think teenagers and young adults are the ones who ought to benefit most from successful (and worthy) role models, including mentors.

---

[57] "In Battle of the Tech Titans, Steve Jobs Most Admired Entrepreneur for Teens, Leaving Facebook's Mark Zuckerberg in the Dust; Junior Achievement Survey Shows Few Teens Esteem Facebook Founder Despite Widespread Use of Social Media," October 6, 2010, http://www.pmewswire.com/news-releases/in-battle-of-thetech-titans-steve-jobs-most-admired-entrepreneur-for-teens-leaving-facebooks-mark-zuckerberg-in-the-dust-104402028.html.

For me, individual role models have been a great way to learn. Sometimes, role models are inspirational. It's the "If they can, so can I" effect. Other times, it's a lesson in character. Their example helps us anticipate the effects of our behavior and the outcomes of our decisions. Role models can also be mentors whose insights and perspectives can be incredibly valuable, especially when facing life-altering decisions. You can ask them for advice or see what other people in your situation chose to do.

> *"There is no one right mentor. There are many right mentors."*
>
> Jack Welch

TYPES OF ROLE MODELS

There are two kinds of role models – famous ones known to everyone and personal ones known only (mostly) to you.

PUBLIC ROLE MODELS

The first type of role model is people in the public eye, typically celebrities, athletes, historical figures and the biggest names in politics, the military and business. They can also be people who have changed the course of history. The constant exposure of these people makes them unavoidable role models, especially for children. Some people become role models by virtue of the positions they hold. The President of the United States, by virtue of the office, is a natural role model, for example.[58] Many people also look up to professional athletes, which is understandable. These are individuals who, through commitment, ambition, and skill, have reached the pinnacle of their sport. The most inspiring role models often include those

---

[58] I have always been a great admirer of George Washington. Of all the people I have known or know about, he is certainly one I would have wanted to have met. As a role model, I think Daniel Webster said it best: "America has furnished to the world the character of Washington. And if our American institutions had done nothing else, that alone would have entitled them to the respect of mankind."

who have overcome poverty, social injustice, or physical challenges.

Many people in the public eye have used their fame for promoting political or social causes, helping charities, and bringing attention to important issues. Of course, all role models are human. No one is perfect and even the best role models make mistakes. Many public figures have been brought down or discredited by their personal behavior.

What professional athlete said, "I think it's an honor to be a role model. If you are given a chance to be a role model, I think you should always take it because you can influence a person's life in a positive light, and that's what I want to do. That's what it's all about." Tiger Woods was considered one of the ultimate role models in professional sports until 2009 when a personal scandal rocked his life, career, and credibility. Certainly, the self-confessed adulterous escapades of golf's superstar make the point.

Even one of the world's most successful people has made mistakes. Take Warren Buffett, for example. Often called the "Oracle of Omaha," Buffett admitted to having done "some dumb things in investments" in 2008. Those mistakes included the acquisition of shares in two Irish banks, as well as the purchase of a lot of Conoco-Phillips Inc. stock when oil and gas prices were nearing peak levels. Energy prices fell dramatically later in 2008. So, no one is perfect, not even Warren Buffett.

Sometimes these mistakes are ones to learn from, while others ruin the role models' credibility completely. When it comes to role models that everyone knows, it may be best to judge them on a case-by-case basis.

For example, there's an often asked question: If you could meet and talk to any three people who have ever lived, who would they be? The first person I would choose would be Jesus of Nazareth. Many people around the world would agree that Jesus made as much of an impact on humanity as anyone who ever lived. My second choice would be George Washington. His impact on mankind also has been far-reaching and enduring. How amazing would it be to listen to the military, political, and personal stories of this man? My third person is still undetermined, because I haven't identified anyone else that fits in the same category with the first two. Everybody's list would be different. In any case, you can learn a lot from a great role model.

Ulysses S. Grant's Vicksburg campaign is considered to be one of the masterpieces of American military history – both strategically and tactically. I was so impressed with it all that I wrote my first-class year paper (like a senior thesis) at the U.S. Naval Academy on the Battle of Vicksburg and Grant's leadership.

Grant has been a role model for me ever since. Grant's focus and determination were extraordinary, even though somewhat obsessive. Over seven months and after several failed attempts to take Vicksburg from the river and by other means, Grant's forces finally captured the town in July 1863 after a lengthy siege. His relentless pursuit of this strategically located town on the Mississippi led to a turning point in the Civil War, as Grant was able to take control of the Mississippi River and isolate the South.

President Abraham Lincoln recognized Grant's tenacity and subsequently appointed Grant as Commanding General of the Union Army. It was under Grant's command that Union forces finally defeated the Confederacy. His resolve left an impression on me that has stuck with me all my life.[59] Grant is truly unique among American military commanders for his

---

[59] I am also a great admirer of Grant's counterpart and opponent, Robert E. Lee. Ironically, both men were graduates of West Point. Abraham Lincoln originally offered Lee command of the Union forces. Lee declined Lincoln's offer. He made the decision instead to follow his allegiance to his home state of Virginia, which chose to secede against Lee's wishes. Lee's surrender to Grant at Appomattox Courthouse on April 9, 1865 marked the end of the Civil War. I have been to the Appomattox Court House and saw where the surrender was signed. I have also been to Vicksburg, Mississippi and visited the views from the town where Union forces established their siege lines, and where the river bends around the town's bluffs. Robert E. Lee is also well known as a brilliant military strategist, but I will always remember him for his courage, honor, dedication to duty, and loyalty to his people of Virginia. He is a special kind of role model for me. I understand the personal loyalties and what they were about, as my great-grandfather, Rufus Houston London, was a Confederate trooper with the 29th Texas Calvary Regiment.

determination, persistence, and unrelenting commitment to success.

Here's a contemporary business example from my own experience. In 1984, I was struggling to pull off a financial turnaround for CACI. I had just become CEO and we were still having serious performance problems. That year, the autobiography of Lee Iacocca was published. The auto industry is nothing like the government contracting industry, but Iacocca was a businessman, like me. Iacocca had risen through the ranks at Ford to become its CEO in the 1970s. I had also risen through the ranks at CACI in the 1970s becoming CEO in 1984. Later, after joining Chrysler, Iacocca engineered a turnaround for the struggling carmaker in 1979. Iacocca was a leader of the first stripe. I read his book carefully and I really liked his way of thinking and talking about the business world. He wanted to deal with people who were "street smart" and had "fire in their belly". Iacocca looked for aggressive, ambitious, and experienced people who wanted to win and win big. His exploits and successes at Chrysler provided a *role model* for me! (I met Lee Iacocca in 1985 at a fundraising luncheon in Washington, DC where he spearheaded President Reagan's overhaul of the Statue of Liberty. I thanked him for his comments).

PERSONAL ROLE MODELS

While well-known role models can be useful, I recommend reaching out to personal role models known to you. You've no doubt met people who have been inspirational or helpful to you in one way or another. This could be a friend who overcame major personal challenges, a teacher who believed in you, a coach who challenged you, or a long-term mentor. On the flip side, you have also likely known certain friends, family members, or authority figures who have disappointed you.

Role models can also be for a specific situation or a period of time. You may have had an academic mentor in school, yet a different one in your professional career. You can look to someone else as an example to help you through a crisis and another who is a life-long inspiration. In any case, you often need look no further than your own life for role models. I guarantee *you already know someone who can be an inspiration to you.*

The most influential role models for me were a certain group of men that were leaders in the Navy in the late 1960s. These were senior officers with senior positions when I started my naval career and who were all veterans of the Second World War. These Admirals, Vice Admirals and Rear Admirals all had a tremendous impact on me because they were some of the finest people that I have ever met. They were consummate professionals. They were men who had been Navy pilots flying planes off of aircraft carriers, engaging in combat over the Pacific against the Japanese. They were true heroes of the Navy's submarine war in the Pacific, with remarkable combat experiences. They were all dignified people, and real gentlemen who treated everyone with genuine respect. It was a wonderful experience to be around them.[60]

As a young Navy officer, I once worked for Admiral J.D. "Jack" Arnold when he was Vice Chief of Naval Material. My Admiral was a real leader and a true hero. He was a Navy pilot

---

[60] Three great men of that era immediately come to mind. ADM Ignatius "Pete" Galantin was a World War II hero that I had the privilege of knowing while I was at Naval Material Command, which he led from 1965 to 1970. He was succeeded by my boss, ADM Jack Arnold. RADM Eugene "Gene" Fluckey was also a World War II hero and a Medal of Honor recipient. I first learned about Gene Fluckey when he was a department head at the Naval Academy while I was a Midshipman. He was also a good friend of my boss, Jack Arnold and submariner Pete Galantin. Gene was a legendary submarine skipper in the Pacific, sinking plenty of Japanese ships. His nickname was the "Galloping Ghost of the China Coast." I met him later in life through Boy Scouts support programs. We became good friends in the 1990s. We also had close ties through relatives who served during the Civil War.

Although I hadn't known Everett Alvarez before he was a prisoner of war in Hanoi, I did meet him in the early 1980s while I was in the Navy Reserve. We became close friends beginning in 2003, when the 30th anniversary of the American POW releases was being remembered and celebrated. CACI assisted with one of these "30 Years After" celebrations. Ev Alvarez was a prisoner of war for over eight years in North Vietnam's infamous Hanoi Hilton complex. He was the first captured and second longest held POW.

Each of these men held values that I learned about and appreciated, including courage, leadership, decisiveness, and commitment. I am both proud and privileged to have known each of them.

stationed at Pearl Harbor on December 7, 1941. He was the only Naval Aviator that day credited with a "kill," while on the ground, for shooting down an enemy plane with a BAR (Browning Automatic Rifle) during a strafing attack. Admiral Jack Arnold went on to lead Carrier Air Group Two flying "Hellcats" from the USS *Hornet* in June 1944 in aerial combat during the decisive Battle of the Philippine Sea.

Jack Arnold was certainly a hero. He set an example as a leader who always gave his best and expected everyone else to give their best, too.

After World War II, Admiral Arnold became the Navy's chief aeronautical engineering duty officer (AEDO). Since I had become a member of that specialty engineering community, I was selected to work as his aide for two years during the height of the Vietnam War. Admiral Arnold would hold regular briefings with officers from various departments on war matters. He expected each officer to be fully prepared at each meeting. If an officer's brief was incomplete, Admiral Arnold would stop the officer and move on to the next briefer. He would do the same thing if he asked you a question that you couldn't answer because you were unprepared. Admiral Arnold expected each briefing officer to be ready and without excuses. He would never humiliate anyone and was professional about his criticism, but each officer – as well as others in that briefing room – knew never to be unprepared.

Jack Arnold was a distinguished man who's military and aeronautical engineering achievements garnered him enormous respect. Everyone who worked for him knew they had to meet his expectations. They were proud to be a part of his team.

Jack also played a part in connecting me with another Navy great who would become a colleague as well as a role model. Admiral Thomas H. Moorer was the two-term Chairman of the Joint Chiefs of Staff during the Vietnam War and with the Nixon Administration until 1974. Before then he had been a two-term Chief of Naval Operations. He was also a veteran of Pearl Harbor and a hero of the Pacific War. He was the quintessential mission-oriented person. Moorer was certainly politically savvy, but it was his unrelenting focus on the Navy's and country's goals that made him someone in whom people believed. Moorer was one of the best known and highly respected men in the Navy. His fine reputation was one reason I put him on a short list of people to fill a vacancy on our Board of Directors.

Nearly all of the interviews for CACI's Board of Directors took place at CACI headquarters. However, in 1988 while trying to interest Tom in our board, I traveled to his office at the Center for Strategic and International Studies on K St. in Washington, DC for the first meeting. This was the policy think tank that David M. Abshire and Admiral Arleigh Burke had founded in 1962. Despite the setting, we quickly hit it off. Not only did we share the common bond of the U.S. Navy, but Tom was also familiar with the type of large-scale Automatic Data Processing/Management Information Systems work CACI performed. Later meetings between Tom and CACI also went well. Yet I'm certain that one reason Tom decided to join our Board was because he knew I had worked for Jack Arnold. Tom knew Jack from their Naval Academy days and the war in the Pacific. I must have gotten an "up check" from Jack, or Tom would have never joined up with us.

Tom served six years on our Board of Directors, from 1988 to 1993. He was a tremendous resource for me during the early 1990s and in CACI's battles for control of the company in proxy contests and in fighting the outrageous class action lawsuits filed by the corporate "raiders."[61] Tom taught me the value of determination and refusing to give in. It was something to see someone in action who was genuinely committed. You wanted to be on his side.

When Tom Moorer left CACI's Board, he gave me a signed photograph of him as JCS Chairman. It reads, "To my friend, Jack London. Top Gun in computer science, business, and legal

---

[61] One of the class action lawsuits against us at the time was filed by the New York law firm of Milberg Weiss. They were notorious for the filing of class action lawsuits – "strike suits" – against corporate boards of directors, making millions of dollars through their intimidation, threats and extortionist-styled litigation strategies and methods. But apparently they believed in double standards. Melvyn Weiss of the firm was convicted in 2008 for fraud and perjury, and sentenced to 18-33 months in prison and home confinement.

combat. With appreciation, Tom Moorer." He even exudes confidence in the photo. You can understand why it's one of my prized possessions.[62]

BEING A ROLE MODEL

Having good examples to follow can be a constructive way to grow. But just as we look up to others, chances are there is someone who looks up to you. It could be someone, like a colleague, who is trying to benchmark their performance. Perhaps, it's an employee who respects your leadership style. Maybe it's a friend or family member who has simply always admired you. Mentors and role models should be important in your life. Pick a good one and be a good one. Someone once told me that to be a good admiral you had to know how to be a good sailor. I believe it!

As a corporate executive, I know I set an example by virtue of my position. In my position I set examples, whether I mean to or not. I do make a point of trying to set a good example in both public engagements and personal dealings. I often have had opportunities to pass along what I have learned.

Upon becoming CEO in 1984, Herb recommended I read three books: *The Prince* by Niccolo Machiavelli, *The Peter Principle* by Laurence J. Peter and Raymond Hull, and *Parkinson's Law* by C. Northcote Parkinson. The first is a classic treatise on 16th century Italian court politics with astute observations on acquiring and using (political) power. The other two were a little newer (1969 and 1957, respectively). Both were humorous, yet insightful examinations of organizational behavior. Herb felt the books would help prepare me for the challenges of the top job. He was right. In fact, the lessons from

---

[62] Tom Moorer passed away in 2004. In his funeral program, I was surprised to see CACI's Board of Directors listed among his affiliations. Mrs. Moorer told me later that Tom had been very proud of CACI and having worked with us. He believed there was a real need for competent companies like CACI in the defense computer software and systems field. In 2007, we decided to name CACI's Boardroom after him. The "Admiral Thomas H. Moorer Board Room" was dedicated that spring at a luncheon and ribbon cutting ceremony attended by the Admiral's family and CACI executives.

these books were so useful, that when I passed the CEO baton to Paul Cofoni in 2007, I gave him the same reading list.[63]

When you are a leader, whether you are aware of it or not, others will watch what you say and do and emulate your behavior. These are likely to be the people with whom you spend the most time. Your example will also communicate to others how you will treat them – and how you expect to be treated. Therefore, another benefit of being character-driven is having the same kind of people be attracted to you and your style.

This has been a leading principle in our hiring philosophy at CACI. One of our three management manuals is called *How to Hire Heroes the CACI Way*. Heroes are the people we enjoy working for and with every day. This helps maintain high employee morale and retention rates. Heroes also bring innovation and knowledge to the way we do business at CACI. With heroes on board, we can continue to deliver "Quality Client Service and Best Value" (one of our mottos at CACI), and build business relationships based on honesty, integrity, and mutual respect for each other.

For example, one of our hiring rules of thumb is not being afraid to hire someone better or smarter than we are. It's how we attract the very best people, achieve our strategic goals and

---

[63] The lessons in *The Prince* are subtle and varied. The two I like best are about avoiding mercenaries and the risks in attempting coups. The reader can reflect upon how these examples relate to corporate America.

The Peter Principle claims that "in a hierarchy every employee tends to rise to his [or her] level of incompetence." People are promoted so long as they work competently, but eventually they are promoted to a position beyond their ability (to their "level of incompetence"). And it's where they remain, being unable to earn further promotions, yet not fulfilling the needs of their current position either.

In *Parkinson's Law,* the central thesis is that work expands so as to fill the time available for its completion. Basically, two people can have the same task. The person with all day to do it will take all day to do it. The person with limited time will complete the task in that lesser time frame. The latter person tends to be the more assertive and busier, and will always want more to do. I have always tried to find and hire the latter.

When Herb passed these books on to me, it was to reach my own conclusions and relate my experiences to the lessons in each one. He never told me what they were about or why he thought they were important. When I recommended the books to Paul Cofoni, I kept with tradition, but I also shared my perspectives about each book.

provide client satisfaction. It also takes courage and self-confidence to hire people with more skills, experience or background than you have. I have this concept in mind every time I hire someone to work for me. I want them to bring something of value to the company that I don't already have! For me, value-add is a big deal.

Role models and mentors are informative and insightful resources to help you learn and grow – both as a person and as a professional. You may be that resource for someone else. So set a good example! That way you can genuinely proclaim: *do as I say and as I do!*

BLUEPRINT: Vision

Strength of character is essential, but it's only the start. Success is an active pursuit, never passive. Vision sets success in motion – it creates momentum, defines what you want to achieve, identifies opportunities to succeed and enables you to distinguish yourself.

More than sensing with the eyes, vision is insight and perception – the ability to anticipate and plan the future, to see what others don't see (from minor improvements to major opportunities), and to discover where and how you can make your mark.

Your character dictates what you envision and how you seek to realize it. Scoundrels, people with immoral character, can also have a strong vision. However, it is the vision of our world's heroes that has inspired us – and inspires us today – to also succeed. In fact, history is full of examples of bad characters who have successfully executed their vision.

What is your vision?

CHAPTER 6

BE A "PRACTICAL VISIONARY"

"Keep your eyes on the stars and your feet on the ground."
Franklin D. Roosevelt

What's next? It's a question we ask ourselves daily. What's next on my "to do" list?

What's the next step in my career? What are the next big opportunities in my industry? What are the next personal challenges I need to address? When making a decision or trying to predict something, we all focus on the *what's next* question.

I wish I could say that I've had a crystal ball on top of my desk all these years. Trying to figure out what comes next is never easy. In fact, it can take great effort.

As a young man, I based my choices on what I liked or what interested me, and then looked at what my options would be as a result. A prime example was my decision to join the Navy. During Christmas break of my junior year in high school (1954), I met the brother of my good friend Perry Wooten.[64] He was in his junior year (his *second class* year) at the U.S. Naval Academy (graduating with the Class of 1956).

The year before, our family visited Annapolis, Maryland. It was the first time I saw the Naval Academy, and it piqued my interest. And when Perry's brother told us about his experience, the Academy sounded like the place for me.

Of course, going to the Naval Academy wasn't that simple. In 1953, I had a vision of what a career in the Navy would be like.

---

[64] Perry's brother was Carl Bramlett Wooten, Jr. from Oklahoma City, Oklahoma and in the U.S. Naval Academy class of 1956. Some 58 years later, Perry Wooten and I now both serve with the Navy Memorial Foundation in Washington, DC. I am on the Board of Directors and Perry is with the Trustees.

To make that vision a reality, I had to apply, secure a nomination and prepare for college boards (the equivalents of today's SATs). I also knew that I had to find a way to get a scholarship for college, since my parents did not have the money to put me through a big name school. I didn't have my own resources to draw from either. But I was motivated and threw myself into the pursuit. In case it didn't work out, however, I made back-up plans and had firm acceptances for the Navy Reserve Officer Training Corps (NROTC) programs at both Princeton University and the University of Oklahoma.

Being a *practical visionary* means knowing what you are capable of now and what you may be capable of in the future. It's about what you can put together today that will get you to where you want to be (or think you want to be) in the future. It's also recognizing if, when and how changes need to be made. Being a *practical visionary* means using common sense, but at the same time being confident about what you see in your future and what you are going to do to make it happen.

We've all heard such advice: *Think before you speak. Look before you leap. If in doubt, don't.* And yet people often act otherwise. A colleague told me that she saw her apartment's front desk receptionist step out of a new SUV, one she was considering buying. She complimented the receptionist on the car, mentioned that she had been looking at the same model, and asked the receptionist if she had got a good deal on it. The receptionist responded, "I don't know. I paid the price on the tag."

This lapse in judgment is not limited, of course, to buying cars. We see it all the time on a serious scale. In business, we often hear about companies hiring a big name executive, acquiring a company, or selling a product line, and wondering later *what in the world were they thinking?*

We also hear of examples that make no sense at all. Did you hear about the car company that bought a large tech firm and an airplane manufacturer? No, this isn't a set up for a joke. In the mid-1980s, General Motors bought, in rapid sequence, information technology firm EDS, Hughes Aircraft and other small technology companies in hopes of creating the high-tech car company of the 21st century. That certainly was some vision, but it was not the least bit practical. After a decade of problems and missteps, GM spun off EDS in 1996 and sold Hughes' assets to Raytheon in 1997. This deal was put together by *impractical* visionaries!

We all make mistakes and misjudgments. Yet it seems hard to believe that organizations that employ highly skilled and accomplished professionals and consultants, who have available the latest research and technologies, can make such moves.

Being a *practical visionary* isn't so easy.

Whether it's personal, professional, or organizational, a *practical visionary* may see a world of opportunities, but stops to recognize which ones are real and worthwhile, and which ones to pass up. It's the combination of enthusiasm and skepticism.

I learned what being a *practical visionary* meant when I began to work with Herb Karr, the CACI co-founder and first President. I first met him shortly after joining the company. Herb was a fascinating man, known for his hard-headed practicality. And yet he was truly eccentric. Herb's favorite holiday was Halloween. It was the only time he would decorate his office. Every Halloween, Herb would dig into a supply closet and pull out a gorilla suit, which he would wear all day. I appreciated Herb's creativity and penchant for innovation and change, but it was Herb's street-sense and realistic approach to business that influenced me most. It was evident in how he looked at proprietary software development projects.

"It's easy to see, hard to foresee."

Benjamin Franklin

Herb knew software and had extensive experience with the evolution of *Simscript,* a simulation and modeling software language on which CACI was started. Herb used to say that people who developed software were never finished, that there was always a little more to be done. After you had tinkered with it, spiced it up and grilled it, Herb derisively said you had to think of software products like you think of dog food. There's only one way to test dog food – put it on the floor and see if the dogs will eat it. He thought that the same was true with

93

commercial software products. Put it out there and see if someone will try it and use it. If a customer is interested enough to seriously ask what it's about, then you just may have something. By putting out this trial or *beta* version, Herb wanted the users – the potential market – to say what they liked and which changes they wanted to see.

PRACTICAL VISION IN PRACTICE

You can put the concept of a practical visionary into action by learning the past, watching the present, and creating the future – combining knowledge, awareness, and foresight. Obviously without the proverbial crystal ball, doing this is not as easy as it sounds. You still need a way to look into the future.

My process for answering the *what's next* question is my version of forecasting. It's *projecting* the future, not *predicting* the future. You take the information available to you, then project it to create an idea of what might happen in the future. This is not technical or analytical forecasting that's all about number-crunching, game theory, or industry reports, although those tools can be valuable. It's a decision-making framework that can be adapted to various scenarios. As I read in *The Peter Principle,* it's an effort to "Calculate the unknown." For example, I am big on trying to read the "trend lines".

In the late 1960s, I attended a two-day seminar in Philadelphia given by Herman Kahn, founder of the Hudson Institute. Kahn came to be known as a premiere futurist and theorist who predicted the rise of Japan as a world power, and was rumored to be one of the inspirations for Dr. Strangelove from Stanley Kubrick's film. In that session, Kahn spoke about issues he foresaw with oil supplies, nuclear weapons and energy, Russia, China, Japan, and even world famine. He was mostly right about everything he said during that brief seminar. Why was he so accurate?

Kahn had developed a concept and methods for reading and projecting trends. As the pioneer of scenario planning (or forecasting), Kahn used a combination of examining long-term trends, determining the causes of these trends, and then comparing scenarios where individual action could make a difference. While forecasting is as much art as science, it's a way of differentiating between what's possible and what's probable. In fact, many businesses and government organizations do scenario planning.

Trend analysis is one of the most valuable lessons I ever learned. The big take-away for me from the Herman Kahn experience was that you could create a framework without hard data that still gives you insights on problem-solving and developing solutions. If you have hard projection data, you can lean into the analysis of likelihoods. For my purposes, though, creating several realistic scenarios and then analyzing what to expect or how to react usually gives me enough insight to make a business decision.

In 1984, I read the book *Megatrends* by John Naisbitt. *Megatrends* reinforced my belief in trend analysis. Using content analysis and other methods, Naisbitt accurately forecasted the inevitable transition to an information economy, which in 1982, was difficult for many to imagine. Email was still a decade away and manufacturing was still central to the U.S. economy. This trend would be accompanied by a change from representative to participatory democracy, the rise of informal networks over hierarchies, and the move towards a global economy. *Megatrends* convinced me that forecasting was not a science, but at best a scientific process that could be useful. Yet Naisbitt also noted: "Trends tell you the direction the country is moving in. The decisions are up to you."

JACK'S FORECASTS

The first step for me in forecasting is *recognizing that the trend lines can be meaningfully read*. I like to think of it as peering into my crystal ball; trying intently to read the future. Whether I have more variables than information, I know that I can gain some insight. This also means I have to work at it. Developing the framework and getting answers takes time and effort. The bigger the question, the bigger the effort.

The second step in my process is *creating checklists.* These are not *to do* lists, but deal with the signs or the questions that may predict direction or establish trends. For example, when I was CEO of CACI, after every presidential election, I tried to identify indicators that were important to the company and our industry. One key indicator was always the President's choice of Secretary of Defense. As a government contractor in the national security arena, CACI is strongly influenced by changes in regulations, policies, and senior executive leadership in the government. The choice of Secretary of Defense is potentially one of the most impactful in our business. One candidate may be reform-oriented, like Robert Gates. Another may be more traditional, like Donald Rumsfeld. By examining a candidate's background along with other indicators, I could develop a fairly accurate picture of the likely changes and opportunities for our company.

"The best way to predict your future is to create it."

Stephen Covey

Then there are events that could have never been predicted. One example is the attacks of September 11, 2001. This event impacted individuals and organizations alike on many levels. There may have been intelligence information about the potential of an al Qaeda terrorist attack on the United States, but that is not the same thing as predicting suicide hijackings of airplanes that were flown into the World Trade Center buildings in New York, the Pentagon in Washington, DC, or a Pennsylvania field.

The third step is to *step out the door,* get out and about, and participate in the world. Technology has made research, networking and exchange easy and convenient; however, the most important and effective learning and sharing can't be done in front of a computer. Job hunting? Professional networking websites are effective tools, but using them is not the same as attending networking events and meeting people face to face. A white paper downloaded from a leading think tank's website may be informative, but not as much as talking with a noted expert at a conference. Some market research can be done online, but it's not as useful as personally talking to your customers.

The final step is to *get advice or input from experts*. As CEO, and even now as Executive Chairman, I've regularly engaged advisory groups or specialist consultants. The most obvious set of advisors pertains to CACI's Board of Directors. Three fellow CACI board members, in particular, have been my sounding board. They have been with me for a very long time. Warren Phillips, an international businessman and former university professor of political science, is the political savvy one and our governance advisor. Charlie Revoile, CACI's former General Counsel, is the corporate legal mind, business and litigation advisor. And when it came to checks and balances, and risk analysis, I looked to Richard Leatherwood, a former transportation and utilities executive, who retired from our board in 2013. I value their input, advice, and counsel. It seems wisdom comes from the experience we gain from difficult times. These men have shared many of these times with me.

There are also experts and professionals with experience and valuable insights into our market. At an earlier time, I would sometimes confer with General Jack Keane, USA (Ret.), a former Vice Chief of Staff of the United States Army. After retiring from the Army, he started his own consulting firm and became a national and military security analyst for a major television network. He was someone whose advice about national security affairs was important to have.[65]

In the late 1990s, when I decided to move the company into the Intel (intelligence community) market, I leaned heavily on a number of freelance consultants that had experience in the Intel-related technology and communications markets, and in the U.S. government. Lieutenant General Jim Williams, USA (Ret.) had been director of the Defense Intelligence Agency (DIA) in the early 1980s. He gave me the proverbial "U.S. Government

---

[65] As a member of the Defense Policy Board Advisory Committee, Jack was also an advisor on Iraq. In 2007, he and Fred Kagan developed and presented to the White House a policy position that became the strategy for the surge in Iraq beginning in 2007.

Intelligence Community 101" course. I had met him in the late 80s through Lee Bryan, who was working for me at the time as my Technical Director. (The vogue term in today's jargon would be "Chief Technology Officer.") Lee was a U.S. Naval Academy Class of '59 classmate and a crack technologist of the first stripe. Besides Jim Williams, Dr. Anthony "Tony" Tether also brought his experience and advice to me in the late 1990s. Tony was later appointed Director of the Defense Advanced Research Projects Agency (DARPA) during the George W. Bush administration. There were other colleagues that shared general information about the market, including long-time friend Tony Spadaro, who had a long career serving the Intel community.

With my decision to acquire Questech Inc., an intelligence and engineering-focused company, CACI moved seriously into the Intel contract market. Questech brought about $90 million in annual sales to the CACI portfolio, but more importantly, it brought serious business contracts with the National Security Agency (NSA), the National Reconnaissance Office (NRO), and the Army's communications and systems engineering community at Ft. Monmouth, New Jersey, the home of the Signal Corps. In 1998, this was all we needed to get going. The rest is history as CACI has become a major contractor participant in the U.S. government's Intel community spanning the past 15 years.

When it comes to forecasting, there are a couple of points to remember.

First, *forecasting is a guidance tool*. It can help develop strategies, but not tactics, the day-to-day part. I make this distinction because I often hear the two terms – strategy and tactics – being used interchangeably when they shouldn't be. When I served as an instructor at the Naval Academy in 1968, I taught a course on Naval Strategy. I emphasized the difference between military strategy and military tactics. I presented it to my midshipmen students in simple terms so they would never forget. I taught them that *military strategy* is about determining your adversaries' geopolitical positioning, capabilities, alliances, assets and weapons, and developing your plan to cope with and respond to or counter them. *Tactics*, I emphasized, boils down to finding the enemy before he finds you and putting ordnance on him before he puts it on you. How does all this translate outside the military? Business strategy deals with the big picture situation, like the economic outlook for your industry, market or commercial sector, as well as your competitors. Tactics deal with operational, circumstantial situations; your business plan for daily or short-term activities. Forecasting and reading the trend lines help shape and define the big picture. This helps identify the market trends and business course or direction you may want to take.

The second point is to *trust your gut instincts*. Gut instincts or intuition are not random, temporary emotions. They are reactions to a situation based on your previous experiences. You have your own knowledge and experience from which to draw. The best advice is often that which you have for yourself. Looking back, I would say that my instincts have served as a very good advisor to me! I've made forecasting part of my personality.

Regardless of whether you are a student, mid-career professional, CEO of a large company or a small business entrepreneur, you need to figure out *what comes next*. That question is never an obstacle, but an opportunity. *So be a practical visionary!*

CHAPTER 7

CHANGE HAPPENS

"Change is inevitable – except from a vending machine."
Robert C. Gallagher [66]

After 20 years, I'm still in awe of the amazing view from my office. On the horizon looking east, I can see the Maryland suburbs of Washington, DC. Closer in the city itself, there's American University, the Washington National Cathedral, and the Shrine of the National Basilica. Even closer are the Lincoln Memorial, Washington Monument and Capitol building all in a row. The Thomas Jefferson Memorial and the Kennedy Center landmark are also in view. In between Washington, the Potomac River, and my office is a panorama of the northern neighborhoods of Arlington, Virginia.

Yet there's something else that catches my eye when I look out the window – construction cranes. In 1991, CACI moved its headquarters to its current location in the Ballston neighborhood of Arlington. Since then, the landscape has changed dramatically. Only two buildings remain at the intersection where CACI stands from when we moved here. The old, low, office buildings have been replaced by stunning new high rise apartments and offices. Down the block are two new buildings where a car dealership and chain store used to stand. In its place are new science and technology facilities for government agencies and a regional university. The high school down the street was recently renovated into a state of the art educational facility. My grandchildren will eventually go there.

---

[66] Gallagher is the retired Chairman, President and CEO of Associated Banc-Corp. He is the Lead Director of Integrys Energy Group, a holding company focused on delivering energy in the U.S. and Canada. Both are multibillion dollar organizations.

CHARACTER: The Ultimate Success Factor

Apart from family photos and career memorabilia, the inside of my office hasn't changed all that much over the years. However, I wouldn't have kept that office for two decades had I not been able to deal with change. In an era where the average tenure of a CEO is about 36 months, I led CACI in that position for 23 years.[67] In that time, I saw five presidential administrations, the meteoric rise of the IT industry, and the transformation of government contracting. CACI also changed during that time. In 1990, we had 2,300 employees and $150 million in revenue. By 2013, we employed about 15,000 people and posted close to $3.8 billion in revenue. During this time, we acquired 59 companies, expanded our technical services, and spread out to 120 offices worldwide.

Benjamin Franklin may have quipped that, "The only things *certain* in life are death and taxes," but I believe the only *constant* in life is change. Some changes we initiate ourselves. Others are forced upon us. Some simply happen without us noticing. Changes can either be positive or negative. The reality is that success is impossible without embracing change. Charles Darwin said that it's not the strongest or most intelligent of the species that survives, but the one that is the most adaptable to change. Of course, in our business we are interested in more than just *surviving*. We want to *thrive*!

Success is a long-term effort. It depends on relationships, opportunities, resources, and circumstances; none of which are ever static. We deal with change in different ways. Being flexible and open-minded definitely helps. Being scared of or intimidated by change doesn't. On the other hand, it's not about being a consummate risk-taker, either. *Change for change's sake* isn't necessarily a good thing. And not all change is good. In fact, some change can be fatal! Yet failing to change or adapt when

---

[67] BP CEO Tony Hayward's tenure would only last 41 months as a result of the Gulf oil spill. Don Thompson, the current CEO of McDonalds, has been in that position since July 2012 (almost 1 year), after 23 years with the company. Although his career with the company has spanned nearly 20 years, Coca Cola CEO, Muhtar Kent, has had the top job since July 2008 (five years). (As of May 2013)

necessary can also be fatal. The point is that change happens, so **make change happen for you**.

By this, I don't mean manipulation either. I'm talking about taking advantage of opportunities, but not taking unethical or illegal advantage of people or circumstances. Scheming and calculating to deceive will only get you so far before it all blows up in your face. You only need to look at the front page news for daily reminders of this flawed way of doing things.

I also don't mean *all* types of change. Most changes don't affect us, and not every change is positive or worth our effort. There are an infinite number of possible things you could be doing. No matter how hard you try, you can only do a few of them effectively. The choice is largely up to you, so choose wisely. Knowing what to do and what *not* to do greatly influences how effective you are. As a shrewd observer once said, "Few things matter very much; most things don't matter at all." Or, as Herb Karr and I used to say, *Don't do most things!*

Realistically, only a handful of changes matter to you. A variety of changes compete for your attention, time and resources. To be successful, you must select and prioritize the changes that offer the most value and concentrate on those prime few. Otherwise, you'll spread yourself and your resources far too thin or, worse yet, come up empty.

THREE WAYS TO MAKE CHANGE HAPPEN

You can make change happen for you in three ways: anticipate, participate and innovate. These three methods merit some explanation.

ANTICIPATE

Anticipate means seeing the change coming. No fortune teller can actually predict things to come. Nor can you put much stock into proclamations, like "I've seen the future, and it is (insert your prediction)."[68] (In Chapter 6, I discussed my approach to looking for trends and developing forecasts.)

What we do have is insight. Through our circumstances, we may even have a special view of things. Or through our experiences, we can perceive things to our benefit. Again, we all possess this capability. Yet few of us tap into its potential.

At CACI, we've had to anticipate changes in our industry. In the early 1990s, we could foresee a networked world. This new world pushed us to expand from a software and systems developer to a systems integrator and network solutions provider. We made this move quickly and successfully, broadening our business offerings considerably.

Perhaps you can anticipate changes in your industry? Not too long ago, if you were in the market for a TV, computer, or other electronic item, you could shop for the best deal at Best Buy, CompUSA, Circuit City or Tweeter. Today only Best Buy remains because they anticipated the changes in their market. As technology grew more complicated, many consumers needed help once they got their purchases home. So in 2003, Best Buy acquired Geek Squad, a small but effective tech support company that made house calls. Best Buy then added in-store Geek Squad centers and support services as the company added new products, like those for home theaters, gaming, and GPS units. Through Geek Squad, Best Buy boosted customer satisfaction and return business long after point-of-sale. Their competitors paid the price for lack of anticipation.

How do you watch movies at home? In September 2010, a month before it 25th anniversary, video-rental chain Blockbuster filed for Chapter 11 bankruptcy protection. Once the leader in home entertainment, Blockbuster lost ground to Netflix, Redbox, and other companies that provided movies via subscription and on-demand services. Blockbuster failed to recognize the changes

---

[68] The saying has been used with many variations, but derives from American journalist Lincoln Steffens. After a visit to the Soviet Union in 1921, he is reported to have (naively) said, "I have seen the future, and it works." In this case, he was as wrong as a person can possibly be! Communism is truly a failed concept of social and economic order.

in consumers' movie-watching habits, specifically the convenience of not having to go to a store to rent movies. In an effort to stay competitive, the company ended late fees and started its own online, on-demand and kiosk services, but it was too little too late.

Once second to Blockbuster in the movie rental business, Hollywood Video filed for bankruptcy protection in February 2010 before liquidating in August.[69] In April 2011, satellite television provider Dish Network acquired Blockbuster at an auction. Under new ownership, Blockbuster continued its online, on demand, and kiosk operations in 2012, but the mighty movie rental giant that once had 4,000 stores worldwide struggled to keep 500 stores open.

If we look for improvement because we know we can have something better, we also look for improvement to avoid decay. Again, physics provides some useful concepts. The *Second Law of Thermodynamics* states that organization breaks down within a closed system and disorder naturally increases. So, if we leave things the way they are, unattended, things will naturally begin to fall apart. If we don't water a plant, it dies. If we don't keep up with the developments in our field, our careers will suffer. For example, would you go to a dentist who hadn't upgraded their equipment or learned new procedures in years? History even makes this point with the rise and fall of empires and nation-states. Kings, emperors, and tribal leaders had to expand their territory and populace through war or marriage, or risk being taken over themselves. It was a kind of Pac Man game on a national level.

Without anticipating change, we risk irrelevance or extinction. Some may say it's akin to the Darwinian idea of *adapt or die*. On my desk is a CACI coaster made to commemorate the opening of our Vision and Solutions Center, a state-of-the-art, computer-based digital simulation and modeling facility. The slogan on the coaster says, "It begins with your vision, it results

---

[69] David Lieberman, "Blockbuster files for Chapter 11 bankruptcy, will reorganize," *USA Today,* September 23, 2010, http://www.usatoday.com/money/media/2010-09-23-blockbuster23 ST_N.htm.

in your solution."[70] This is a profound statement that still motivates me. So keep an eye out. Watch for the change that's coming – and make it work for you!

PARTICIPATE

Even when the change is not of your own doing, don't ignore it. In fact, refusing to acknowledge that change is happening can be fatal. At times, you can even participate and become part of the change!

Success is a combination of initiative and innovation. Sometimes, you don't even know a need exists. Other times, you simply don't see the change coming until it is upon you. That doesn't mean you still can't take advantage of it.

Look at the cupcake, for example. I always associated cupcakes with kids. You either made them or bought them at the bakery. Many have been eaten at my grandchildren's birthday parties. Driving through the Georgetown neighborhood of Washington, DC one day, I noticed a line outside a corner store. Imagine my surprise when I learned it was a cupcake store – a bakery specializing in cupcakes. I later learned that cupcakes had become the latest food trend. Local publications had "cupcake wars" to pick the tastiest cupcake in DC.[71] The trend didn't start in Washington, but several smart small business owners picked up on it and became very successful.

In my experience, there are two (business) models for participatory change: 1) change is internally generated; and 2) change is externally forced upon you.

Change is internally generated. The technology industry is innovation-driven, and yet not every successful tech company

---

[70] One of CACI's earliest employees was Joe Aninno. Joe managed simulation technologies and products for some three decades. Simscript may have been CACI's earliest product, but through Joe's efforts to anticipate future simulation software needs, Simscript always stayed one of the company's freshest products, too.

[71] I later found out that the store that regularly won the taste test battles was the very one I had seen with the long customer line. The store, Georgetown Cupcake, soon earned its own reality TV show, called *DC Cupcakes*, and has risen in popularity. The lines now are longer than ever. Their cupcakes must be worth the wait!

invents their products. Nor is every inventor or first-mover at the top of their business—or even still in business!

Before DVDs, we recorded and watched everything from our personal memories to Hollywood movies on video tapes. There were originally two kinds: Beta and VHS. Beta tapes were smaller and lighter, while VHS had longer recording times. Although Beta was considered the superior format, its smaller size made it incompatible with full size VCRs. Manufacturers soon recognized the consumers' dilemma. Sony, who championed the Beta format, could not duplicate the functionality that VHS offered. Their competitor, JVC, did. By 1980, JVC's VHS format dominated 70 percent of the North American market. By 1988, Sony gave in and switched from Beta to VHS.

Timing is key. You can't wait too long to take advantage of change because the barriers to entry become too high. The costs may be too high; in fact, out of reach. Take the MP3 player market. Apple's iPod dominates the field with all competitors lagging as a distant second. I don't think anyone would think about jumping into that mix.[72] The longer you wait, the lower the benefits will be. For example, many people go back to school later in life, but few older students become doctors because it would be a decade before they could start practicing on their own.

At CACI, we picked up on this need to participate in change early. Our culture has already been developed to drive the positive changes we need to make to stay at the top of our business. For example, a key contributor to CACI's growth has been our Mergers and Acquisitions program. By acquiring firms with skills, people, and contracts in developing markets, we take advantage of change without having to start from scratch every time. We can also reposition the company faster this way. In our

---

[72] Microsoft introduced the Zune portable media player in November 2006. Despite being the second most popular player, its market share was only 9%, Apple's market-leading iPod's already had 63% market share. By 2008, some retailers had stopped selling the Zune because of low demand. Microsoft finally discontinued the Zune in October 2011.

industry, you have to get in at the early phases of change. You won't get anywhere just bidding government contracts without a distinctive, innovative solution. In fact, you'll waste your money and quickly go out of business.

We also stay abreast of changes that our customers face. Currently in our industry, cyber security and military health care IT systems are two big national security trends. CACI is already well positioned in many solution areas within these trends, like information assurance and intelligence analysis and systems. How these trends will develop is uncertain, and we're still developing them as a business practice. Wherever our customers need to go, we'll be right next to them with well thought out solutions.

Another reason for not waiting too long to take action is that the *change will itself change*. For example, in the video tape market, just a decade after VHS defeated Beta, a new competitor emerged – DVDs. The new digital technology not only recorded and played media, it could also store data. These discs were smaller, lighter, and had larger capacities. Similarly, CDs replaced albums in the music industry. Getting in early definitely increases your chance of success.

Change is forced on you. Let's revisit a previous example – music sharing and downloading. Record companies may have stopped Napster and others by claiming copyright violations, but it couldn't stop the trend started by them. Digital music was what consumers wanted. Other file sharing tools emerged and artists even began selling their music directly to consumers. Music industry executives had to accept that their business models no longer worked. They had to change – or go out of business!

CACI had a similar situation. Our marketplace had always been highly competitive, but informal. We always had to hustle to find deals and to convince clients that our solutions were the best. It was a competitive sales environment, but without any specific rules. Then in 1984, the government enacted the Competition in Contracting Act (CICA). Our world was turned upside down. The act required government agencies to *formally* compete most contracts. At that time, the majority of CACI's business came from single-source contracts. As a result of CICA, our selling methods became obsolete. It was a real wake-up call. Before CICA, we had done business largely by convincing clients to hire us for additional work, by pitching our services to new clients with urgent needs, and by touting our excellent performance and innovative solutions. With CICA, we now had to aggressively chase down and evaluate bid announcements or Requests for Proposals (RFPs). We weren't used to that. CICA, however, meant that CACI had to adapt or die. If we couldn't figure out a way to change, we would jeopardize the livelihoods of several thousand employees and the projects of numerous clients. So we got with it! We created a new business development group dedicated to changing how we marketed our offerings. We worked hard to make the change – we had no choice.

In 1984, CACI's competitive wins only accounted for 7 percent of revenue. By 1986, competitive contract awards grew to 70 percent of our revenue. Today, virtually all of our contracts are competitive awards. CACI would not be around today if we hadn't adapted rapidly and effectively to the changes that CICA placed on us.[73]

In an ideal world where foresight is perfect, we wouldn't be blindsided or endangered by change. In the real world, however, it's adapt or die. At the start of the 20th century, most of the 10 largest U.S. firms were in natural resource extraction (e.g. mining and exploration). At the end of the century, most of the top 10 were high tech companies. Only General Electric appeared on both lists!

Challenges show us what we're made of. Just as there are no guarantees, there's no way to avoid change either. Sometimes, you decide when it's necessary. Sometimes, you just have to play the hand you're dealt. It's up to you to play your hand well – or fold.

---

[73] When I first noted the newly enacted (1984) legislation's title, CICA, I was horrified. It seemed as though someone had played a bad joke, specifically on us. It had appeared that they had taken our own name, CACI, and in true bureaucratic fashion, scrambled the letters to CICA, and pitched our business methods out the window at the same time.

There is one caveat about change, however. Dealing with change may challenge personal as well as organizational values and standards. There's never a good enough reason, no matter how tempting or acceptable, to compromise integrity. Organizations can be flexible and opportunistic without relaxing time-tested performance standards, values and practices. Once you let those standards or your principles slip, there is no recovery. Imagine a drug manufacturer cutting corners, rushing through quality controls to beat a competitor to market. Such actions endanger public health as well as company viability. What if an employee who catches the error is offered a promotion to look the other way? Compromising integrity to deal with change only makes things worse.

INNOVATE

Innovate means to make the change. A change can be as simple as trying a new route to work or it can be as significant as an industry-creating invention. The Edisons and Fords are hard acts to follow. Yet innovation simply means the introduction of something new or different.

Today, Post-Its® are incredibly useful products found in every office. Yet they started out as a reusable, pressure sensitive adhesive accidentally developed by a scientist at the 3M Corporation in 1968. It took five years of unsuccessfully promoting the adhesive within the company before a colleague thought it would be useful in anchoring his bookmark in his hymnbook. It wasn't until 1978 (and one failed product launch) that Post-Its took off, and another two years before the product was sold nationwide.

"Be the change you want to see in the world."

Mohandas Gandhi

The three most visited websites in the world today are Google, Facebook, and YouTube. Google began as a research project by two Ph.D. students (Larry Page and Sergey Brin) at Stanford University in January 1996. Facebook was founded in 2004 by Mark Zuckerberg with several college classmates during his sophomore year at Harvard. The idea for Facebook came from an existing directory unofficially called the "face book."[74] Video sharing website, YouTube, was created by three former PayPal employees in February 2005, who supposedly came up with the idea after having trouble sharing videos from a dinner party.

Who knows what the next big thing will be. These and other web-based tools show that more innovations are on the way. Thinking outside the box is not that difficult an idea. We all can see things in a new way or do something that hasn't been done before. Creativity doesn't know class, race, or any other distinction – it's within all of us. Luckily, it's also a trait that grows as we get older.[75]

Innovation is in our nature. When do our creative juices get flowing? When we perceive a need. (Needs create *visions*). Until the 20th century, most manufactured goods were individually made. However, leaders at the Ford Motor Company thought there had to be a better way to produce their new Model T cars. Although the concept of mass production had been around for centuries, technology and other factors wouldn't make it a practical reality until the early 1900s. The assembly line, as conceptualized and introduced by Ford between 1908 and 1915, was an innovation that allowed manufacturers to more efficiently and less expensively produce their goods.

Modern technology has evolved to meet increasing consumer needs. Cellular phones in the 1980s were clunky luxuries for those who could afford the novelty. Today, cell phones are as common as land line phones and include a variety of communications, productivity and entertainment features. The need for larger data storage capacities in smaller portable forms has evolved from floppy disks to flash drives in less than a few decades. Dial-up service has long given way to high speed

---

[74] Although there is controversy between Zuckerberg and Cameron and Tyler Winklevoss about Facebook's origins, Zuckerberg retained control of Facebook.

[75] Studies on creativity show that, unlike other traits such as memory, our ability to be creative actually increase as we get older, peaking around middle age. It's no surprise then that innovators, such as Michelangelo and DaVinci, had their greatest successes later in life.

broadband, wireless and fiber optic services to meet the needs for faster and more reliable Internet access.

Innovation also occurs when we have to look for alternatives to existing options. The negative effects (high cost, pollution, and foreign dependence) of fossil fuels have yielded numerous innovations in energy, including solar, and wind power. Just look at these examples: hybrid cars, ethanol fuel, wind farms, and smart grid infrastructures. In this case, necessity really has been the mother of all inventions, even if the economics involved have not yet come into line.

Someone once told me that their former boss was famous for saying, "The answer is yes. What's the question?" For him, there was no doubt that whatever needed to be done, could be done. Sometimes you just hadn't yet thought of how to do it.

We also get inventive when we look for improvements. I bet that the TV in your house isn't a clunky, black and white unit with a "rabbit ear" antenna and that your telephone doesn't have separate mouth and ear pieces and a hand crank?[76] Do you listen to music on a gramophone?

The Gillette brand is ubiquitous for disposable safety razors. In the 1890s, King C. Gillette, its inventor, was a salesman for the Crown Cork and Seal Company. There, Gillette saw that opened bottle caps from the cork seals he sold were thrown away. At the time, razor blades were expensive and needed continuous sharpening. Gillette, having seen the value of a discardable product, thought that dull razor blades could be thrown away and replaced. Razors, therefore, could be sold at low profit margins while creating an ongoing market for the blades.[77]

---

[76] I can clearly remember the old hand cranked phones. To reach my grandfather in Geary, Oklahoma in 1945, all you had to do was find a phone (not everyone had them back then), call the operator, and ask for his number, 10F112, which I remember to this very day. Not exactly speed dial!

[77] The Gillette Safety Razor Company was founded in 1902. It is a great and familiar example of the power of the branding concept. By 1999, Gillette was reportedly worth $43 billion. Gillette's brand value alone was estimated at $16 billion. Gillette sold to Proctor & Gamble in 2005 for $57 billion. King Gillette got it right!

If what we had in life was good enough, we would never have change or progress. Just as we update our home appliances, we look to update our lives. Our careers, for example, follow an up-or-out course. Most people look for greater responsibilities and challenges to grow. In turn, they may seek more education and training to get those opportunities. If you want to lead larger initiatives and manage project teams, you may want to get a Project Management Professional certification. I've always supported the education, training and self-improvement approach. It's the formula I have used in my life. In many ways, it's the path toward making the American dream come true.

> *"If there is no struggle, there is no progress."*
>
> Frederick Douglass

Maybe you need a change of scenery? If you want to pursue a performing arts career, you'll definitely have more opportunities in New York or Los Angeles. Are you dreaming of becoming a Senator, then a stint in Washington, DC might do you some good. Do you want to become fluent in Mandarin Chinese? Spend some time in Beijing.

There's no better example of the importance of innovation to success than the history of the United States. American pioneers and early settlers were looking to build a better life. Over 100 pilgrims made the treacherous passage on the *Mayflower* in 1620 in search of religious freedom. Three hundred years later, millions would make the same journey through Ellis Island in New York City in pursuit of building their American dream.

These immigrants all knew that you must take some risk to make things better. Doing more of the same won't give you anything different.

The willingness to make changes, to innovate, takes self-confidence. It's the desire and faith that you can do something different and the perseverance to make the change over time. It can take repeated attempts and failures before success. Thomas Edison is said to have conducted some 10,000 experiments in the process of inventing the light bulb. After every failure, Edison would note what had gone wrong and what parts he had used. After making adjustments, he would try again. Each failure took him one step closer to success and the rest of us to electrical lighting. Innovation requires ongoing attention and commitment – *refusing to fail*. [78]

Of course, innovation alone does not yield success. I attended the Northern Virginia Technology Council's annual awards banquet in October 2010. The keynote speaker was John Chambers, CEO of Cisco, the international networking equipment and services company. His talk covered several points relevant to rapid changes that take place in the IT and communications industries. What grabbed my attention was his emphasis that significant, sustained growth only comes when innovation is balanced with operational excellence. Long-term success requires achieving both in equal measure.

Innovation, of course, is necessary in becoming a builder, inventor, or entrepreneur. To make positive change happen, you have to have a serious appetite for it. There are two myths, however, about innovation and entrepreneurship.

The first myth is about resources. There is a belief that new ventures can only happen with lots of money. I've never been in a business environment where a good idea needed lots of capital to get started. If the idea does, it may not be a good idea anyway. (There are some serious exceptions, however, like FedEx, which required large start-up capital.) CACI may be a multi-billion company now, but we started on a park bench in Los Angeles, California in 1962. The company conducted business from a nearby phone booth. At least most entrepreneurs today have laptops and cell phones!

The second myth is that innovation has to be big. The modern jet airliner didn't happen overnight. And even if an apple really fell on Sir Isaac Newton's head, inspiring the theory of gravity, it still took him some 20 years to develop the full theory. And what about Albert Einstein's theory of special relativity? In

---

[78] Some people use the phrase "fear of failure," but it doesn't quite do it for me. I have known a number of great people who have succeeded in life, simply because they "refused to fail." That's the more powerful idea.

1905, Einstein talked to a friend about a puzzle that had bothered him for a decade. To Einstein, the two pillars of physics, Newtonian mechanics and James Clerk Maxwell's equations, were incompatible.[79] While he was riding home on a streetcar in Bern, Switzerland, and looking back at the city's famous clock tower, Einstein imagined his streetcar moving away from the tower at the speed of light. He realized that as he rode away at that speed, the tower's clock would appear to stop, while the clock on his streetcar would be working as usual. Einstein suddenly had the answer: time moves at different rates throughout the universe depending on how fast you are moving. Einstein had a *eureka* moment, but it had taken 10 years of pondering and several centuries of physics research to make it happen.

Most of the time, innovation is a series of mini-Eureka moments. Change truly doesn't happen overnight. It's often an evolutionary process. So, be patient yet persistent. When you know there's a better way out there, innovate – make change happen!

I still have the same corner office where I worked as President and CEO beginning in 1984, but it's no longer the Office of the CEO. That office is now down the hall in another corner of the building with other senior CACI executives nearby. I stepped out of the President and CEO role in 2007, and have never looked back. My office is now the Office of the Chairman. Over the years, my office has seen many challenges and opportunities, numerous faces and personalities, and a few surprises, including some ugly ones as well as some great ones. Some were changes we wanted, some we created, and some we never expected. In every case, we made change work for us, knowing full well that no matter what, *change happens.*

---

[79] Einstein felt that Newton's theory of absolute time and space violated Maxwell's theory of the constancy of the speed of light.

CHAPTER 8

OPPORTUNITY COMES IN SOME OF THE UNLIKELIEST PLACES

"The pessimist sees difficulty in every opportunity.
The optimist sees the opportunity in every difficulty."
Winston Churchill

We often hear: *When life throws lemons at you, make lemonade.*
There's a silver lining in every cloud. It's always darkest before
the dawn. There's a reason why they're clichés—they're true.
Such advice is meant to encourage people through adversity. Yet
it's good advice, applicable in all challenging situations.

Starting a new business is tough, especially during a
recession? In the first half of 2010, more than a quarter of newly
unemployed workers considered starting their own businesses.
Most people would think it's crazy to start something as risky as
a new business during the worst of economic times. Don't tell
that to General Electric or Hewlett Packard. Both companies
were started during recessions. So were Hyatt Hotels, Sports
Illustrated, Burger King, FedEx, Microsoft, CNN and MTV.

How about having to restart your life at 42? That's what
happened to business moguls Paula Deen and Gert Boyle. In
1989, a divorced, broke and agoraphobic Deen started a catering
company to makes ends meet. After opening a Savannah,
Georgia restaurant six years later, Deen and her sons parlayed
the popularity of her comfort food into a frozen foods company,
cookbooks, a magazine, and several TV shows. When Gert Boyle
was widowed in 1970, the housewife and mother of three had to
take the helm of the outdoor apparel company her parents had
started 33 years earlier. Boyle and one of her sons proceeded to

take Columbia Sportswear from $800,000 to nearly $1.7 billion in annual revenue by 2011.[80]

These examples show that life doesn't always go as planned, but it can go in a different, sometimes even better, direction if you're open to it. This is a hard perspective to accept because we tend to focus on the negative when faced with a problem. If you can open yourself to the possibility of something good in a difficult situation, then you have already begun solving your problem.

What would you do if you lost your job today? Most people would jump into a job search, but during tough economic times when jobs are scarce, some people decide to go out on their own.

Accidental entrepreneurs is the nickname given to people who start their own business after losing their jobs.[81] For these folks, they found opportunities and success in franchising, freelancing, and starting small businesses. In fact, unemployment increases rates of self-employment. In the recessionary year of 2008, more new businesses were started than during the more prosperous 2007. A leading online legal document service company reported that the number of new businesses it helped to form was up 10 percent in the first half of 2009 compared to the same period in 2008. Many small businesses fail within the first two years, but what about the ones that don't? Did you know that Starbucks, Intuit and PetSmart were also started during a recession? In fact, more than half of 2009's Fortune 500 companies were founded during a recession or bear market.

---

[80] Michelle V. Rafter, "7 Second-act Entrepreneurs," *Entrepeneur.com*, August 7, 2012, http://www.entrepreneur.com/slideshow/224116.

[81] I like to think of CACI co-founder, Herb Karr, as an accidental entrepreneur. After leaving RAND, Herb joined Planning Research Corporation (PRC). There he was fired by his boss, PRC's founder Bob Kruger and Herb subsequently vowed never to work for anyone else ever again. In fact, Herb used to say that getting fired by Bob was the best thing that ever happened to him because it pushed him to start CACI. Bob and Herb later buried the hatchet and made peace, with Herb even asking Bob to consult with me on mergers and acquisitions. Herb still respected Bob and thought I might learn a few things from him, which I surely did.

Today, Fairchild Semiconductor is a leading global provider of semiconductor technology delivering energy-efficient solutions. It is a $1.6 billion company with 9,000 employees. It was founded by employees pushed out of their previous jobs! In 1955, William Shockley, co-inventor of the transistor, started Shockley Semiconductor Laboratories in California. Shockley won the Nobel Prize for Physics the next year, but his management style and changes in research focus compelled eight young scientists to leave the company.

> *"Opportunity is missed by most people because it is dressed in overalls and looks like work."*
>
> Thomas Edison

The eight scientists wanted to continue working together and turned to a friend at a New York investment banking firm for advice. The bankers told the group to set up their own company instead and offered to help find financial backing. The idea clearly appealed to the scientists, as they could keep working as a group and stay in California, where most had already put down roots.

After scouring *The Wall Street Journal* and the New York Stock Exchange listings, the group identified about 30 companies that might be interested in supporting a semiconductor venture. True to their word, two bankers went to talk to each company, but were turned down cold. A fortuitous run-in with Sherman Fairchild changed their luck. Fairchild, an inventor and serial entrepreneur, was a technology buff. He had invented the flash camera as a college student. He eventually dropped out to start his first company, which would later become Fairchild Camera and Instrument. Fairchild introduced the bankers to the company's chairman who decided to support the scientists' new venture. So in 1957, each scientist put up $500 (a month's salary) and Fairchild added a whopping $1.3 million. Hence, Fairchild Semiconductor Corporation was born.[82]

It's easy to look at these examples and statistics, but what about when it happens to you? My path from the Naval Academy to corporate America was never designed as such. Rather, it came about from opportunities that presented themselves as a result of emerging challenges. My challenge came during my second year at the Naval Postgraduate School (NPS) in Monterey, California. I was almost finished with my master's degree and was determined to go to Vietnam. With my aviation and operations background, I felt I could go as part of a helicopter gunship squadron. I even appealed to my squadron commander from my old ship, the USS *Randolph*. In all, I sent letters requesting this duty three times and was denied each time. Instead, I was ordered to the Naval Academy to teach operations analysis to Midshipmen. It made sense from the Navy's perspective; the assignment at the Naval Academy would be a payback for the Masters degree in Operations Research.

Not going to Vietnam, however, started changing my perspective about a full Navy career. It seemed to me that after the war there would be two kinds of officers; those who had been to Vietnam and those who had not. I would be in the latter category, which I believed would be limiting. Realizing that my Navy career would not likely be what I wanted it to be, I pondered what I could do to realign my career or what I could do with my remaining time in the service. While at NPS, my studies included learning about operations analysis and advanced engineering methods, as well as early programming languages and simulation modeling. This triggered a shift to an aeronautical engineering and logistics focus soon afterward. Then on duty at the Naval Academy, I also decided to go for a doctoral degree in business administration, and soon enrolled in a postgraduate program at George Washington University in Washington, DC under the GI Bill.

---

[82] Fairchild Semiconductor became a Silicon Valley leader. As an incubator, it would spawn several leading technology companies, including Intel, Advanced Micro Devices, and National Semiconductor.

Although I had been assigned to duty at the Naval Academy as an instructor in operations analysis, this new interest led me to my next assignment. My interests and ambitions along these lines were picked up in the Navy in Washington, DC, and soon I was interviewing for a front-office job in the Naval Material Command (NMC). I was selected for a great position and became the Aide and Administrative Assistant to the Vice Chief responsible for all Navy material acquisitions. NMC was the acquisition and procurement organization of the U.S. Navy. This would be my first exposure to the Department of Defense world of government contracting and procurement. It seemed like a great opportunity. I was motivated and thought I could be of real service.

After a lengthy emotional and internal struggle that lasted two years I finally decided to leave the Navy in 1971, and the defense contracting world was a good fit. I looked nationwide for six months for my first job as a civilian. Knowing that my family didn't want to leave the DC area, I began interviewing seriously in the local market. Jobs were few and far between; business was slow, and the national economy was in a recession.

My first job out of the Navy that year was with a small company called Challenger Research Inc. located in Rockville, Maryland. Challenger's focus was submarine search and detection systems, including advanced and sophisticated work on sonar systems for submarines, surface combatants and anti-submarine warfare aircraft.

I had experience during the Cold War tracking and chasing Russian submarines. So I knew the problems the Navy faced. The Soviets had a large and growing nuclear submarine ballistic missile fleet that was a serious threat. I also had good logistics systems and IT experience, which made me marketable. I had a positive, can-do, get-it-done attitude.

After a year at Challenger, I got a cold call from Ron Steorts at CACI. He had seen my resume in an old proposal that Challenger had submitted to a client with whom CACI was working. Ron called me to arrange an interview. At first, I wasn't interested in this research-focused position in a small unknown company. However, the role would focus more on computers and information systems, and it offered the opportunity to do marketing, business development, and project management. After several intensive back-and-forth interviews, I was made an offer I couldn't refuse. So in 1972, I joined CACI as a project manager making a whopping $1,835 per month ($22,020 a year). As to my decision to accept the opportunity with CACI, the rest, as they say, is history.

Too many people accept the setbacks in their careers, and in their lives believing that they can't change their circumstances. Many people also dismiss ideas and opportunities without giving them serious consideration. They could be passing up their next big opportunity because they don't take a closer look.

Had I stayed in the Navy, I believe I would have had a successful career. While I might even have made flag rank, I would never have made the top rank of a four star Admiral since that level isn't open to engineering specialty officers. By embracing the change I knew I had to make, I could work my way up to the top spot of CEO at CACI. Being CEO of a small $100 million, independent and publicly-owned company in 1985, in my view, was every bit as challenging from a leadership perspective as being the commanding officer of a naval aviation squadron.[83] A positive attitude is part of embracing unexpected changes. And I approached all of these career-changing experiences with a positive attitude and an enduring love and respect for all that is the U.S. Navy.

In my case, it didn't matter if the glass was half empty or half full – it was knowing that I could get a refill, or even something else to drink.

Personal change is never easy because it taps into our insecurity. What happens when change threatens your security, and everyone else for whom you're responsible?

After a year as CACI's CEO, I began to realize that I would be dealing with a steady stream of challenges since all of the bad news and serious problems come directly to the CEO's desk. But

---

[83] Just for clarity and candor's sake, I would never compare leading a commercial company as a CEO to being a squadron commanding officer during combat operations. They are quite different chapters in the book of leadership.

making the best of a bad situation can become an advantage. Once you embrace the potential opportunities that come from challenges, the easier it becomes to do it.

In the late '80s, a couple of opportunist shareholders tried to derail the company. The first one bought a little over 5 percent of CACI's stock (and thought he *owned* the company). He then spearheaded an effort to make Herb Karr and the rest of the board of directors sell the company. Herb would have none of it and fought off the attempt. After Herb died in 1990 and I assumed the Chairman's position, another dissident shareholder came after me (presumably joining forces with the former). Had CACI ever had any serious legitimate offers, we would, of course, have seriously considered them. That's a board's duty; the fiduciary duty to act in the best interests of *all* shareholders. However, both times the intentions were purely short-sighted, selfish, and grossly naive to our future prospects. Their intentions would have been to the detriment of the company and all of its shareholders. In the midst of these battles, the board and I made a decisive move. We bought back from the Karr estate just over two million shares and stock options of CACI's stock at a slight premium to the market and then retired it into the corporate treasury.[84] With that one move, we settled the market and raised the value of the company. It was one of the best deals I ever negotiated – ever made – and everyone benefitted, especially our shareholders (many who continue to benefit).

I know that not every cloud will have a silver lining. Not every step back will lead to two steps forward. But knowing and believing that the potential exists is important.

We've all heard that *opportunity comes when you least expect it.* Did you ever think that *you can create an opportunity when you least expect it?*

---

[84] The purchase price of $3.25 was a 25¢ premium above the market at the time. By comparison, CACI stock was trading around $60/share by June 2006, fifteen years later. This would have been a $120/share price on the pre-split basis (2 for 1) that we instituted in spring 2002, and over 40 times the price in 1991!

CHARACTER: The Ultimate Success Factor

What would you do if you were asked to take over a project at work reputed to be the "kiss of death?" In fall 1984, Microsoft employee Tandy Trower found himself in that predicament. In the three previous years, Trower had managed several high-profile Microsoft products, including their flagship product, BASIC. He had loved working on products geared to wider PC audiences. Then during a project review meeting, Bill Gates directed Trower to devise a strategy to deal with a new competitor to BASIC. Frustrated by Gates' narrower, highly technical task, Trower sought counsel from his boss and head of Microsoft's product marketing group, Steve Ballmer (CEO of Microsoft in 2010). Ballmer suggested that Trower may have been the wrong person for the job. He would later suggest that Trower take over the Windows project, thinking it would appeal to Trower's end-user product experience and interests.

Once Microsoft's star project, Windows had become a bit of an embarrassment. Windows had been announced with much anticipation and support from PC vendors the year before, but it still hadn't shipped. Some within Microsoft questioned if it would ever ship. Ballmer even went on a PR tour to reassure the industry that the product was on its way. There were more problems. Favoring its own application windowing product, Microsoft failed to get IBM to license Windows. With IBM ruling the PC market, Microsoft would have to market Windows directly to IBM PC users. That kind of direct marketing and sales had never been done before.

At first Trower thought Gates and Ballmer were trying to push him out because of challenges with another project. Windows had already had four product managers who had been either reassigned or were no longer at Microsoft. It earned the moniker *vaporware* for its career-ending reputation. Trower was even advised by colleagues against taking the job. Gates and Ballmer reassured Trower that they had confidence in him and that the offer was sincere.

Trower accepted and transferred to the Windows team in January 1985. The challenges were considerable. Trower was given only six months to finalize the product and get it out. The Windows lead developer had been reassigned and getting developers to write Windows software was difficult. In the meantime, Macintosh had also been announced. Apple and other competitors would be offering a small bundled set of applications, including word processing and drawing, which Trower knew had to be matched. Windows would also require a keyboard interface. To add to the challenge, Ballmer wanted Windows' system requirements to match a standard IBM PC. Over the summer, a critical defect in the memory management code was found and the testing process would have to start from scratch.

The Windows team would persevere, working tirelessly into the fall. In November of 1985, Trower and his crew did what others before him had failed to do, release Windows 1.0. Over the next three years, Trower would either lead or advise on the

"The secret of success in life is for a man to be ready for his opportunity when it comes."

Benjamin Disraeli

development of newer versions of Windows. By the 1990s, Windows would become a dominant operating system. In 2010, Windows celebrated its 25th anniversary. Trower not only created an opportunity from what was considered a career-killing project, he paved the way for a successful 28 year career at Microsoft.[85]

Trower's example is extraordinary, to be sure. Yet it shows that even the most daunting circumstances can be turned to one's advantage. Most opportunities don't have to be created from a potential disaster. Usually, it's simply fulfilling a need by adding some ingenuity and innovation!

A number of years ago, when CACI's client, the Navy's Military Sealift Command (MSC) began outfitting ships activated to support Persian Gulf troops, the command discovered a shortage of machine-gun mounts. The client casually mentioned

---

[85] Trower's career as an engineer and software developer covered over 25 Microsoft products. In 2005, Trower formed the company's Robotics Group. Trower resigned from Microsoft in November 2009 to pursue his own entrepreneurial interest, a new robotics venture aimed at improving assisted living care.

this situation to the CACI logistician in the course of discussing other project tasks. Our logistics analyst was quick to recognize an opportunity to help his client. He thought about it and came up with a great game plan.

He located some army friends and they jumped into his pickup and were off to Ft. Eustis, Virginia, to the James River "Ready Reserve" Fleet of decommissioned ships. The men were allowed on board the decommissioned ships to look for salvageable gun mounts. They commandeered, with permission, all the available mounts and loaded them into our analyst's pickup. The next weekend, he and his team visited the Army Reserve Unit in North Carolina to retrieve nine more mounts located there. He then contacted managers of inactive fleets in another six states to request any remaining gun mounts. He found a dozen workable gun mounts for MSC, saving his client and U.S. taxpayers thousands of dollars and enabling the command to meet mission goals on schedule.

Here's another example. One CACI professional has spent over 20 years at CACI supporting an ever-evolving Navy aircraft program, starting as a software developer and working his way up to program manager. Among other remarkable leadership and innovative qualities, the CACI engineer was known for staying on top and ahead of the latest technologies in his field. Recently, the CACI engineer and his customer discussed a new piece of equipment that would fit well into the customer's lab, which would not only make their work easier, but substantially lower costs. A month later, the CACI employee came back to the customer having researched the equipment, and the customer remarked that "the government is excited about adding this innovation into the lab. I never have that sort of thing from other companies." This innovative effort provides serious value-add for the U.S. Navy and is an example of how a dedicated *individual* can make a difference. It shows our people really care.

In both cases, our professionals created the opportunity. The decommissioned ships had been sitting in Virginia. The lab equipment already existed. Our attentive employees matched them with our clients' needs – they created their own opportunity!

Some opportunities are expected, some are earned. Some are modest, some are industry reshaping in scope. Often, they're simply hiding from us. You have to look for them – or create them yourself. It will take some imagination and persistence, but the result could be better than anything you could imagine because *opportunity comes from the unlikeliest places.*

CHAPTER 9

CREATE DISTINCTION EVERYWHERE

"One who walks in another's tracks leaves no footprints."
Italian Proverb

Bread is one of the oldest prepared foods in recorded history. It comes in many varieties and is a staple of every country's diet. For thousands of years, the process of making and selling bread remained relatively unchanged. That is, until a Missouri jeweler and part-time inventor revolutionized bread as we know it.

In 1912, Otto Friedrick Rohwedder knew how much bread was hand-sliced in American homes. He also took note of how much people liked toasted bread, but hand sliced pieces didn't fit well into early toasters. So he built a prototype of the first loaf-at-a-time bread-slicing machine. Confident he was on to something, Rohwedder sold his jewelry stores to work on his invention. Unfortunately, a factory fire in 1917 destroyed Rohwedder's blueprints and prototype. A decade later, Rohwedder bounced back with an invention that not only sliced the bread, but also wrapped it. In 1928, he sold his first machine to a friend and baker in St. Louis. By 1930, Wonder Bread had come across Rohwedder's machine and became the first mass-marketer of sliced bread as a product. Shortly thereafter, Wonder Bread launched an ad campaign touting the innovation featuring the now famous saying, "the greatest thing since sliced bread."[86]

---

[86] The impact of sliced bread was remarkable. Bread and toaster sales skyrocketed by 1932. Sliced bread became such a household staple in the U.S. that a World War II ban on the machines only lasted two months. The ban was intended to reduce bread prices and manufacturing costs, and free up metal for military purposes. Although the government stated the reason for the repeal was lower than expected savings, it is widely believed that it was the ban's unpopularity with housewives and bakeries. Bread knives were also in low supply during the war.

People had been eating bread for thousands of years by either tearing off pieces or cutting slices with a knife. Yet Rohwedder thought there had to be a different and better way of serving bread – and that changed everything.

Creating distinction is not necessarily striving to come up with the greatest thing since sliced bread (although kudos to you, if you do). **Creating distinction is the capacity for making something different and better**. It comes down to one question: What sets you apart?

Asking this question forces you to assess yourself: *What do you do different and better? What unique skills and insights do you have? What do you bring to the table? What else is possible?*

Many people fear being distinctive. They want to be like everyone else, like one of the herd, and find security in conformity. There's nothing wrong in knowing other people think and feel like you; or that you are just as capable as the next person. Yet for many people, it's a self-imposed constraint. They feel it's wrong to think differently or that expressing differences will have negative consequences. The irony, however, is that no one ever really thinks the same. In fact, as George S. Patton once noted, "If everyone is thinking alike then somebody isn't thinking."

This insecurity also manifests itself in actions. Some are habits, like taking the same route to work every day because that's how you've always gone even though there's a shorter way. It could also be complacency, like following specific steps in a career path even though your career hasn't progressed as planned or even if you're unhappy in your current field.

Of course, with many things there are tried-and-true methods to getting things done. Best practices, in general, are the most effective way to achieve particular outcomes. However, life isn't static. Herb Karr and I used to say *consistency is the bugaboo of small minds*. What worked best yesterday may not be as good today. A decade ago, the best way to play music was from a CD. Now it's MP3 files. Data storage went from floppy disks to mini discs to CDs to thumb drives – in less than 20 years. If we stuck with what always worked before, we'd still be slicing our own bread. So don't be *one of the herd* – only the wildebeest makes out in a herd.

Worse still is the fear of thinking. For some people, everything needs to be regimented. They want an instruction sheet instead of thinking for themselves. This problem manifests itself in many mindsets: I have to be married and have kids by a certain age. I shouldn't bring ideas to my boss unless he or she asks for my opinion. I wish someone would just tell me what to do here.

It amazes me how people resist relying on their own judgment and insight. In conjunction with that insecurity is the lack of creative thinking and the belief that they lack this ability altogether. In all my years, I've never met anyone who didn't possess some degree of creative thinking. Thinking outside the box, after all, is not a remote idea. Why? Curiosity and insight are part of our nature. From the child who asks why the sky is blue to the scientists who asked the same question and found out why, we instinctively know there's always something more.[87]

> "And it ought to be remembered that there is nothing more difficult to take in hand, more perilous to conduct, or more uncertain in its success, than to take the lead in the introduction of a new order of things."
>
> Niccolo Machiavelli
> *The Prince*

The beauty (and difficulty) in our capacity for creative thinking is the variety of perspectives it creates. For example, I've always had a curiosity about how things began. This includes many aspects of history and science, as well as genealogy (family history). In high school physics, we learned about Sir Isaac Newton and his discoveries. These include the relationship of force as a function of a body's mass and acceleration as described

---

[87] Why *is* the sky blue? As light moves through the atmosphere, the shorter blue wavelength light is absorbed by gas molecules while longer wavelengths of other colors are unaffected. The blue light is then scattered in different directions in the sky, thus making it appear blue.

in his *Laws of Motion* that predicted the orbit of Halley's Comet.[88] Newton's work made possible our modern day search for the origin of the universe by focusing on *the world around us.*

Then there's Charles Darwin. His observations and theories that living species change through mutations to adjust to their environment was groundbreaking. In fact, his theory of evolution still sparks debate today. Yet Darwin's work made possible our modern search for the origin of life by focusing on *the world inside us.*

Here is the same question – *where do we come from?* – pondered from two different perspectives. Both Newton and Darwin, two men I greatly admire, were thinking creatively and differently than the prevailing norm of their time to find better answers to their questions. Their insights were also based on their personal knowledge and experiences.[89] What set them both apart was their ability to think and act differently. That's distinction!

My point is not to encourage contrarian thinking at every turn, but to empower original thinking. Distinction starts with the belief that different can be okay and that better is possible. Don't let anyone restrict you from thinking or seeing things differently. Experience teaches us that there is often more than one way to do things.

---

[88] Newton's laws of motion describe the relationship between the forces acting on a body and its motion due to those forces. The First Law states that every object remains in a state of rest or uniform motion unless it is acted upon by an external unbalanced force. The Second Law states that the relationship between an object's mass (m), its acceleration (a), and the applied force (F) is $F = ma$. The Third Law finds that for every action there is an equal and opposite reaction.

[89] You can learn a lot by studying their lives and their pursuits of the world of science and physics. For an interesting review of distinction in human history, I recommend Daniel Boorstin's series, *Knowledge Trilogy.* The first book in 1983, *The Discoverers,* chronicles the curiosity, inventiveness and achievements of man and his desire to understand the universe and his place in it. The second book in 1992, *The Creators,* is the story of mankind's creativity, highlighting great works of art, music and literature. It examines both the ideas and the people behind those ideas. Both Darwin and Newton are discussed in the first two books. The third volume published in 1998, *The Seekers* examines man's social, political, and religious development.

INDIVIDUAL DISTINCTION

How is individual distinction possible? First, it's understanding that distinction is not about *being the best, but what you're best at*. Too many people let themselves down by failing to recognize this difference. Of course, it's wonderful when your best is better than everyone else. Not being the best, however, should not be considered a failure. As the old U.S. Army ads used to say, "Be all that you can be."

The distinction I'm talking about is personal, circumstantial, and dynamic. It's personal because distinctions are both inherent and learned. Your personal qualities, education, and experiences can never be duplicated. Others may share some of those attributes, but it is still something unique to you. Take hiring, for instance. Sometimes you will have a situation where two candidates seem about the same. Both have the same degree and 10 years experience at comparable firms. Despite the similarities, the differences are bound to be greater. Perhaps one candidate has a better attitude, more engaging personality, or is the more effective communicator. There will always be something personal, different and better about you, because you are you.

Second, distinction is circumstantial. It's having or doing something that fits at the right time and right place. Take those two candidates again. At the time of the interview, the company may be seeking to enter a new market where a candidate with stronger sales skills would be better. Or perhaps the position had been held by someone who tended to criticize their colleagues, so a more positive personality is preferred. The trick is recognizing and creating those circumstances for yourself.

Third, distinction is dynamic. Circumstances change and so do you. You can learn new things or discover abilities you never knew before. Have you ever helped anyone with their homework, and then turned it into a multi-million dollar global non-profit organization? The answer is yes, if you're Salman Khan. In 2004, Khan began helping his teenage niece with algebra. Because Khan lived in Silicon Valley and his niece was across the country, he created his tutorials on Yahoo's Doodle

133

Notepad, then later on YouTube. Then, unexpectedly, strangers began using Khan's lessons on YouTube. By 2009, Khan's tutorials became so popular that he quit his job as a hedge fund analyst to focus on producing more lessons. Khan converted a closet in his apartment into an office and began the Khan Academy with the mission "to provide a free, world-class education for anyone, anywhere."[90]

Little did Khan know how many people he was helping. At the 2010 Aspen Idea Festival, Microsoft co-founder Bill Gates said, "There's a new website that I've just been using with my kids recently called Khan Academy. K-h-a-n. Just one guy doing some unbelievable 15-minute tutorials."[91] Khan couldn't believe Gates was using his lessons. Two weeks later, Khan got another surprise: a phone call from Gates' chief of staff inviting him to Seattle for a visit. In 2012, the Gates Foundation and Google provided more than $15 million in funding to help the Khan Academy hire the country's most talented engineers and designers, and develop the tutorials even further. The site boasts over 3,100 lessons and practice tools on math, science, history and more.

Online education isn't anything new, however. "Stanford University's engineering school rolled out gratis video lectures, handouts and assignments for several of its courses. Meanwhile, UC Berkeley has been posting classes online since 1995, on iTunes since 2006 and on YouTube since 2007. The university is fast approaching the 100 million download mark."[92]

So what makes Khan Academy different and, arguably, better? Why is it distinct? It's simplicity. As Khan explains, "I'm 95 percent of the time working through that problem real time. Or I'm thinking it through myself if I'm explaining something. And to see that it is sometimes a messy process, that it isn't always this clean process where you just know the answer. I

[90]Khan Academy, www.khanacademy.org.

[91] David A. Kaplan, "Gates' Favorite Teacher," *CNNMoney*, August 23, 2010, http://money.cnn.com/2010/08/23/technology/sal_khan_academy.fortune/index.htm.

[92] James Temple, "Salman Khan, math Master of the Internet," *San Francisco Chronicle*, December 14, 2009, http://www.sfgate.com/cgi-bin/article.cgi?f=/c/a/2009/12/13/BUKV1B11Q1.DTL#ixzz1tYToCCki.

think that's what people like, the kind of humanity there."[93] By working through the problems, "he showed people the right way to do video content – the wrong way being the 'talking head' or the 'professor at the blackboard.'"[94]

Khan Academy boasts some impressive numbers. It's visited more than four million times every month worldwide. In one 24-hour period in early 2012, students worked out some 1.8 million problems. In an 18-month period, the site had 41 million visits from the United States, 1.7 million from India, and another 1.4 million from Australia.[95] The effectiveness of these programs is now being tested in American classrooms, where some 23 schools are piloting Khan Academy's math program. The program includes a dashboard where teachers can monitor each student's progress in real time, including how long a student spends on a problem and where they are lagging. Teachers step in when the dashboard shows a student having problems on a particular question or subject. As one teacher explained, "I feel like I'm using my time more effectively with my students because instead of making the assumption that the entire class is weak in this area, and I need to spend time reviewing this, I can pull those three, four, five kids, do a mini-workshop, address those needs, and allow those other students to move on to problem solving activities, or project-based learning with their peers."[96]

In 2012, *60 Minutes* profiled Salman Khan and the Academy. Later that year, Khan was listed among *Time* magazine's Most Influential People of 2012. As Bill Gates wrote in his *Time* profile for Khan, "Sal Khan is a true education pioneer. He started by posting a math lesson, but his impact on education might truly be incalculable."[97]

---

[93] Sanjay Gupta, "Khan Academy: The Future of Education?" *60 Minutes*, March 11, 2012http://www.cbsnews.com/8301-18560_162-57394905/khan-academy-the-future-of-education/?tag=currentVideoInfo;videoMetaInfo.

[94] James Temple, "Salman Khan, math Master of the Internet," op.cit.

[95] Sanjay Gupta, "Khan Academy: The Future of Education?"op.cit.

[96] Ibid.

[97] Bill Gates, "Salman Khan, Educator – The 2012 Time 100," *Time*, April 18, 2012, http://www.time.com/time/specials/packages/article/0,28804,2111975_2111976_2111942,00.html.

History is full of stories of distinction. Here's one I particularly like. At the beginning of the 19th century, battles at sea were fought by two sides engaging each other in single parallel lines. Prior to that, fleets mixed and ships fought in a disorganized and uncontrollable battle. Both tactics often led to inconclusive outcomes. Vice Admiral (Lord) Horatio Nelson believed there was a different and better way to fight at sea.

In 1805, the Battle of Trafalgar during the Napoleonic Wars pitted the British Navy against the combined French and Spanish fleets. Nelson, in command of the British fleet, knew the battle needed a conclusive result. And orthodox tactics would not do against the enemy's larger fleet. Inspired by tactics used by British admirals in two separate battles five years earlier, Nelson decided to attack head on. He divided his fleet into two columns and perpendicularly confronted the French and Spanish fleets, which were horizontally aligned. This way, Nelson divided the enemy's fleet, surrounding half of the ships and forcing them to fight. Also, by dividing the enemy's line in front of their flagship, the isolated ships couldn't see the flagship's signals and were taken out of the battle until they reformed. Nelson's unorthodox tactics led to a decisive victory for the British and reconfirmed their naval superiority.[98] This success was a distinction!

---

[98] It should be clear by now that I have been a big fan of Lord Nelson for many years. His prayer from the morning of the battle, with the enemy fleets in sight, further epitomized Nelson's distinction for me. He prayed: "May the great God, whom I worship, grant to my country and for the benefit of Europe in general, a great and glorious victory: and may no misconduct, in any one, tarnish it: and may humanity after victory be the predominant feature in the British Fleet. For myself Individually, I commit my life to Him who made me and may His blessing light upon my endeavors for serving my Country faithfully. To Him I resign and the just cause which is entrusted to me to defend. Amen. Amen. Amen."

I have been to visit HMS *Victory* in Portsmouth, England twice in my life. The first time was as a 19 year old Midshipman from the Naval Academy. We had sailed to England on the battleship USS *Iowa* (BB-61) in the summer of 1956. The second visit was with my wife, Jennifer, in the fall of 2008. A large etching of Nelson made in 1845 hangs in my library and a beautiful high quality museum model of HMS *Victory* set in a glass case is there also. Anyone who has visited London, England surely has been to the huge plaza at Trafalgar Square that has the tall column where Lord Nelson, the most famous of all English naval greats, stands triumphantly at its top.

Distinction also is shown in the legend of German mathematician, Johann Carl Friedrich Gauss (1777-1855). Gauss was a child math prodigy. One account had Gauss correcting his father's computations at age three! According to one story, Gauss' teacher assigned the class to add up the numbers from 1 to 100. Thinking the long task would occupy his students, the teacher was shocked when the 10-year-old Gauss placed his slate on the teacher's desk just moments later. Instead of adding up each number, Gauss saw things differently. If he "folded" the series of numbers in the middle, then added them in pairs (1 + 100, 2 + 99, 3 + 98, etc.), the sum of each of the pairs would be 101. There are 50 such pairs. Gauss figured he could simply multiply the two numbers (50 x 101), giving an answer of 5050. By following his insight instead of a process, Gauss is said to have discovered the formula for the sum of consecutive integers![99] Gauss was definitely thinking outside of the box. His new method was certainly different and better!

These examples may seem extraordinary, but **distinction is always realistic and tangible**. How you cultivate those advantages is up to you, just as long as you don't stop yourself from doing it. Remember, if you won't be better at something, someone else will.

ORGANIZATIONAL DISTINCTION

Distinction is also what sets your organization apart. It can be a single act or gesture, or a strategic advantage. Organizational distinction is more complicated than individual distinction and requires a different approach to achieve and sustain.

In the fall of 2003 on a visit to CACI staff and customers at the Naval facility at Yokosuka, Japan, I noted the old Navy Jack flag flying from the stem of the USS *Kitty Hawk (CV-63)* as I boarded. The Navy Jack flag bears 13 horizontal alternating red and white stripes, but is most easily recognized by the diagonal rattlesnake and the "Don't Tread on Me" motto. It struck my attention because the American Union Jack, a maritime flag

---

[99] This is also known as the sum of the first n integers, namely $\Sigma = n(n+1)/2$.

bearing a blue canton with 50 white stars, is typically flown on Naval and other U.S. government vessels. It turned out that in May 2002, the Secretary of the Navy issued a directive ordering all U.S. Navy ships to fly the first Navy Jack flag during the Global War on Terrorism.[100] I'm in support of this. I have a *Don't Tread on Me* flag in my office and one that I fly from a flag mount outside of my house.

Why was this so distinctive? In the post 9/11 months, the Navy Jack flag was a unique way to symbolize American fortitude.[101] It was especially empowering to the men and women of the U.S. Navy who would be at the forefront of the Global War on Terror.

There's only one way to stay in business and make good profits – supply your customers with distinctive solutions, products, and services. In their book *In Search of Excellence,* Tom Peters and Bob Waterman found that the most successful companies are ones with strong track records of innovation and entrepreneurial spirit. Creativity in thinking up new products and getting them to market was common. Innovation, entrepreneurship, and doing things with distinction make the difference.

Any marketer will tell you that creating distinction is hard. As advertising guru David Ogilvy said in *Confessions of an Advertising Man,* in business, creative, original thinking is useless unless you can sell it.[102] You need an offering with distinction that meets a market need. More specifically, it must meet your customer's needs and create value from their

---

[100] The Secretary of the Navy is the only Navy Department executive with such authority.

[101] The idea was especially important in announcing the fact that America wouldn't put up with attacks on her own territory. Japanese Admiral Isoroku Yamamoto learned this lesson after his attack on Pearl Harbor, Hawaii on December 7, 1941 when he said, "I fear all we have done is to awaken a sleeping giant and fill him with a terrible resolve."

[102] In the late 1970s, I read – and re-read – Ogilvy's book. It is loaded with excellent business insights and lessons on how to successfully manage a services business. He also had good advice about public relations, advertising, branding, and hiring great people.

perspective. You also need to find the key factors or positioning that makes your offering distinctive in your market. Or you need to know what your existing and potential customers value most and then come up with the best value proposition that embraces your distinction!

Just ask American automakers. Years of making look-a-like cars with little distinction left them wide open to the competition from Japan. Subsequently, Detroit manufacturers suffered from lower labor productivity, the perception of inferior initial quality and reliability, and a lag in bringing new vehicles to market. Add higher employee costs due to labor unions (non-competitive wages and benefits) and strategic mistakes, like the focus on SUVs in the 1990s versus the smaller, fuel-efficient foreign cars, and the Big Three car makers had considerable challenges to overcome. Today, American automakers are still in trouble as recent setbacks (including government bailouts) show that their future is still in question.[103]

On the other side of the spectrum are the folks at the Korean auto maker, Kia Motors. Kia caters to budget-minded consumers. In the U.S., Kia models were first imported and marketed by Ford in the late 1980s. Early success led the company to operate here under its own name a decade later. By the late 1990s, Kia had dealerships in every state except North Dakota. However, the Asian financial crisis of 1997 led to Kia's bankruptcy. In 1998, Korean rival Hyundai acquired Kia and helped the new subsidiary with improvements in quality, refinement, and customer service. The result has been over 14 consecutive years (through 2010) of increased U.S. market share. With competitive pricing, high feature content, and a substantial

---

[103] In 2008, the big three American auto makers, General Motors, Chrysler, and Ford, all testified before Congress about the need for a multi-billion dollar bailout plan to keep them from going into bankruptcy. In 2009, Chrysler filed for bankruptcy protection and sold most of their assets to a new Chrysler company. The federal government provided $6.6 billion in financing for the transaction. General Motors also filed for bankruptcy in 2009 and transferred assets to a new corporate entity. The U.S. and Canadian governments loaned General Motors $8.6 billion. On the other hand, Ford was able to secure a commercial line of credit for a bridge loan, if necessary.

warranty program, Kia now boasts 730 retail dealers nationwide with more than 14,700 employees.

Being competitive and providing value in meeting market demand gives you a path to success – any other course is likely to fail. Distinction must not only be created, it must also be maintained. Every solution, product, and service, from the moment it's delivered, starts aging, deteriorating, or growing obsolete. Failure to create a steady flow of new offerings with ever better value propositions to our markets will have us sliding into mediocrity or bankruptcy! (Think about GM, Chrysler, and Ford in 2008-09.)[104]

Since competitive forces and obsolescent forces are always at work, you have to keep innovating and improving what you do. Hence, you must devote much of your quality time to: (1) maintaining the distinctions you have, (2) listening to your customers and meeting their needs, and (3) creating new distinctive products and services with better value for the future.

For example, the CEO of Gillette was once asked about the company's business strategy. He said that Gillette's strategy is simple; create a steady stream of new products. Those that sell, the company supports. Those that don't sell are closed down. Gillette has followed this strategic game plan since the company was founded.

We do the same thing in our business. Mainframe computers, floppy disks, Zip drives, and wired networks are all history or on their way out. CACI's customers want and expect new and better ways to use IT to gain tangible business value. They all want to reduce costs, raise productivity, increase their competitiveness, or gain significant military advantages. They want value. Our job is to find new and better ways for them to do these things and demonstrate that value. This is the arena where we find our distinctive difference, in delivering better solutions,

---

[104] There is a lesson here – a big lesson – for our political leadership. Do everything you can to help American businesses be competitive, both on the domestic and international market scene. Competition in the capitalist setting is what has made America one of the greatest economic powers in the history of mankind. We have to work at it, to keep America at the top. There is nothing automatic or preordained about it!

Character Can Be a Way of Life. J. Phillip "Jack" London's parents, Laura Evalyn (Phillips) and Harry Riles London, taught him the principle of "doing the right thing" and made him recognize this as an important part of his life. London's father, born in 1903 before Oklahoma statehood in 1907, and his mother, born not long after in 1913, were descended from colonists and early American adventurers, pioneers, and settlers in the 1600s and 1700s. This spirit of independence, accountability and self-reliance is part of a person's character that can be passed on through the generations. Jack and Jennifer London formed an iron-clad partnership as they worked to overcome false allegations about CACI's work in Iraq. Doing the right thing is a value that can also be shared. (Courtesy of J. Phillip London)

In the Navy. Stories told by a friend's brother in 1954 about his experience at the U.S. Naval Academy set a young J. Phillip "Jack" London on a path to his future. London graduated from the Academy in 1959, served 12 years on active duty as a naval aviator and another 12 years in the Naval Reserve. Character development and integrity were at the core of the Academy's curriculum at the time and have always been an integral part of Naval service. (Courtesy of J. Phillip London)

CHARACTER: The Ultimate Success Factor

Character. There is nothing more timeless and universal than the importance of character. Johnson and Johnson, led by James Burke shown here presenting new packaging, based their response to the 1982 Tylenol poisoning crisis on unprecedented corporate integrity. (Bettman/Corbis) Alfred Krupp's attitude was evident in his relentless determination for his company's long-term success. Dean Smith told college basketball star Michael Jordan (with teammate Sam Perkins) that if he couldn't pass, he couldn't play; proving the team and the game was not all about him. (Robert Willett/AP Photo/Raleigh News and Observer) Lee Iacocca has served as a role model not just for his business savvy, but his activism and philanthropy. (Bettman/Corbis/AP Images)

The Rewards of Responsibility. Chris Gardner, whose life was depicted in the 2006 movie *The Pursuit of Happyness*, overcame obstacles such as poverty, homelessness and single parenthood to become a successful businessman, motivational speaker, and philanthropist. Gardner attributes his achievements to taking personal responsibility for his life – the ultimate depiction of character. (Courtesy of David B. King)

No Reservations About It. With over 3,700 properties in 73 countries, Marriott is one of the most successful hotel chains in the world. However, founder J.W. Marriott, noted that, "Success is a combination of many things, but a good character is the foundation of the kind of success that will bring you real happiness." (Courtesy of Marriott International)

143

CHARACTER: The Ultimate Success Factor

An Ancient Lie Detector. The Bocca della Verita is a 1st century sculpture located in the church of Santa Maria in Cosmedin in Rome, Italy. A legend arose in the Middle Ages that if a person told a lie with their hand in the mouth of the sculpture, it would be bitten off. It's unknown if anyone actually fell victim to the Bocca, but the story shows the timeless importance of integrity.

All For One and One For All. One of the most complex operations in the Navy is an aircraft carrier operating at sea, requiring a fully coordinated team, as shown here on USS *George Washington* (CVN-73). Working under these dangerous conditions means every member of the team must be trusted to do their job to the best of their ability – and flawlessly – at all times. (U.S. Navy photo by Mass Communication Specialist 3rd Class Jacob D. Moore)

The End of an Epidemic. Dr. Jonas Salk developed the first successful polio vaccine at the University of Pittsburgh in 1955. Salk was clearly not motivated by profit. When asked in a televised interview who owned the patent to the vaccine, Salk replied: "There is no patent. Could you patent the sun?" Salk's attitude reflected his selfless motivations for making the historic discovery.

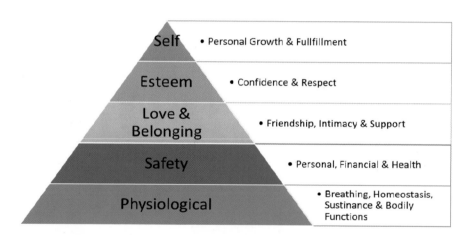

Organically Grown. According to Maslow's Hierarchy of Needs, people are motivated by unsatisfied needs. At the top are self-actualization needs – the need to grow – which stem from a desire to fulfill one's potential. Goals and the actualization of these goals, however, are determined by a person's choices and character.

Stellar Revelations about Revolutions. The collective and interdependent research of scientists Nicolas Copernicus, Galileo Galilei, Tycho Brahe and Johannes Kepler proved that the sun was the center of the universe, and confirmed details about the orbits of Earth and other planets. The singular efforts of each scientist would have never been enough to prove these important facts. This is an excellent example of how achievements of great and personal importance often require a group effort.

Corporate Teams Work and Win Together. In 2010, CACI's General Services Administration (GSA) Program Management Team was selected by the Coalition for Government Procurement (CGP) and the GSA as "Most Valuable GSA Schedule Contractor." The award recognized the CACI team's tireless efforts to promote the GSA Schedules program, maintaining an outstanding reputation with GSA's Federal Acquisition Service and serving the customers' needs. CACI's highly successful project teams are essential in achieving both client and company goals. It's a long-enduring part of the company's culture. (CACI photo by Steve Gibson)

146

The Roles of a Lifetime. George Washington, Ulysses S. Grant, Robert E. Lee, and Admiral Thomas H. Moorer may be key historical and political figures, but they are also some of Jack London's personal role models for their displays of character, integrity, determination and patriotism, as well as their accomplishments.

CHARACTER: The Ultimate Success Factor

Vision. Everyone's potential is either empowered or limited by their vision. As a young man, the author's goal was to attend the prestigious and competitive U.S. Naval Academy, which he achieved by taking the practical steps to qualify as a successful candidate. (U.S. Navy photo by Mass Communication Specialists 2nd Class Alexia Riveracorrea and 1st Class Chad Runge/Released) Albert Einstein may have changed our understanding of the universe, but he had to change how he looked at the universe first. (AFP/Getty Images) Gert Boyle of Columbia outerwear embraced opportunities after personal setbacks. (AP Photo/Don Ryan) And "the greatest thing since sliced bread" was possible because Otto Rohwedder came up with the distinct idea that bread could be sliced and packaged before it was sold.

A Visionary Practitioner. CACI co-founder Herb Karr (left) often referred to himself as a 'practical visionary'. He felt the unique mix of innovation and practicality was essential to keep both his personal success and CACI's growth moving forward. Jack London (right) has worked to continue this approach as a practical visionary in sustaining company growth. (CACI photo)

Not Your Typical Forecast. Herman Kahn was a premiere futurist and pioneer in scenario planning who developed methods for reading and projecting trends. Kahn co-founded Hudson Institute in 1961 where he predicted the rise of Japan as a world power, issues with oil supplies, nuclear weapons and energy, Russia, China, and even world famine. He was also rumored to be one of the inspirations for Dr. Strangelove from Stanley Kubrick's film. Kahn also inspired a new generation, including Jack London, to try his valuable forecasting methods.

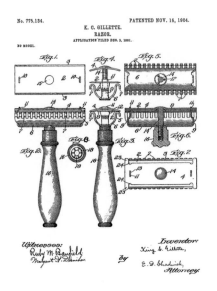

A Sharp Turn. King C. Gillette came up with the idea of disposable razors after seeing bottle caps from the cork seals he sold thrown away. Realizing that dull razor blades could also be thrown away, Gillette envisioned selling razors at low profit margins while creating an ongoing market for the blades. This clever idea transformed the shaving market.

Geeks to the Rescue. Companies, like CompUSA, Circuit City and Tweeter, fell victim to the competitive consumer electronics retail market. Anticipating customers' needs for help with increasingly complicated products, in 2003 Best Buy acquired Geek Squad, a small but effective tech support company that made house calls. They later added in-store Geek Squad centers and grew its range of support services. The strategic move boosted Best Buy's customer satisfaction and return business. (Tim Boyle/Getty Images)

A Conducive Connection. Fairchild Semiconductor was born when eight young scientists decided to start their own company in the nascent industry. Turned down for financial support by the 30 companies they had targeted from *The Wall Street Journal* and New York Stock Exchange listings, a fortuitous run-in with inventor and entrepreneur Sherman Fairchild helped get them started. By taking the chance to form their own company, they also opened the door to further opportunities. (Wayne Miller/Magnum)

Fifth Time's a Charm. Once considered Microsoft's *kiss of death* project, Tandy Trower led the successful development and launch of Windows in 1985. He had succeeded where four previous product managers had failed. Trower's perseverance helped make Windows the dominant operating system within a decade. His career at Microsoft would go on to span 28 years where he also headed Microsoft's Robotics Group. (Reuters)

151

CHARACTER: The Ultimate Success Factor

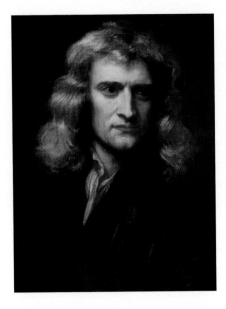 

Where Do We Come From? By examining the world around us, Sir Isaac Newton's discoveries, like the *Laws of Motion,* made the search for the origin of the universe possible. Focusing on the world inside us, Charles Darwin's groundbreaking theories on evolution made the search for the origin of life possible. Newton and Darwin pondered the same question from two distinctly different perspectives.

A Direct Hit. At the Battle of Trafalgar in 1805, Admiral Horatio Nelson broke from traditional naval tactics by taking on the larger enemy fleet head on instead of the usual horizontal alignment. Nelson was able to cut the opposing Franco-Spanish fleet in two, forcing half the ships to fight and the other half to scramble. Although mortally wounded, Nelson's distinctive victory reinforced British naval superiority.

Action. All good intentions stay as intentions unless they are put into action. One of the original celebrity chefs, Julia Child's career started not in a kitchen, but in advertising and espionage. (AP Photo/Jon Chase, File) Former U.S. Air Force and commercial pilot Chesley Sullenberger's expertise in aviation safety came in handy when he had to make the extraordinary decision to land his damaged plane in New York City's Hudson River. (Photo by NY Daily News Archive via Getty Images) Tim Hortons may not have become a household name in Canada had Jim Charade not persuaded Horton to switch from the hamburger business to coffee and donuts. (CP Photo/Stuart Nimmo) Renowned leaders, like Jack Welch and the late Gen. Norman Schwarzkopf, epitomized character and passion in their roles. (U.S. Army; General Electric)

CHARACTER: The Ultimate Success Factor

An Original Software Startup. In 2012, CACI celebrated its 50th anniversary with nearly 15,000 employees in 120 offices worldwide, and $3.8 billion in annual revenue. When the company was started in 1962, co-founders Herb Karr (right)and Harry Markowitz (left) used a California park bench and phone booth as their first office with only $1000 on hand for a direct mail campaign. Like many other large companies, CACI began with a simple idea and product – selling the simulation software language Simscript®. (CACI images)

From a Rocky Start to a Rock-solid Strategy. After CACI's co-founder Herb Karr's several failed acquisitions of software companies in the early 1970s, it took his successor CEO Jack London years to convince him to give the strategy another try. Although it took London and his team several years to develop and refine their Mergers and Acquisitions' process, it was well worth the effort. Between 1992 and mid-2013, CACI had made 59 successful acquisitions. Known in the industry as a strategic consolidator, CACI's persistence paid off and Mergers and Acquisitions became a cornerstone of the company's growth. (CACI photo by Z. Selin Hur)

The Original Decider. President Harry S. Truman understood accountability in decision-making, represented by the iconic image of the "The Buck Stops Here" plaque on his desk. In terms of monumental decisions, Truman's decision to drop the atomic bomb on Japan was a difficult, but necessary choice. Few decisions have had such far-reaching consequences. Virtually all other decisions seem easy in comparison.

The Truth Will Out. In 2004, an *illegally-leaked* military report falsely accused a CACI employee of culpability for abuses at Abu Ghraib prison in Iraq. CACI was often wrongly associated with the iconic photograph of the "hooded man," taken by Staff Sgt. Ivan "Chip" Frederick, shown here in another photo taken moments later. (Frederick and ten other soldiers were convicted for the abuses, with several serving prison terms of up to seven years.) What ensued was a hypercrisis management campaign by CACI to refute the unfounded allegations and media onslaught, as well as set the record straight. Months after the shocking headlines, nine government investigations found CACI had no role in the abuses. *Our Good Name – A Company's Fight to Get the Truth Told About Abu Ghraib* was published in 2008 by Jack London to provide a factual narrative of events. (Book image by Stan Poczatek)

155

CHARACTER: The Ultimate Success Factor

"Sink the Bismarck". During the Battle of the Denmark Straits in World War II, the British Navy was shocked when the German *Bismarck* sank the HMS *Hood* in a decisive battle. Despite the damage to Britain's confidence about winning the war, an undaunted Winston Churchill issued his famous command to "sink the *Bismarck.*" Just three days later, the British Navy, led by the HMS *Rodney* and HMS *King George V,* put the *Bismarck* under the sea. Churchill's decision became a goal that the British Navy was determined to achieve.

"Make it Happen!"

"Remember: at CACI we are looking for team players, not people who have to be a one-person band!"

A Culture to Draw From. CACI co-founder Herb Karr enlisted the famous single-panel cartoon humorists, Virgil Partch (left) and John Dempsey (right), to illustrate some of the principles behind CACI's culture. Partch, known for his syndicated comic strip *Big George*, drew several dozen cartoons for CACI and added the company's name to his familiar abbreviated signature. Dempsey, who took over after Partch died, was featured in the *Saturday Evening Post, Look, Playboy*, and *Collier's*. These Partch and Dempsey originals for CACI reflect the effective and entertaining way their cartoons communicate CACI's corporate culture to its employees. (CACI images)

A Big Deal. When Serge Godin, head of the Canadian IT firm CGI, looked to acquire the faltering Virginia-based American Management Systems (AMS) in 2004, he needed to find a third party who would be willing to buy AMS' Defense and Intelligence Group – a division CGI could not own as a foreign company. Despite being advised against the $415 million deal, CACI's then-CEO Jack London seized the opportunity to build the company through the transaction. The deal was later named the "Hottest M&A Deal of the Year" and was a resounding success for both companies. (The Canadian Press/Ryan Remiorz; CACI photo)

Another First in Flight. Frederick W. Smith started FedEx in 1971 based on an economics paper outlining overnight delivery service in the computer age that he had written nearly a decade earlier. Inspired by the bank clearinghouse network, Smith created the hub-and-spoke model for shipping. The 29-year old Smith raised nearly $90 million in venture capital. FedEx struggled for four years before showing a profit, but today FedEx is a worldwide leader in priority shipping. (Landov/James R.Reid)

157

Resolve. No success can be achieved without the resolve to see things through. When Apple first offered an exclusive deal to carry their new iPhone, Verizon Wireless didn't want to take the risk of a unique profit-sharing agreement. AT&T successfully took the risk and Verizon Wireless would have to wait for a second chance. (Ramin Talaie/Bloomberg via Getty Images) In the late 1990s, a widespread panic was created by the Y2K bug that failed to cause any trauma to computer systems worldwide. (Photoshot/Getty Images) While many investors and companies did well in the Internet bubble of the 1990s, others didn't know when to hold back and pushed their luck with unviable businesses. Starting as a wood pulp mill in 1865, Nokia diversified and innovated for over a century before entering the telecommunications industry, proving adaptability is part of success. (REUTERS/Jussi Helttunen/Lehitikuva)

A Good Return on Their Investment. Christopher Columbus told Spain's King Ferdinand and Queen Isabella that he could find a new, direct Spanish route to the Orient with its abundant treasures of silks and spices. Ferdinand and Isabella didn't have much to lose if Christopher Columbus failed, but everything to gain if he did. The discovery of the Americas in 1492 created a whole 'new world' of opportunities.

If It Ain't Broke. Trying to boost sluggish sales, Coca-Cola reformulated its popular soft drink into *New Coke*. Despite favorable market research, loyal Coke drinkers fervently responded with their disapproval. Within 80 days, the company introduced *Coke Classic* and New Coke was never heard from again.

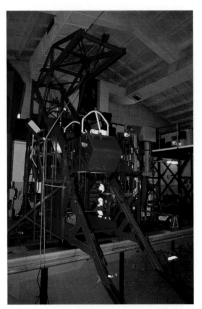

In Case of a Water Landing. A Dilbert Dunker drill simulates an aircraft crash into water. Used in Navy drills to train and test crisis reaction skills, participants must brace for impact, free themselves from harnesses, and swim to the surface. Nerves are considered a natural part of the process, but participants are taught how to manage their emotions and overcome their fears to prevent mistakes in their escape. (U.S. Navy photo by Photographer's Mate 2nd Class Michael B. W. Watkins)

Ready to Soar. The Blue Angels, the U.S. Navy's flight demonstration squadron, have been the world's premiere aerobatic team for over sixty years. Intensive preparation and practice helps the pilots overcome the anxiety of performing these risky maneuvers. After all, there's very little room for fear in the air! (U.S. Navy/Blue Angels photo)

The End and The New Start.

In 1985, CACI's new CEO Jack London and Chief Counsel, Jim Berkson, had to take the difficult steps of shutting down the company's poorly performing European offices. The closings included removing the executive in charge of this division, who ironically had hired London at CACI 12 years earlier. A positive outcome of the closings was the turnaround of CACI's UK operations. Greg Bradford, CACI's top contracts and legal counsel in

London at the time, asked for the opportunity to take charge. The UK division with Bradford at the helm has been performing well ever since. The closings were a significant test and display of character and determination. (CACI photo by Sarah Berresford; Fabrice Coffrinu/AFP/GettyImages)

What Seemed Like a Good Idea.

The merger of AOL and Time Warner in 2000 was considered to be the ultimate partnership; a leading content company joining forces with a primary distributor of online content. However, the arrangement quickly fell apart. Synergies were never established between the two companies. Many executives on both sides didn't know about the deal until it was announced.

The two companies had distinct and clashing cultures. In 2002, AOL Time Warner had lost $99 billion (including a fourth quarter charge of $45.5 billion related to the depreciation of the America Online unit). In 2007, Time Warner's new CEO proposed splitting the companies. When the split happened in 2009, the combined value of both companies was one-seventh of what it had been the nine years earlier. The split was a hard, but necessary decision that acknowledged the

merger's mistakes. (AP Photo/Stuart Ramson; Henny Ray Abrams/AFP/Getty Images)

161

CHARACTER: The Ultimate Success Factor

City of Champions. This is the moniker for a city when two or more of its professional sports teams win the top prize. In 2009 it was Pittsburgh whose Steelers won Super Bowl 43 and whose Penguins won the Stanley Cup. Success is contagious in Pittsburgh, where professional and collegiate teams have won nearly thirty major championships, including the Steelers' six Super Bowls – more than any other football team. (Sporting News Archive)

Washington's Bold Move. In December 1776, it looked like the new United States of America was losing its War of Independence. General George Washington knew a bold move was necessary to reinvigorate their cause. A surprise attack on Christmas night pushed back Hessian and British troops and led to several empowering victories in New Jersey and Pennsylvania. America was on its way!

A Culture of Success. The tenets behind CACI's culture of ethical and operational excellence have been documented and distributed since the early 1980s. CACI's corporate culture is introduced at new employee orientations and reinforced through internal communications, awards programs, compliance initiatives, and philanthropy. CACI also has received numerous recognitions for its culture. For example, in 2009, CACI received the top rating of "Best Overall Government Contractor Ethics Program" in the 2008 Government Contractor Ethics Program

Ratings released by the Ethisphere Institute. The Greater Washington Human Resources Leadership Awards has annually conferred the "Dr. J.P. London Award for Promoting Ethical Behavior" since 2002. (CACI image by Stan Poczatek)

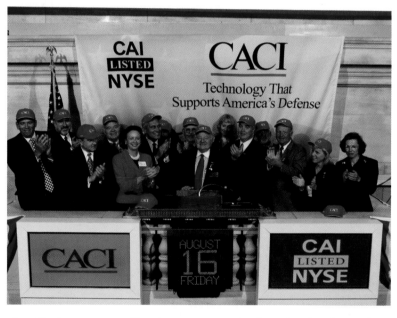

A Ringing Endorsement. Nearly 34 years to the day after first becoming a public company, CACI joined the New York Stock Exchange on August 16, 2 002 when Dr. J.P. London, CACI's then-CEO, rang the opening bell. After the Exchange changed the rules on trading symbols, the company modified theirs to read "CACI." In 2012, the company celebrated its 50th anniversary. Character has been at the center of CACI's success story. (CACI photo)

163

CHARACTER: The Ultimate Success Factor

Character-based Success Stories. *Jane Goodall's* lifetime of work in wildlife protection and education has garnered her numerous awards and accolades. Today, Goodall is still active in her late 70s, giving university lectures, meeting with government officials, and fundraising for the Institute. Thousands of doctors and staff members who work for *Medicins Sans Frontieres*, aka Doctors Without Borders, give up the comfort of a lucrative practice to work in some of the most volatile and impoverished parts of the world for a small stipend. At *UPS*, corporate responsibility includes a foundation for charitable donations and community activities, as well as a safe driving campaign. (Michael Nichols/National Geographic/Getty Images; Thony Belizaire/AFP/Getty Images; Courtesy of the UPS Foundation)

offering specialized domain knowledge, enabling customers to stay on the edge of new and emerging technologies, and meeting rapidly changing requirements, such as today's unprecedented national security demands. This is just the start. Distinction can reside anywhere. It's our job to seek it out, promote it and reward it.

If you don't believe me, just ask former General Electric CEO Jack Welch. Under Welch's twenty year tenure, GE's revenues increased by nearly five times. The company's market value went from $14 billion in 1981 to more than $410 billion at the end of 2004.[105] Welch championed many business practices, including differentiation. He believed that certain products, services, and people worked better for the company. Those that fell to the bottom had to be removed. "Running your company without differentiation among your businesses or product lines may have been possible when the world was less competitive. But with globalization and digitization, forget it."[106] Not focusing on what you do better is counterproductive.

I think that the most overlooked element in distinction is people. In CACI's management manuals, we explain the importance of this point. At CACI, we insist that we only hire heroes. 'Heroes' are people we enjoy working for and with every day. Heroes can bring innovation and knowledge to the way things are done. Our heroes concentrate on delivering great solutions and services to our customers.

"If each of us hires people who are smaller than we are, we shall be a company of dwarfs. But if each of us hires people who are bigger than we are, we shall become a company of giants."

David Ogilvy

How do we hire heroes? We say at every recruiting opportunity, hire the very best you can get and afford, even if the

---

[105] Welch was CEO from 1981 to 2001. GE's market value reached $410 billion a few years after Welch's departure. At the time, GE was the most valuable and largest company in the world. Now that was real distinction!

[106] Jack Welch, *Winning* (New York: Harper Collins, 2005).

person greatly exceeds your immediate requirements. If the candidate really is too good for the job, in no time he or she will surpass the job description, expand into new responsibilities and challenges, and become a greater asset to the company. Unless you can predict the future, you'll never know what kind of opportunities or challenges you'll face. These so-called overqualified employees may have the know-how and experience to help tackle unforeseen prospects and problems. In our business, no matter how clever you may be, if you hire mediocre people, you will fail. If you surround yourself with talented, high-powered people, they'll see that you succeed no matter how many messes you face. Ogilvy's words, quoted here, say it precisely.[107] Heroes make work life a whole lot easier and operations will be stronger and more effective than ever.

Whether individual or organizational, creating distinction isn't automatic or instant. Even if you know what your *edge* is, it will take time to implement it into actionable steps. Big, positive transformations happen with persistent pushing in a consistent direction, sustained over time. Success is a long-term effort.

So if you know what you do – and can do – different and better, start now. Your best approach is to *create distinction everywhere!*

---

[107] Ogilvy's quote about a company of dwarves or giants was inspiring to Herb Karr and me. In April 1985, we took a photo of a set of Russian *matryoshka* nesting dolls all lined up in a row. We put the photo, Ogilvy's quote and our own quote in a picture frame. Our quote read "Let's make CACI a company of giants." The point was to surround ourselves with talented people. We had several of these made and distributed them among our senior staff. These pictures can still be seen in several offices at our headquarters building. It was a great idea then and it still is. Mine hangs in my office to this day.

STRUCTURE: Action

Knowing who you are and what you want to achieve are important steps to success. The most important step you can take, however, is the one going into action. And that starts with changing your behavior. The biggest obstacle to success is choosing not to do something – anything. Nothing changes when you choose to do the same thing over and over again. Most people don't realize how much they can accomplish by simply making different choices and trying different things. These are often simple actions, like speaking up and stepping up.

The one thing you should never change is your character (except to improve it!). The challenges and opportunities you face may tempt you to cut corners, work around the rules, or even knowingly break the rules. If you compromise your character (even simply by failing to do the right thing), you will surely compromise your chances for success – whatever your goals may be. Everyone imagines what they could do. Only a few choose to actually do it.

Which are you?

CHAPTER 10

EVERYTHING HAS TO START SOMEWHERE

"Do what you can, with what you have, where you are."
Theodore Roosevelt

The next thing you do will start something. If you join a gym, you'll start exercising. If you go after a new job, you'll be starting a career. If you join the military, you may end up on the Joint Chiefs of Staff. If you run for local office, you may eventually run for President.

I'll bet there is at least one thing nearby that you have been meaning to do, but haven't yet started. A report? A job search? Remodeling? Writing a novel? Starting your own business? A groundbreaking invention?

In 1752, an enthusiastic 20-year old surveyor applied for the command of one of Virginia's regional militias. In 1789 the same surveyor, George Washington, was elected the first President of the United States.

A young man with only three months formal education may have disappeared into obscurity had he not saved the life of a train station agent's child in the 1860s. The grateful agent trained the unwitting hero as a telegraph operator, a job that would allow him to read and do experiments during the night shift. That man, Thomas Edison, would later invent the phonograph, light bulb, and start General Electric, among other accomplishments.

After a career in advertising and in the Office of Strategic Services (the precursor of the CIA) during World War II, a 38-year old housewife who relocated to Paris with her husband's job would use her new free time to take French cooking classes. Julia

Child's culinary career became legendary and even the subject of a popular 2009 movie.

In 1976, two twenty-something guys in the bedroom of a suburban San Jose, California home created a fully-assembled circuit board. By 2011, the early tinkerings of Steve Jobs and Steve Wozniak had become technology giant Apple with 60,400 employees worldwide and annual revenues of $108 billion.

For 23 years, I was CEO of CACI International. Yet both CACI and I had very humble beginnings. One of my first jobs was a paper route.[108] Even when I started at CACI, it was on a project team. I joined the fledgling company as a project manager, eventually working my way up and building my business over 12 years to make the top spot. From there it took another 20 years to lead the company to a Tier 1 status.

That first step can be a no-brainer, or it can be a doozy. However, anything worth doing requires you to take that first step, and few things of consequence are accomplished in just a few steps. Even fewer people start at the top or close to achieving their goals. For the rest of us, reaching goals are longer, more complex efforts that take time and multiple steps, sometimes a lifetime. You don't run a marathon the first time you put on sneakers, but at some point you have to put on your running shoes and attempt that first mile.

Once you've started moving, you build forward momentum. New opportunities arise and new people are met. Think of it this way. You are at a career crossroads and you want a new job, a new direction. Do you sit at home and wait for a "fairy job-mother" to magically appear with the next great position? Hardly. No one, especially employers, will know you are in the job market unless you tell them. So you post your resume on job boards and apply to a few openings. Just like thousands of other job seekers. Not very useful, is it? (Only 3 percent of jobs are found online.) Successful job seekers will step it up. They contact everyone in their network to inquire about

---

[108] Like many of my friends in the late 1940s and 1950s, I had lots of odd jobs as a youngster growing up in post-World War II Oklahoma City: car hop, janitor, paper boy, junior artist for a high school yearbook publisher, and delivery truck driver.

opportunities, set up informational interviews, or ask to be kept in mind if they hear of anything. They attend networking events and other activities where they can meet people. The broader the net is cast, the more the opportunities. Of course, economic conditions and other factors may challenge even the most highly motivated job hunter, but employers will at least know you are looking and available.

Waiting for the right time to make that first move? After the holidays? When there's more money in the bank? When you get a promotion? When things get less busy? We've all made or listened to these excuses at one time or another. Unfortunately, **excuses are self-made obstacles**. Remember: If there's a will, there's a way. Want to learn a foreign language? There are classes available. Crunched for time? Take a second look at your schedule. Conflicting obligations may be shorter term than the language course. Things can be moved around. What's on your schedule that you want to do more, or less, than the language classes? Are classes a financial stretch? Why not start with online resources, commercial language products, or books from the public library? The point is, if you want to do something, start now, even if it's a smaller step than you wanted to make. Create a "to do" list to get things going.

Another reason to not put off your start is that you may lose out. In business, there's something called *first mover* advantage – the idea that the first company to move into a market segment will gain market share, resources, brand recognition and other advantages that the following companies will lack. Not only do follower companies have a competitive disadvantage, they can be pushed out of the market altogether.

Just look at the iPod by Apple. While it wasn't the first digital audio player in the world, it was the first one with mass appeal that also offered licensed music through iTunes, an application for buying, organizing and playing digital music. The iPod and iTunes were introduced in 2001. By 2009, Apple had nearly 74 percent of the MP3 player market and iTunes became the top retailer for music in the U.S. with 26.7 percent market share. While being the first mover doesn't guarantee success, if you work it right, maintain focus and momentum, your odds skyrocket.

Being a first mover also applies to your career. Imagine that you and a coworker both seek the same promotion. Should you speak to your boss about the opportunity or hope that your record will speak for itself? Do you wait to see what your coworker does first? The person who shows initiative and determination is far more likely to get the job.

Of course, there are legitimate challenges that keep us from starting new endeavors – health, money, time, and other resources. We also all have responsibilities to ourselves, families, and jobs that make our lives an ongoing balancing act. But I can guarantee that you can do one thing right now that will get you on your way to achieving a goal. It doesn't have to be complicated. You can't learn how to cook until you learn how to boil water. If you want to declutter your home, start with one closet. If you want to start a business, write your plan (what will you sell, to whom, and how). Don't exaggerate what you need to do. The simpler you keep the process, the more likely you'll get started – and do it.

Even when you're up and running, what happens next isn't always certain. The first step may not be the right step. An opportunity may turn out to be a dead end. There can be surprises. You may even detest what you thought you would like doing. You will make mistakes, but all is not lost. You can learn from what goes wrong. Perhaps you should be doing something different. Setbacks and failures teach you what to do and what not to do, where you can improve, and how you can change your plans for the future. So take advantage of the process. Learn from it and make your mid-course corrections.

We may also start down one road and end up somewhere else. At age 18, even age 28, I thought I would always have a career in the Navy. I could have scarcely imagined the corporate career that I have had or the struggles, unknowns, and the ups and downs that so often went with it.

Nothing happens unless you take action. Every large business started as a small business. Every small business started as an idea in someone's head. AT&T, IBM and Microsoft didn't spring up overnight. Neither did the local bakery. They all started with an idea – ideas that were acted upon.

Starting a business is not some kind of lofty venture that only rich, adventurous or very smart people can do. It is challenging, yes, but not unattainable. The number of people who call themselves entrepreneurs is a small fraction of those people who actually are entrepreneurs. Even though he's considered to be one of the best-known technology entrepreneurs ever, I doubt that Bill Gates started his career in 1972 with the goal of being

"The beginning is the most important part of the work."

Plato

an entrepreneur. In fact, he turned a lifelong interest in computers into a profession, which led him and Paul Allen to eventually start a venture called Microsoft.[109]

Celebrity chef and author Rachel Ray started her career managing the candy counter and later the fresh foods department at Macy's in New York City. After helping open a market in New York, she moved upstate to manage a resort hotel restaurant. While working as a buyer for a gourmet food store, she came up with the idea of teaching reluctant cooks how to make quick and tasty meals. The result was a course showing how to make meals in less than 30 minutes. That course led to weekly segments on the local TV news, which led to a public radio appearance, the publication of her first book, and a *Today* show spot. It wasn't until 2001 that the Food Network offered her the show that would become *30 Minute Meals*. Now she boasts a food empire! I bet she didn't see herself as an entrepreneur at the Macy's candy counter.

An entrepreneur is one who organizes, manages, and assumes the risks of operating a business or enterprise. It is motivated by the desire to do new and different things, to tap

---

[109] Gates took a leave of absence from Harvard in 1972 to work with a microcomputer company in Albuquerque, New Mexico. He never returned to Harvard. Although a good education is always useful in being an entrepreneur, the entrepreneurial spirit is not necessarily a function of education.

into your creativity, to implement an idea. The focus is about having the entrepreneurial spirit.

Whatever your goal is, nothing starts happening until you do something. And in business, as Thomas Watson, Sr., founder of IBM famously said, "Nothing happens until something is sold." So get started!

Professionally, I've always enjoyed starting things. I did not start CACI, but I did get a lot of things started there! Most of the lines of business that I personally initiated in the 1970s and 80s are still a part of the company. Virtually all of CACI's current growth lines of business were started in the late 1990s when I was CEO. In fact, many in the industry credit me with being the founder of the modern-day CACI, taking it as CEO from a troubled and declining $100 million company in 1984 to a nearly $2 billion enterprise in 2007 with a more than commensurate increase in profit and shareholder value.

Here's one example from my experiences. In the late 1990s, CACI had some investor relations challenges. Being both an IT company and a government contractor, we found that investors did not always understand what CACI did or how we created value. We also had some challenges in the way we communicated to our shareholders. All of this was happening in the middle of the crazy dot.com and Y2K era. It seemed CACI's investors, management and board were not on the same page. So we decided to overhaul our investor relations program. I knew what I wanted to do – and I got started on it.

CACI initiated a new investor outreach program and a method to evaluate its effectiveness. We wanted to clearly communicate the company's strategic goals and initiatives. The new program would also help identify potential shareholder issues and concerns that could impact investment appeal.

The program consisted of a quadrennial perception study targeting 50 of CACI's largest shareholders, sell-side analysts and former shareholders who knew the company best. In addition, we implemented a process after each quarterly earnings conference call (four times a year), where our investor relations (IR) consultants would gather feedback from call participants and then present them to CACI's management and board. As a result, we have an ongoing process to monitor the financial community's perception and reaction to our message and performance.

All of this information is presented to the Investor Relations Committee – and sometimes to the entire Board – by our Investor Relations officer. This way, the Board understands the current thinking of the financial community's position on CACI as well as the market issues influencing our investment appeal.[110] To this day, CACI is perhaps the only company on the NYSE that has a formally constituted Investor Relations committee of its board. We've had it in place since the mid 1990s. Setting it up was another one of my more important board-level innovations.

Not everything that gets started works out right the first time. Lee Iacocca, the former head at both Ford and Chrysler, said it very well, "So what do we do? Anything. Something. So long as we just don't sit there. If we screw it up, start over. Try something else. If we wait until we've satisfied all the uncertainties, it may be too late."

Here's a prime example. Since 1992, CACI has made 59 acquisitions (about 59 more than most companies ever make). Our Mergers and Acquisitions (M&A) program benefits the

---

[110] The perception studies are pretty substantial. We ask participants to candidly respond to a series of detailed questions on such value issues as strategy, performance, governance and investor relationships. We also ask our upper level management and our directors to respond to a subset of the same questions to compare external and internal perceptions.

The interviews are conducted by an independent market research firm, ensuring confidentiality and encouraging candor. The results, verbatim comments, and recommendations are presented uncensored to our board and management team. Over the last ten years, we have conducted four comprehensive perception studies (1999, 2003, 2007, and 2009). We use the studies' results and recommendations as input to our investor relations (IR) initiatives. They have also become an important part of our board development and training program. In 2012, I chartered another such study as part of our ongoing IR program.

The primary benefits from our ongoing IR program have been more control and continuous improvement of our message; improved communications between the company and the financial community, including current and potential shareholders; and, rather importantly, increased board understanding of all of this.

company because we have a comprehensive and seasoned process that assesses the potential of each deal and helps us make the right decision.

Did we have this full-blown process when we did our first acquisition? You bet we didn't! It took many years of getting ready, studying the process and looking for takeover candidates, before we did our first deal. People think that because we've been successful with M&A that it must be easy to do. Even with our experience, these deals are not easy. Yet everything, including CACI's M&A program, had to start somewhere. It was a business strategy we put in place over twenty years ago. Now it's a time-tested and highly successful core capability in our company.

My predecessor at CACI, Herb Karr, loved software. He was a software guy himself and believed that if you could run a software project, you could run anything. That's probably why his first acquisitions were several small software companies in 1970-1971. While the companies had some interesting products, they were not the best match for CACI's portfolio at the time.

Herb was upset with the acquisitions' poor financial performance. The truth was they were disasters. As a result, he quickly lost all interest in ever doing another acquisition. Even the idea was painful to him. For years he would emphatically refuse to even consider the idea of an acquisition, but I knew it was a strategy we couldn't permanently abandon.

A few years after I became CEO in 1984, I felt it was time to take another look at acquisitions. The same year I got the top job at CACI, the Competition in Contracting Act (CICA) changed the landscape of the government contracting industry. Companies needed to gain competitive advantages wherever they could, and acquiring companies with lucrative contracts, skilled workers, and promising technologies was an excellent way to do so – if you could pull it off! I felt we needed to give M&A a fresh try.

Herb, still Chairman of the Board, had always felt 5 to 10 percent of the CEO's job should be dedicated to *exploring* – in the entrepreneurial sense. So I convinced Herb that it was time to re-explore M&A as a growth strategy. That led me to a three day M&A seminar by Peat Marwick (now KPMG) at the historic

Mark Hopkins Hotel at the top of Nob Hill in San Francisco. I combined the seminar with visits to the Oakland office which CACI had back then. The course itself was fascinating. It covered nearly everything anyone needed to know about M&A, including how to structure a deal, negotiating, accounting, and all the possible pitfalls. There was not a single other attendee from the consulting industry there, let alone the government contracting business.

Herb also recommended that I contact his former boss at Planning Research Corporation (PRC), Bob Kruger. Bob had built PRC single-handedly in the 1960s and 70s through a series of acquisitions.[111] I had several visits with Bob at my office, each one lasting the entire day. He taught me several key things that had not been covered at the Peat Marwick seminar: how to hunt for companies in our industry, best ways to value and price companies, and proper due diligence methods. Bob was also the person to teach me one of the most important factors to focus on in a successful acquisition – the employees. Even though this was the late 1980s, the concept of culture was still evolving and absent from many M&A approaches.

Bob taught me that while the numbers may look promising, the acquisition could still easily fail if you ignore the roles and interests of the employees. This lesson became a cornerstone of our acquisition program and still sets our approach apart.

Now that I was armed with all this new M&A knowledge and confidence, I was ready to do a deal. The opportunity presented itself in 1989. We saw potential in a small local company that had interesting naval aviation engineering contract opportunities. As a former Navy Aviator, I also had a technical expertise advantage. We had developed a sound M&A process and I took each step carefully. But in the end, it just didn't work

---

[111] PRC would later end up on the other side of the M&A equation. Connecticut-based Emhart Corp. bought PRC in 1987, and then was in turn acquired by Black & Decker as part of its 1989 takeover of Emhart Corp. In 1995 Black & Decker sold PRC to California-based Litton Industries. Litton PRC was formally acquired by Northrop Grumman in 2000 where it has been absorbed into their operations.

out. The board and management team at the target company apparently got cold feet. In any case, they changed their minds. They decided they didn't want to sell and would continue to operate as their own company. Although the deal fell through, it taught me that our process would work and what we could do better the next time.

The next opportunity wouldn't come again for three years. In the meantime, CACI and I faced many challenges. In 1990, Herb Karr passed away, and I was elected to the position of Chairman of the Board. A few short-sighted shareholders used Herb's passing as a chance to try to force the company to be put up for sale. The battle for control became a CACI priority for several years.[112]

By 1992, with the company succeeding, we resumed looking for new M&A opportunities. Despite carrying the three top titles at CACI (Chairman, President, and CEO), I still, properly, had to convince the board that it was time to try another acquisition. So, that year we pursued a company called American Legal Systems under the belief that we could create a commercially focused, computer-based legal and litigation services line of business similar to the one we had been delivering to the U.S. Department of Justice.

This acquisition was not terribly successful as its own stand-alone enterprise, but after we folded their operational capability into our business with the Department of Justice it finally worked out well for everyone. It was a difficult transaction, but we took what we learned to improve our M&A process. The lessons we learned were all about business *fit*, people (motivation and retention) and earn-outs.[113] This due diligence and integration process we developed included computerized tools, and economic and financial analysis models that CACI still uses today. The lessons learned from American

---

[112] Control would also be an up-and-down issue through 1998 and into our ugly proxy fights and tit-for-tat lawsuits in November 1999.

[113] Earn-outs are payments to the sellers of the company over a period of time after the deal closes. Amounts paid are based (contingent) upon achieving ongoing performance factors, such as profit and sales growth.

Legal Systems have served us ever since. It was an extremely valuable, real-life learning experience.

So CACI's highly successful M&A program all started with Herb Karr's unsuccessful acquisitions, years-long hiatus, a learning process, a passed-on deal, and another several year hiatus before we finally completed a deal. Along the way, we had to learn from some failures, and start over twice before we got it right. Determination, persistence and a fine-tuned feedback and learning process paid off handsomely for the company and its stakeholders.

As you evolve, you may have to change along the way, start again, or even take a step back. Nevertheless, to get somewhere other than where you are now, you have to make the first move. So, take those first steps. *Everything has to start somewhere.*

CHAPTER 11

YOU DECIDE

"Nothing is more difficult, and therefore more precious, than to be able to decide."
Napoleon Bonaparte

In the 1984 movie *Moscow on the Hudson,* comedic actor Robin Williams plays a Russian musician who defects at Bloomingdale's department store in New York City during a trip to the U.S. Williams' character is taken in by the store's security guard and his family while Williams' case is reviewed.

Wanting to be useful to his new American family, Williams' character offers to run errands. He winds up at a grocery store with a list that includes coffee. Williams stares in amazement at the size of the store. He asks a manager for coffee and is directed to "aisle 2." Williams asks him for the coffee line. The manager tells him, "Aisle 2, no line." As Williams strolls down the coffee aisle, he's astonished by the variety of coffee brands; "Taster's Choice, decaffeinated, Maxwell House, El Pico, Chock Full of Nuts, Espresso, Cappuccino, Café Francais, Sanka, Folgers, Cafe Caribe, coffee, coffee, coffee, coffee ... !" Overwhelmed by all of the choices, he hyperventilates and collapses.

This scene highlights the importance of decision-making. Having the ability to choose – to decide – is powerful and sometimes daunting. Even small moments of indecisiveness can be frustrating. Have you ever read a menu at a restaurant and not been able to decide what to order? Do you have trouble deciding what to wear? What to watch on TV? For some people, even simple decisions can be challenging. It's no wonder that the larger decisions in life – such as education, career, housing, travel, health, and relationships – are difficult to make. Imagine the challenges of making such decisions for families, organizations, and countries!

Having the ability to make decisions can be a double-edged sword. We want the freedom to choose, but can be intimidated by the choices. Sometimes, indecisiveness can even lead to inaction or paralysis.

WHY DECISION-MAKING CAN BE INTIMIDATING

First, thanks to our insecurities, we question our qualifications and judgment. We wonder if it's even our responsibility. We worry about the consequences of our choices. We fear making the wrong decisions and taking the blame more than we believe we can make the right decision and accept the credit. We're also afraid of what our decisions will say about us. Circumstances may warrant deciding one way, but it may not represent us or our intentions overall.

Second, we face endless variety. Having too many choices is both a blessing and a curse. The Robin Williams coffee example shows how having many options can intimidate some people. Fewer choices are manageable. Chicken or fish? In or out? Coke or Pepsi? Now or later? More options require more complex decision-making processes.

Evaluating our options takes time, requires prioritizing, means assessing value, or determining the impact on others. Then there are the consequences. It's common to see people fail to decide anything at all when the options are endless – perhaps because it's too overwhelming or too complicated to evaluate the outcome.

Third, we think that decisions are final – that once we make a decision, there's no going back. Unlike some TV game shows, however, there rarely are any final answers. While one decision may have a major impact on our lives, it's not the only one that decides how our lives will turn out. Even then, the result is rarely permanent. The thought of having to live with their choices is hard for some people to bear. For others, it's the thought of what they would need to do to change the results.

Whether it's uncertainty, the plethora of choices, or irrevocability, **indecisiveness prevents success**.

We like to think we make the best choices we can at the time, but when choices are made under fear, obligation or duress, we can make poor choices. Not all decisions can be made under optimal conditions, but they can be made with the right mindset.

For example, suppose you have two job offers. You want to pick the one with the best professional opportunities and compensation package. Other factors may play into your decision as well. You want to make the right choice, but with the wrong mindset you may feel that you're setting yourself up for failure with your decision.

DECISIONS ARE OPPORTUNITIES

The right mindset means that having a chance to decide between two offers excites you because you see decisions as opportunities. It's an opportunity to take control over things that are important to you.

EMPOWERING

First of all, decisions are empowering. You have decision-making power in any situation. You decide whether to get out or take a pass. You decide your attitude toward the decision-making process.

For example, today you don't have to accept a doctor's word as final – you can question your doctor's recommendation or diagnosis, get multiple opinions, and even do your own research online about your medical conditions. By being an informed patient, you can take some control of your health, perhaps even come up with an amazing breakthrough.

In 1984, a six-year-old boy, Lorenzo Odone, was diagnosed with adrenoleukodystrophy (ALD), a rare genetic disorder that attacks complex fatty neural tissue covering a good part of the nervous system. His parents, Michaela and Augusto Odone, frustrated by the lack of information and treatment options at the time, took matters into their own hands. With the help of a research scientist and many hours of research and study, the Odone's created a treatment. Called Lorenzo's Oil, the treatment helped slow the clinical progression of the disease and in some cases delayed death from the disease. The Odones had no prior medical experience, but they had motivation and a sense of urgency.[114] That was enough.

Decisions are also empowering because they can *build our self-confidence*. By making decisions, we reinforce our skills, logic, and experiences. When our decisions work out favorably, we are encouraged to tackle more or bigger decisions. For example, deciding to leave an unfulfilling job can lead to other changes, like switching careers.

What if your decision doesn't work out? Most of the time, it really won't hurt you. You could say what doesn't kill you makes you stronger. Despite the wrong choice, your confidence grows because you were bold enough to try. And if you can deal with the consequences, you are empowered to keep at it. Of course, you want to be careful in your decision analysis and make sure you can live with a potentially unfavorable outcome – the downside risk.

Sometimes your decisions can empower others. In 1969, African-American star center fielder Curt Flood decided he would rather not play baseball than be traded to a city considered unfriendly to blacks, even for a hefty salary. Flood's objection wasn't merely about the location of the trade, but the trade itself. Under baseball's reserve clause, owners could trade players like cards. Players had no choice in where they played and were banned from seeking out other teams for themselves. Flood challenged the system and later lost his case in court. However, Flood's stand for his principles paved the way for others. In 1975, two pitchers mounted another challenge against the reserve clause and won. As a result, the era of free agency was

---

[114] The 1992 movie called *Lorenzo's Oil* depicts the Odone's family struggle.

born. Ball players today can thank Flood for his decision to fight for his rights.[115]

EDUCATIONAL

Decisions are also educational. Could you ever imagine Western Union as your local phone service provider? For Alexander Graham Bell, 1876 was a momentous year. He successfully tested his new invention, the telephone, received a patent for it, and planned to marry the following year. That year Gardiner Hubbard, Bell's future father-in-law, also presented an offer to Western Union to purchase the patents for $100,000. Western Union, the dominant player in long-distance communications at the time, seemed to be the obvious customer for Bell's new invention. The value of this new technology, however, was lost on Western Union's president, William Orton, who proclaimed the telephone to be nothing more than a toy. Within a year, Western Union's customers were replacing teletypes with phones from the newly established Bell Company. Within two years, Orton admitted that it would be a bargain if the patents would be available for $25 million. To add insult to injury, Western Union was later forced to lease telephone equipment from Bell. Mr. Orton learned an important lesson the hard way, but it wasn't fast enough to reverse his actions.

The results of our decisions are lessons learned. They teach us what was right, what was wrong, and what could have been better. If we live and learn, then we learn through our choices.

EVOLUTIONARY

Decisions are also evolutionary. Through experience, we learn how to make better choices and avoid bad ones. Good decisions can lead to greater opportunities and challenges. By

---

[115] Flood's career suffered as a result of his decision to challenge the professional baseball system. Sitting out all of 1970, Flood played 13 games for the Washington Senators in 1971 before retiring at age 31.

1914, Henry Ford was already a successful businessman. In 1914, Ford announced that he would offer workers an unprecedented $5 a day for an eight-hour work day – twice the prevailing wage paid for a nine-hour day. What critics proclaimed "an economic blunder" was actually a shrewd move. Ford's assembly line was revolutionary, but resulted in an annual 370 percent turnover rate for workers. The staggering wage was not only meant to retain workers by paying a premium for the repetitive work, but also enable workers to afford cars. The initiative only lasted four years, but it changed employer-employee relations forever. No longer was a job performed solely for wages. By the 1950s, the relationship evolved to include, for example, pensions and dental insurance.

As we make decisions in our lives, we can better address future questions and issues. Not only does our decision-making ability evolve, so does our way of thinking.

DECISIONS ARE RESPONSIBILITIES

Decision points may be inflection points for personal growth and contribution, but they are not without effect. Decisions also carry responsibilities. They require follow through and action. Sometimes, they require flexibility. Sometimes, they call for taking further risks.

Decisions are harder to make when there's more at stake. Actually, the decision is not hard – it's the consequences that can be difficult! How tolerant are you? You can test yourself. Always know (or estimate) the worst that can happen to you as a result of a major decision. In these situations, I try to assess the *maximum downside risk*, and the likelihood of it occurring. This is one of my hard-and-fast rules in making big decisions that carry major consequences. If you can't take (or survive) the hit, don't commit.[116]

These decisions are not solitary acts. They involve the interests and actions of others. The responsibility is even greater

---

[116] Of course, I also consider what the potential positive outcomes may be and their "value-add."

when you're not just deciding for yourself, but when you are deciding for others.

In the 1970s, tales were told around Ford Motor Company that the Pinto, the popular new compact, exploded in rear-end collisions. At first the recall committee lacked the evidence to prove there was a systemic problem. A year later, evidence emerged from pre-production crash tests. The recall committee decided that small cars were inherently unsafe, but that the car's design was legal and fixing the problem would reduce storage space. By 1977, *Mother Jones* had gotten wind of the story. Citing Ford's own studies, the magazine reported that Ford decided that paying off victims and their families cost less than recalling all cars with rear-mounted fuel tanks, including the Pinto.[117] Public outrage at Ford's choice of money over lives was a blow to consumer trust in product safety.

Such moral dilemmas still challenge leaders today. In 2007, Secretary of Defense Robert Gates learned from a newspaper article about mine-resistant, ambush-protected vehicles (MRAPs) that the Marines were using. What caught his attention was that the MRAPs had taken about 300 attacks without losing a single Marine. When he inquired as to why the Army was not using MRAPs, he learned that the vehicles weren't in the Army's program and that buying them now might mean sacrificing something else in the future.[118] I heard this story in DC circles from reliable sources who added that someone in the top ranks asked: "Is Marine blood more valuable than Army blood?"

> *"It's not hard to make decisions when you know what your values are."*
>
> Roy Disney

---

[117] The Pinto was recalled in 1978 and discontinued in 1980.

[118] Kris Osborn, "Gates urges ramping up MRAP acquisition," *Army Times*, May 9, 2007, http://www.armytimes.com/news/2007/05/defense_mrap_070509/.

Luckily, Gates' intervention led to the addition of 5,000 MRAPs in Afghanistan over the next three years. Sadly, some people along the way thought there was no need.[119]

I have little patience with people who can't, don't, or won't face up to their responsibilities and do the right thing. We can't forget the decisions made in the chain of events that led to the 2008 Wall Street financial crises or the BP oil spill of 2010. Think of all the people along the way who chose not to speak up – or who chose not to listen to those who did.

We all like to think our decisions reflect our values and morals. Making the right choices – ethical decisions – is not always easy or obvious. Imagine that a group of children are playing near two railway tracks; one still in use and the other not in use. One child plays on the unused track, while the rest play on the operational track. Suppose that you are standing by the track interchange and see that a train is coming. If you change the train's track, you could save most of the kids – but sacrifice the one child playing by the unused track.

Would you change the track, or let the train go its way? Would you decide to divert the train and sacrifice one child to save many? The kids playing on the operational track should have known better. And perhaps they'll run when they see and hear the train coming. And why sacrifice the child who chose to play on the safer unused track? Should that child pay the price for the other children's bad judgment? Also, by diverting the train to an unmaintained track, you could be putting at risk the lives of all of the passengers. By diverting the train scores of people could be sacrificed (injured or killed) to save the children.

History is full of real examples of this kind of hypothetical situation. Harry "The Buck Stops Here" Truman is one of my decision-maker role models. In his 1956 memoir, Truman wrote, "As President I always insisted on as complete a picture as

---

[119] I wonder if those decision-makers who chose against the MRAPs would have made a different decision if they had a family member or close friend serving in the Army in combat operations in Iraq without the safer vehicle as our family did. If that were the case, I'm sure the answer would have been different. Unfortunately, the answer too often seems to depend on who controls the money, not who needs it.

possible before making a decision..." Truman was so insightful and thorough in his decision-making, that many mistakenly felt it was automatic. For Truman, it was more than getting all the facts and making up his mind – it was making the right decision.

The first time Harry Truman learned about the atomic bomb was after his first cabinet meeting on the day he took the oath of office in April 1945.[120] There was no denying the bomb's power and potential. By July 1945, the bomb had been successfully tested in an isolated corner of the Alamogordo Bombing and Gunnery Range some 230 miles south of Los Alamos, New Mexico. Truman discussed the bomb's possible role in the Pacific war with five-star Generals of the Army, Dwight Eisenhower and Omar Bradley.[121] Throughout July, high-level military leaders and scientists weighed in with arguments and opinions, both moral and military, for and against using the atomic bomb.

Before the atomic bomb, there were two options for ending the Pacific war. The first was continuing conventional bombing and a naval blockade that would likely drag on for over a year. The second was an immediate, massive invasion of Japan that would also likely be a year-long effort. In both cases, casualties would range from tens of thousands to hundreds of thousands both for the Allies and Japanese. Truman also knew that military defeat would not lead to a complete Japanese surrender. The staggering numbers of casualties and the duration of an already prolonged war began to outweigh the objections to using the bomb. By the end of July, Truman understood that the bomb could immediately end the war and save countless lives on both sides.

On August 6, 1945, an atomic bomb was dropped on Hiroshima and after receiving no response from the Japanese

---

[120] Alan Axelrod, *Profiles in Audacity, Great Decisions and How They Were Made* (New York: Sterling Publishing, 2006).

[121] I once met Army General Omar Bradley in the 1970s. His daughter, Elizabeth Dorsey, attended the same parish as I did and one Sunday she brought him to church in a wheelchair. I was honored by the opportunity to meet and talk with this fine man under whose command in Normandy during 1944, my uncle 2nd Lt. Gordon Phillips had fought and died.

another was dropped on Nagasaki three days later. On August 10, the Japanese sent word that they were ready to surrender. Following five days of behind-the-scenes negotiations, the surrender was official. Truman had made the right decisions and done the right thing given the situation, as awful as it was.

Perhaps Truman was influenced by another decisive move earlier in the war. Although the Allies started planning a cross-channel assault right after France fell to the Nazis in 1940, a plan for such an invasion only became a reality at the Quebec Conference in August 1943. In late 1942, the Germans had been stymied in Eastern Europe, North Africa, and Italy – and Allied navies had contained the German submarine threat. American and British bombers had also begun to strike Germany's industrial cities. Military operations for the cross-channel assault were planned, and forces and equipment assembled. Clever deceptions were devised to throw the Germans off.

By May 1944, nearly three million Allied troops in southern England were preparing for the cross-channel attack. Over 4,000 American, British, and Canadian ships and 1,200 planes were also ready.

The Allied forces were commanded by General Dwight D. Eisenhower of the U.S. Army. Despite the complexities of such massive preparations, uncertain weather forecasts, disagreements over strategy, and timing problems about tidal conditions, Eisenhower took bold action. Early on the morning of June 5, 1944, he made the decision to proceed with the attack. Eisenhower also penned a private note to the Army Chief of Staff, General George C. Marshall, later that day assuming responsibility for the decision to launch the invasion, as well as to take full blame if the Allied landing failed to establish a beachhead at Normandy. The next day, June 6, 1944, Eisenhower and Allies landed in northern France. After a long day of hard fighting, the long-awaited "Second Front" foothold in France was established. And the allies marched on to victory.

The passengers of United Airlines Flight 93 that crashed near Shanksville, Pennsylvania on September 11, 2001 also had to make a tough decision. They could either watch the suicide high jacking unfold or take a chance to regain control of the plane. The decision to act is best remembered from the recording that captured passenger Todd Beamer as he exclaimed: "Are you guys ready? Let's roll!" Although the day would end in tragedy, the heroes of Flight 93 chose to fight back.

Today we hope never to face such daunting ethical dilemmas or such horrendous life-and-death decisions. Yet our personal character, values, and the process that we use for other decisions are the same, including those of the direst circumstances.

John F. Kennedy's 1955 Pulitzer Prize-winning book, *Profiles in Courage,* illustrated these lessons in ethical decision-making and was an early inspiration for me.[122] The book is about the bravery and integrity of eight senators in American history who did what they believed to be right despite public opinion and party politics.

I particularly remember the case of Edmund Ross. A Kansas Republican, Ross cast the deciding vote that ended the 1868 impeachment proceedings against President Andrew Johnson. The "Radical Republicans," a group in control of the Senate, passed the Tenure of Office Act to prevent a president from firing cabinet members without the Senate's consent. Specifically, they wanted to stop Johnson from firing Secretary of War Edwin Stanton, whom Johnson believed was controlled by the Radicals who wanted to establish a military dictatorship in the South. Johnson fired Stanton, which led to calls for the President's impeachment. The Republicans, it seemed, had no intention of giving Johnson a fair trial in the Senate. But Ross, a partisan Republican who had little sympathy for Johnson, said he would do his best to see that Johnson was fairly tried. Ross believed that if a president could be forced out of office by insufficient evidence that was based on partisan disagreement,

---

[122] My mother had been a staunch Democratic Party worker in Oklahoma for John F. Kennedy in 1960. I voted for JFK in my first presidential election. After JFK's inauguration, through her party connections to the White House, my mother asked the President to autograph a copy of his book *Profiles in Courage* for me, then a junior officer in the U.S. Navy. I still have the Kennedy book autographed to Lt$_{jg}$. J. Phillip London, along with the correspondence to and from the White House in early 1961. It is one of my most cherished possessions.

the presidency would then be under the control of whatever congressional faction held sway.[123]

Despite criticism and abuse within his own party, as well as from the press and public, Ross voted against convicting Johnson. The impeachment measure failed to reach the required two-thirds majority by one vote. Ross' decision had made the difference, but he also paid for his decision. He and other Republicans who voted to acquit Johnson lost their reelection bids. Ross and his family suffered ostracism and poverty when they returned to Kansas in 1871. The U.S. Supreme Court posthumously vindicated Ross when they declared the Tenure of Office Act to be unconstitutional in 1926. Ross, who died in 1907, was praised for having saved the country from dictatorship.

Ethical dilemmas happen every day. The right choice isn't always clear. Sometimes, we have the luxury of time to make a thorough ethical examination. Other times, we don't. Yet we all have a moral compass. In fact, at CACI we call our *ethics-based culture our compass.* If there's any question as to what we should do, we only need remind ourselves of what we believe in and what we stand for. As Albert Einstein once said, "Relativity applies to physics, not ethics." So choose wisely.

PITFALLS OF INDECISIVENESS

INACTION

Apart from ethical dilemmas and moral lapses, another pitfall in decision-making is inaction. You can spend a lot of time on designing your strategy and finding the best course of action for your efforts. Indecision can be a fatal flaw. Indecision cost IBM the chance to control the personal computer market because they failed to act on Bill Gates' offer to handle their software for them. Barnes and Noble could have remained the world's biggest bookseller had they not waited to start online sales. Now Amazon.com has the top spot.

---

[123] John F. Kennedy Library Foundation, http://www.jflclibrary.org/Education+and +Public+Programs/Profile+in+Courage+Award/Profiles+in+Courage.htm.

The Blackberry smart phone had been a resounding success for Research in Motion, but indecision killed its chances in the tablet market. Research in Motion executives were split on how to market Playbook, the company's new tablet. Some wanted to target their business clientele with a tablet closer in functionality to the Blackberry, while others wanted a flashier product, like the iPad, for a younger demographic. Unable to determine the appropriate market, the Playbook has not been able to compete with the iPad or Kindle Fire.[124]

I agree with Jack Welch, former CEO of General Electric: "When it comes to strategy, ponder less and do more."[125] Set a course and go for it, making corrections and adjustments along the way. Inaction can be devastating. So carpe diem! Seize the day!

CONSENSUS

Another pitfall is confusing a decision with consensus. It's one thing to be open and receptive to other people's ideas. It's another thing to let the flock tell the shepherd what to do. You simply can't get decisions day in and day out by consensus. Why? Consensus is simply what's acceptable to everybody (or to most everybody), and not necessarily what's in the group's or organization's best interest. Consensus can be safe, which is important, but in my experience rarely leads to progress or excellence.

Sometimes someone else's ideas can change your direction or decision for the better (or worse). And sometimes – even frequently – you have to make your own decision setting aside others' counsel.[126]

---

[124] Abe Brown, "RIM's PlayBook Failed Because of Marketing Indecision," *Inc.*, October 3, 2011, http://technology.inc.com/2011/10/03/rims-playbook-failed-because-of-marketing-indecision/.
[125] Jack Welch, *Winning*, op.cit.
[126] When I was CEO, there was always an endless stream of employees, shareholders, board members, and well-intending friends telling me what I ought to do and what I should have done. Some had good ideas and valid points, but most of them had never run a small business, let alone had the CEO position in a much larger public

CACI's acquisition of American Management Systems in 2004 transformed the company dramatically into a top tier performer in our industry. Many of CACI's senior executive team initially advised against the deal and didn't want to do it. I had the same challenge in the proxy fights of 1991 and 1999. The consensus would at times want to go one way when I wanted to go another way. For me, *going with my gut* has always been better than *going with the herd*. And you have to take the responsibility for whatever happens when you go against the herd. In business, few things are as counterproductive as the process of decision-making by consensus. Compromise – good, bad, and ugly – often will amount to mediocrity – and who wants to be known as mediocre?

A corollary of decision by consensus is *decision by sycophants*. A chorus of *yes men* may seem supportive and build your confidence, but it will always be misleading. As Warren Buffett once said, "Of one thing be certain: if a CEO is enthused about a particularly foolish acquisition, both his internal staff and his outside advisors will come up with whatever projections are needed to justify his stance. Only in fairy tales are emperors told that they are naked." The emperor has no clothes![127]

SNAP JUDGMENTS

Another pitfall is making snap judgments. Most of us don't see the harm of impulse purchases for items like a pair of shoes or a few DVDs. Yet most of us would not be so impulsive

---

corporation. Usually, people had no idea of the resources and time needed to implement their ideas. In most cases, I could only think "easier said than done." In those cases, I would politely ignore all the chatter and carry out my existing plans.
[127] In Hans Christian Andersen's "The Emperor's New Clothes," two swindlers promise a fashion-obsessed Emperor a new suit of clothes invisible to the unfit or stupid. Although no one can see the finished garment, everyone pretends to see it to avoid trouble until a child innocently proclaims that the Emperor is wearing nothing at all. Although embarrassed, the Emperor proudly continues the procession. The moral of the story is always be honest with yourself and don't let your staff or anyone else lull you to sleep or lead you down the primrose path of poor decisions! Don't drink the Kool-Aid.

when buying a car or a house or making any other significant life decision! Nor would we make a major financial decision with a salesman over the phone. So why are so many major business decisions made in haste or on the spur of the moment, or without serious scrutiny?

Sure, events in life may force us to make big choices quickly, but I've never found this to be true in business. Hardly anything we do of major consequence in business forces us to decide instantaneously and on the spot.

Yet again and again, people knee-jerk their way through decisions that can change their future opportunities. Then you see them working like mad to get out of the corner in which they put themselves. For major business decisions, you always have to take the time to study each decision carefully. You need to consider your alternatives and to assess the maximum downside risk.

In our business, I'm referring to key decisions, such as pricing large fixed-price contracts, hiring a key executive or technical superstar, entering a big long-term facility lease, making a major capital commitment, starting a new proprietary product development, or acquiring a company! These decisions all have momentous implications for our company. And they all take time to do well. Of course, there are even much more monumental decisions, like hiring or firing a CEO, and whether or not to sell the company.

Many years ago, I was on a business trip with Herb Karr when we got a call from a senior staff officer. If we moved quickly, he told us, we could take advantage of a low-rate line-of-credit deal being offered by a Swiss bank. The catch was that we had to move within 24 hours to get the low interest rate. After studying the matter for a few minutes, we said "no." We decided that we did not need to make a decision that important that fast. Even if the deal was as good as it seemed, we didn't like being forced into it on the spot. And we weren't about to upset a dozen years of successful dealings with our current banker, all for the promise of some out-of-the-blue, snap-decision discount deal from Switzerland! I had a serious discussion with that senior staff officer when I got back.

So, if it sounds too good to be true, it probably is. That's why spur-of-the-moment decisions are usually just that: spurious.

FEAR OF MISTAKES

The final decision-making pitfall is the fear of making mistakes. Peter Drucker, sometimes called the father of modern management, noted years ago that the saying, "If at first you don't succeed, try, try again" was nonsense in business. Instead, he contended, "If at first you don't succeed, maybe try one more time; then drop it fast and try something else." I'd say that's a good decision in any aspect of our lives.

No matter what you do, you won't make every decision correctly. Mistakes are unavoidable. You just don't want to make very many and, hopefully, no real big ones. That's why optimizing your approach to decision-making is crucial. But when methods and procedures aren't enough, judgment, instinct, and common sense are paramount. What's usually the most sensible thing to do? Rely on your experience.

Just ask Chesley "Sully" Sullenberger. Sullenberger was a US Airways pilot, flight safety expert, and accident investigator with several decades of experience in commercial and military aviation. On January 15, 2009, his experience and quick thinking made him a hero (and saved the lives of 155 grateful people). After taking off from New York's LaGuardia airport, Sullenberger's plane hit a flock of birds, disabling both engines. By radio, he quickly discussed with air traffic control about returning to LaGuardia or attempting to land at nearby Teterboro Airport in New Jersey, but neither option was feasible under the circumstances. Sullenberger then determined that landing on the Hudson River was the only choice.

The moments before the crash were, "the worst sickening, pit - of - your - stomach, falling - through - the - floor feeling," according to Sullenberger. Despite all this, he and his co-pilot calmly worked the emergency. He informed passengers and crew to brace for impact and smoothly glided the airplane onto the river. After the best possible water landing imaginable, the plane was evacuated. Sullenberger then walked twice through the plane, retrieved the plane's maintenance logbook, and was the last person off the plane. Sullenberger's actions and decisions saved the lives of all 155 people on board. Talk about a cool decision-maker with a lifetime of experience being put on the line.

In a television interview, Sullenberger later said, "One way of looking at this might be that for 42 years, I've been making small, regular deposits in this bank of experience: education and training. And on January 15 the balance was sufficient so that I could make a very large withdrawal."[128] Sullenberger's experience came largely from years in the cockpit, training and best practices.

BEST PRACTICES IN DECISION MAKING

Good practices take much of the trauma and fear out of the decision-making process. So what are some time-tested ways I've found to make good decisions?

PRIORITIZE

First, sort and define your priorities very carefully. What's the most important thing for the mission? What resources are most available to you? What tasks *must* be accomplished? When and in what order? What is your timeframe? You can't do everything yourself or take every little thing into consideration. So quickly weed out the extraneous and less important factors. It's easy to get lost in the details and miss the big picture. Getting the big picture correct is the first thing and, frankly, it's overwhelmingly the most important.

---

[128] Sullenberger retired from US Airways after 30 years of commercial flying in March 2010. He is currently an international speaker on airline safety and has helped develop new protocols for airline safety. Sullenberger was ranked second in *Time* Magazine's Top 100 Most Influential Heroes and Icons of 2009.

EXTERNALIZE

Second, get out of your head. Have you ever noticed how much easier it is to remember something after you have written it down, even if you don't look at it again? Or why many of us, like me, are constantly writing *to do* lists? We're visual thinkers, that's why. Having information physically in front of us makes it easier to analyze.

Think about the simplest decision-making tool, the *pros versus cons* list (sometimes known as the *Benjamin Franklin T-chart)*. If you're buying a car, you likely have reasons for and against the car in question. The same is true if you're hiring a senior or C-level executive or buying a company. You have reasons for and against the candidate or the company (pros and cons). When you put them side by side, you can better focus on the criteria leading to the decision itself. In making a physical written record, you free your mind from having to both remember the factors and analyze them. By the way, I have always made my own records or diaries for key (major, crucial, life-changing, career-focused, fortune-making, company changing) decisions. I gather much of the data myself and always score it myself. If you are in the data, you'll have a far greater feel and understanding about your decisions. I wouldn't think of doing it otherwise.

Another great and useful tool is the simple matrix. A decision matrix arranges criteria and factors in rows and columns. Various options are then placed in the most appropriate category (where criteria intersect). Although this approach tends to assess options in their most general aspects, it is an easy to use and effective evaluation aid. The graphical format also captures multi-dimensional decision factors. I use them all the time and they can be especially useful with a large number of decision criteria.[129]

---

[129] When I think of decision matrices, I remember the story about Napoleon who supposedly categorized his forces into four types of soldiers. "The first are the dumb and lazy. These I make my infantrymen. The second are the smart and energetic. These I make my field commanders. The third type is the smart and lazy. These I

SOCIALIZE

Next, get out and about. There's only so much information at your disposal, even with the Internet. So, make an effort to talk to people and see things for yourself. Some refer to this approach as *management by walking around* (MBWA). It makes sense because it's the only way to understand the business and see what's happening. This is especially important when making decisions for large organizations. MBWA was an important part of my routine as CEO. It forces you to get out of your chair and from behind your desk, walk out of your office, and go out and talk to people. (I always enjoyed this part of the job the most, and looked forward to being out in the field.) Written reports are important, but there's no substitute for hearing it directly from the source. Personal interaction is far more informative. There is nothing like checking things out for yourself. For me, this meant lots of travel since our operations were located all across the country and in many parts of the world.

Once, I was proceeding with an M&A deal with a California company that was based at the south end of San Francisco Bay. My senior operations staff, the CFO, and General Counsel were all excited about the deal and had met with the target company's people several times. I also met their CEO at our offices and discussed the deal with him at great length. Just as we were preparing to go to CACI's board of directors for the *go ahead* decision, I asked our COO and CFO how the target company's facilities looked and how they were put together. No one said a word; they just looked at me with eyes open wide.

---

make my generals." An inquirer is said to have asked, "That's just three types. What of the dumb and energetic?" Napoleon's reportedly quick-witted and tongue-in-cheek response was "I have them shot."

Chief of the Prussian General Staff, Helmuth von Moltke – a student of Napoleon's methods – is said to have categorized the entire general staff into four similar categories: the active and smart, the lazy and smart, the active and dumb, and the lazy and dumb. Moltke's preferences were for officers who were lazy and smart because they would find the easiest way to do something, and to dismiss the active and dumb because of their potential for trouble.

None of our senior management team had actually gone to the target's facility to check it out! The next day I was on a plane with a couple of my senior team to do an on-site inspection and survey. Our team *never* made that mistake again!

> *"Be willing to make decisions. That's the most important quality in a good leader."*
>
> George S. Patton

I also believe in *informational interviewing* – talking with people who are working in the field to better understand an occupation or industry, to build a network of contacts in the field, and to better gauge market factors or movements in the industry and identify opportunities. It allows me to tap into expertise specific to my decision or interests.

I've also used the *Delphi method* to get a sampling of information from a group of experts. For me, it is a systematic, interactive decision-making process. Formally, it's where a panel of experts answers questionnaires over several predetermined rounds. On the other hand, I frequently use a more informal approach where the experts and consultants seldom know or are aware of each other. Where appropriate, a facilitator can provide an anonymous summary of the experts' recommendations as well as their reasons after each round. The experts can then revise their earlier answers with the other panelists' insight and information. Over several rounds, the experts tend to converge towards an optimal answer or recommendation. The caution here is that you are *not* looking for consensus, but the best, or optimal, answer or course of action.

For the most part, I've used these approaches in making technically-oriented decisions; where organizationally to place the internal IT systems department or how best to implement a large-scale technology demonstration center and facility. I've also used it in the past for decisions about internal promotions, major realignments, and decisions about recruiting into C-level positions.

Again, you are not after consensus, per se. Further, it may not even be possible to get a group of experts to help you with your decisions. You can, however, modify this method. For example, research the opinions of several experts on the issue at hand and analyze where their opinions overlap. Based on what you find, you can do several more rounds of research and analysis. It won't necessarily give you the answer, but I always find the insight gained to be valuable. I do this kind of research myself in order to *know* the data.

You can try different tools, too. For example, CACI's growth has been partly due to what I have called the *Z-curve* strategy of sales used in our business development plans. The idea is to start with the *what* and *who* that you know, and work into new things and new people. The Z-curve strategy is to sell more of your current products to your current customers first, new products to current customers next, then current products to new customers, and finally new products to new customers comes last.[130]

In running a business, sell your proven products to clients you know before trying to sell new products to a customer you've never met! I try hard to discourage the latter! As a decision-making tool, the Z-curve can help you focus on information and factors that you are familiar with before trying to ascertain the many unknowns of new markets and new products.

I've also tried several unconventional tools in decision-making. *Personality profiling* has helped me appraise candidates for certain positions. At one time, I also used *handwriting analysis* to gain a different perspective. For several years during the 1980s I had a psychologist consultant that was good in handwriting analysis and rather accurate in assessing personality

---

[130] The factors of "new and current products" versus "new and current clients" are placed in a 2x2 matrix. The top row is current clients and the bottom row is new clients. The left column is current products and the right is new products. It's called the "Z-Curve" because your business development priorities flow from the upper left (current products, current clients) to the upper right (current client, new product), down to the lower left (current product, new client) and then to the lower right (new clients, new products) – tracing a "Z". The last stop on the "Z" is what characterizes start-up firms; selling new products to new clients. CACI is not in the venture start-up business.

attributes. His assessments were accurate enough that I took them as serious inputs for a number of personnel decisions.[131]

COMMIT

Making important decisions is a challenge. The key to successful decision-making is commitment. And that commitment has to come on several levels.

First, you have to commit to the process. Coin flips work for sports. They don't for decisions that have great significance and impact. Take recruiting. You have two candidates for a position. You review their resumes, check references, and bring them in for interviews. You wouldn't ask them to simply meet you in the lobby, bring a quarter and flip for it? This example never ceases to amaze me as to how cavalier some people are about making hiring decisions. They simply fail to think things through or fail to do their research – such as background and reference checks – before making a decision.

For example, I once had a person working for me who decided to leave the job, the company, and the city. They had surprised me by giving me their resignation letter and an early date of departure. Before the person got out the door, and without telling me, the individual had a change of heart and applied for a job in one of the company's field offices. While this move was surprising in and of itself, what came next was astonishing. I found out later that the field office hiring this person (or approving the transfer) failed to do any reference check or check on the employee's job performance in their previous position. That's always a big mistake – even when hiring inside the company. I was disappointed by this discovery. That's not how hiring is supposed to be done at CACI.

There is only one time that I can ever recall where I did not conduct a thorough background reference check. I can say

---

[131] We ran double-blind experiments on several of our team, including one on me, to see how accurate we believed him to be. He got me right on. When the analyst was suddenly killed in a traffic accident, I tried for a couple of years to find a qualified replacement, but was never able to do so. He was truly one of a kind!

the person turned out to be an absolute disaster and I will leave it at that. Since then, I have *never* made another hire without a double-checked background review. I have never deviated from the process after that awful experience. While reference checking will not guarantee a successful hire, it will surely improve the odds.

Second, commit to the decision. There will always be second-guessing and perfect vision in hindsight. However, you decided a certain way because you believed it was the best option or course of action. So follow through with it. It's like a long road trip. You map out a course, noting traffic disruptions, sites you want to see, and the best times to get on the road. Yet there are people who would throw out your plan and try another route. They might hear about a shortcut or other things to see or do. Unless you have time for an adventure, is there a good reason to give up on your plan? Flexibility is important. But sometimes Robert Frost's "road less traveled" is the most rewarding. Why go through the process of decision-making only to abandon it without a real reason?

The story of Hernan Cortes, the Conquistador, demonstrates both decisiveness and commitment. In 1519, Spaniard Hernan Cortes was commissioned by the governor of Cuba to go on an expedition to explore the Yucatan coast. Realizing the fame, fortune and political advantages in Spain that would come with the conquest of Mexico, there were many parties interested in preventing Cortes from succeeding. The governor himself even tried twice to stop Cortes from leaving. After arriving in Mexico, Cortes allied with local forces and planned the conquest of the Aztecs. Cortes was then appointed chief administrative officer of the region by the King of Spain. However, some of his men still wanted to remain loyal to the Cuban governor. They even tried to steal a ship and sail back to Cuba. To ensure that such a mutiny would not happen, Cortes ordered all but one of the original 11 ships scuttled (deliberately sunk) – leaving the one for communications with Spain. This dramatic move effectively ended all ties to Cuba and strengthened Cortes' mission. For his soldiers, it meant there was no means of escape or retreat on the campaign to conquer

Mexico. For Cortes, there was no going back. Figuratively speaking, he had burned his bridges!

Winston Churchill was a very decisive and committed man. In the Battle of the Denmark Straits at the start of World War II, the British Navy was shocked by the loss of the HMS *Hood*. On the *Bismarck's* first outing, the Germans sank the *Hood* in a decisive battle. The ship's loss severely damaged Britain's confidence about winning the war. Undaunted, a decisive Winston Churchill responded by issuing his famous command, "sink the *Bismarck*." While destroying the *Bismarck,* Germany's premiere battleship, would have been a great naval victory, it would also be sweet revenge for the *Hood* and a major morale boost for the British. Under Churchill's order on May 27, 1941, the British Navy lead by the HMS *Rodney* and HMS *King George V* put the *Bismarck* under. Churchill was absolutely committed and determined, and the British Navy knew it.

You also need to commit to the decision-makers. "Because I said so" may work to get children to follow decisions. And not everyone can scuttle their ships, even figuratively. For the rest of us, it's associating ourselves with people we trust, who are knowledgeable and accountable. When I became CEO of CACI in 1984, I had already worked with Herb Karr, the Chairman of the Board, on and off for seven years. Now, as my chief advisor and direct boss, I would work with him very closely. Or so I thought. Herb had told me that he was 100 percent behind me or, as he said, until that point came when he was not. He also said if he ever had a change of mind about me, he would let me know straightaway. To me this meant that he trusted me to make the best decisions I could for the company. Herb simply said, "I don't want to have a boss, and I don't want to be the boss." Herb knew that he would not know all the factors or details behind my decisions, but he trusted that I would do my homework in detail. Herb also expected me to keep him up to speed on company activities and let him know about any problems we might be having. He would only jump in if he felt there was something serious enough to warrant his involvement. As I look back, his confidence in me was truly empowering. Now as Executive Chairman to a third successor CEO, I've made that same commitment. I am 100 percent behind him. In fact, I believe that there is no one else on this planet, except perhaps for his family, that wants to see him succeed as much as I do.

Empowering people is an absolutely necessary condition for building a company of any serious consequence or size. In life we make virtually an infinite number of choices. Most are easy, some are significant, and some transform us and completely define our futures. Each is an opportunity to take control of our lives, improve ourselves, and create new experiences. Yet there are many people who let their fears, insecurities, or laziness prevent them from taking the advantage. Think of it this way. When we go to the grocery store, we're often prepared with a list and maybe even coupons. We read the labels to choose between products. We heed food recalls and safety information. What we eat is important to our well-being as well as our wallets. Yet many people put more thought and effort into food shopping than they do for life-defining decisions.

Success doesn't come to the apathetic. It comes to those who value the right to choose – to make big decisions – and accept the responsibilities and consequences that come with them.

If you think you have some weighty decisions to make, recall President Harry Truman's decision to drop atomic bombs on Japan. Decisions don't come any tougher or monumental. And while he made the right choice at the time, it was not without future consequences. Are you capable of making tough decisions, big decisions? Where do you fit in? *You decide.*

CHAPTER 12

TALK IS NEVER CHEAP

"Say what you mean and mean what you say."
George S. Patton

In the game *Telephone,* the first person whispers a statement to the second person, who then whispers it to the next person. This chain continues to the last person who states aloud what they heard to the whole group. It's never close to what the first person said! Now add actual telephones, cell phones, text messaging, instant messaging, faxing, emails, voicemails, video messaging, and video conferencing to that mix. It can quickly get very confusing!

There has never been as many technical means and modes of communication as there are today. Yet, we struggle with the actual act of communicating. *Communication is an art.* There are often many ways to say the same thing or, conversely, one statement can have multiple meanings. Sometimes there is no meaning. People will rattle on without realizing they're not communicating at all. Communication is also dynamic. There are subtleties in communicating with different kinds of people. Language seems to evolve as quickly as do the methods of communication.[132]

It's also not what you say, but how you say it. Researchers say that only 7 percent of human communication comes from words; 38 percent comes from the tone of voice; and 55 percent comes from body language – over half! Modern communications can mask or misinterpret meanings and tone. Once, words typed

---

[132] It is much easier in this age of the ubiquitous internet and 24/7 worldwide media to obfuscate and distort the facts, fogging up reality in ways that permit people to put their own bias or spin on the issue. And then there really is a thing called propaganda, the intentional distortion of facts and information for political purposes.

in all capital letters meant the writer was trying to emphasize something; now, using all capitals denotes anger and shouting.

Adding to the confusion are advances in technology, and the explosion of social networking and media. Social networks and blogs now account for nearly a quarter of time spent on the internet.[133] Two-thirds of adults who are online use social networking platforms such as Facebook, Twitter, MySpace or LinkedIn."[134] From blogs to tweets, social networking to e-zines, communication has become all about *being heard*. You wonder if anyone is *listening* – the other half of communication

Communication is being able to express yourself – to articulate your thoughts, needs, and goals. It's about the transfer of knowledge and perception. It's also about listening, the other aspect of communication. In communication, *perception is reality*. What we sense (see, hear, feel) is what we believe to be true – even if it may not be. And we seem to accept this distortion as reality. Take a look at a glamorous magazine cover. Most people know that's not how the cover model looks in real life. The question these days is how much airbrushing and Photo Shopping was done. However most people still treat the doctored image as realistic – even when it's not!

This lesson in distortion hit home with me with our Abu Ghraib crisis in 2004. Within the first two weeks after having a CACI employee's name appear in an illegally leaked army investigation report alleging serious abuses, the media, pundits, special interest groups, and even much of the public had concluded that CACI was among those responsible for the abuses at the Iraqi prison. Yet no piece of evidence – not one – had even been presented in the report or anywhere else, to substantiate the terrible allegations. CACI's logo was shown by the media next to one of the abuse photos in which *none* of our employees

---

[133] Nielsen, "The State of the Media: The Social Media Report Q3 2011," September 13, 2011, http://blog.nielsen.com/nielsenwire/social/.
[134] Aaron Smith, "Why Americans Use Social Media," *Pew Internet,* November 15, 2011, http://pewinternet.org/Reports/2011/Why-Americans-Use-Social-Media/Main-report.aspx.

appeared. This was editorializing taken to the level of outright malicious propaganda![135]

Miscommunication and misrepresentation are sometimes the result of human error or inadvertent misunderstanding. However, all too often, miscommunication is intentional or willful. From putting a spin on an issue to creating full blown propaganda, there are far too many people out there who find value in misleading and lying.

Communication is a work in progress, for individuals and groups alike. As a skill, it is a vital success factor. So it's mandatory that we keep working at it.

There are many dimensions and nuances in communication, and yet the key points in mastering communication for success are clear.

INTERPERSONAL COMMUNICATIONS

Interpersonal communication can be one-on-one or one person in a small group. One advantage of interpersonal communication is the absence of complicating factors, like scale and scope. For example, it's much easier to talk to one person than to 100 people. It's also easier, for example, for a manager to talk to one office than to talk to all locations. Another advantage is the direct interaction. The absence of an intermediary – someone between you and your audience – greatly reduces the chance of miscommunication.

It is important to emphasize that in both verbal and written communication, we often fail to fully articulate the complete thought or message we want to convey. Our message can be further diluted by the audience because they either don't hear everything that is said to them or they filter what they hear.

---

[135] Despite the media onslaught, there was not one bit of evidence to support the headlines and accusations. For example, no one from CACI was in any of the notorious photos. Furthermore, no charges were ever filed against anyone from CACI and no supporting evidence of any kind has ever come to light. Beware the media witch hunts, kangaroo courts, and lynch mobs. Today's media is more interested in headlines and political spin than facts when it comes to matters of this kind. At CACI, I saw it up close, personal, and ugly!

Fortunately, technology provides many more communication tools. Unfortunately, it also complicates it. Not only have we become more dependent on these ubiquitous means of communication, it seems people are increasingly hiding behind them. For example, studies show that the generation born after the mid- to late 1980s – which will comprise more than half of the workforce by 2020 – would prefer to use instant messaging or other social media than stop by an office and talk with someone.[136]

The biggest problem in interpersonal communication is the unwillingness of people to communicate at all! I call this the *call reluctance syndrome*. It happens when an issue needs to be dealt with, but the person can't deal with it. Instead they put it off. They could resolve the issue with one phone call, but they can't even pick up the phone. In the end, they finally make the call and realize it was much easier than they had anticipated. Or they lose a sale because someone beat them to it. Or they find out that their delay has caused even more problems.

Whoever said *silence is golden* wasn't very opportunistic or very bright.[137] You won't get anywhere in life without *knowing how to speak for yourself*.

If perception is reality, then take control of how you want to be perceived. Ask for what you want. Conversely, state what you won't accept. By expressing your needs and interests, you can create opportunities. Auto executive Lee Iacocca noted, "You can have brilliant ideas, but if you can't get them across, your ideas won't get you anywhere."

Tim Hortons is a Canadian quick-food chain, offering coffee, doughnuts, sandwiches, and soup. In 2009, the chain operated 3,527 restaurants, including 2,971 in Canada, 556 in the U.S., and even one in Kandahar, Afghanistan. Tim Hortons dominates 60 percent of the Canadian coffee market (Starbucks

---

[136] Susan Tardnico, "Is Social Media Sabotaging Real Communication," *Forbes*, April 30, 2012, http://www.forbes.com/sites/susantardanico/2012/04/30/is-social-media-destroying-real-communication/.

[137] The origins of this phrase, "silence is golden", are believed to go back to Ancient Egypt! It came into English usage in the early 19th century.

has 10 percent). Had one person not spoken up, Tim Hortons could have easily been another short-lived small business.

Despite being a major hockey star in the 1950s and 60s, Canadian Tim Horton knew his playing career and earnings were only going to last so long. Horton's first foray into the food industry was opening several hamburger restaurants in Ontario. Horton quickly discovered that he couldn't compete with McDonald's and the venture went bust.

Meanwhile, Jim Charade owned a small, yet faltering doughnut store in Toronto. Confident Horton's name would boost a doughnut shop, Charade suggested to Horton and business partner, Ron Joyce, that they launch a coffee and doughnut chain. Tim Hortons opened their first store in 1964 in Hamilton, Ontario. Several thousand stores later, Tim Horton's signature, the company's logo, has become a Canadian fixture. Royce later noted, "Jim [Charade] was... behind the concept... Without him, it never would have happened." I'm sure thousands of Tim Horton's customers are glad Charade spoke up![138]

No one will know you have something to offer unless you put it out there; furthermore, not speaking up can be disastrous. The explosion of the space shuttle Challenger in 1986 was a shock worldwide. All seven astronauts aboard were killed. Yet a subsequent investigation found that several engineers had questioned the safety of the launch. It turned out their concerns were largely ignored because a few people were afraid to speak up when many others wanted to move on with the launch. The result was a terrible tragedy. So speak up! Do the right thing![139]

You also need to be able to *stand up for yourself*. During CACI's Abu Ghraib crisis, not one person or group called us up and offered to defend us.[140] Had we not aggressively put forth

---

[138] Tim Horton died in a car accident in 1974 while traveling from a game. At the time, there were 40 Tim Hortons stores, but the brand was taking off.

[139] In the period after the 1986 *Challenger* disaster, CACI had an information technology project to support the Department of Justice (DOJ) in its litigation investigation and proceedings over the tragedy.

[140] After the height of the crisis, several individuals (including military personnel) came forward to say how CACI's performance and support in Iraq had been above board and by the book. Several thanked us for our work in support of the troops.

our side of the story, as well as the facts of the situation during the crisis, there might not be a CACI today. In 2008, we published *Our Good Name, A Company's Fight to Defend its Honor and Get the Truth Told About Abu Ghraib*. We felt compelled to write the book to set the record straight about CACI, our work in Iraq, and the whirlwind of unsubstantiated and unchecked allegations surrounding the CACI employee who was wrongly accused.

Our Good Name is a thoroughly documented examination of how we pushed back by ourselves and prevailed against the allegations made against us. In its 780 pages, there are 40 chapters, 15 appendices, and over 700 footnotes. Our sources were official U.S. government records, sworn public testimony, and other factual public records. We used the facts to make our points and counter the accusations made against us. We wanted all of our employees and future employees as well as our clients and shareholders to know the truth about CACI and Abu Ghraib. I am very glad we wrote the book. I am also confident that we achieved our goal of setting the record straight.

The key to successful interpersonal communication is creating the relationship. What do I mean by this? It's the knowledge that you have the ability and interest in engaging others, and that you are receptive to being engaged by others. More simply, you are willing to talk and be open to conversation. That perception is essential. For myself, I don't much care to talk to people who don't listen to what I say, or worse, talk so much I can't get a word in edgewise. Some people talk so much and so loud that dealing with them is like trying to take a drink from a fire hydrant. Then there are those who seem to think that interrupting you when you're trying to say something furthers their point on the matter. At some point, enough is enough. You simply give up and walk away.

Take my relationship with CACI co-founder Herb Karr as an example. Some might think that communications between a company's two top honchos would have been relatively easy. Not only was it somewhat difficult, our communications were always a work in progress – but we were probably better executives because of it. When Herb was Chairman and after I became CEO, we used to hold three-day long one-on-one brainstorming and work sessions five or six times a year. The process was key for these sessions to be productive. First, our sessions could not simply be in a boss-to-employee format. We had to be completely honest with ourselves and the issues at hand. The company wouldn't benefit from one of us simply deferring to the other or holding back because of our positions. In fact, we had to be candid, frank, and honest, sometimes excruciatingly blunt with each other. We knew that it had to be okay to ask each other the uncomfortable and confrontational questions; the toughest questions we could imagine. Finally, this process had to be explicit as well as private. There could be no doubt that candor was expected inside and confidentiality outside the workroom. Herb and I would bat around ideas and intellectually spar with each other. Yet when all was said and done, we had to come out of our sessions on the same page and going forward.

What were the benefits of our process? By removing rank and pecking order from our process, we tried to ensure that our communications were uncontaminated by ego or pride of authorship. It's empowering; a confidence booster when people feel they're on an equal footing (intellectually) while expressing their views. Some people can't believe such communication is possible. While it greatly improves communication, it can't guarantee 100% successful communication. By challenging each other and asking provocative questions, our process pushed us to better understand the issues CACI faced and how we would shape the company's next steps.

You need vigorous debate to have any chance of avoiding bad or foolish decisions. Perhaps our arrangement worked because there was genuine mutual respect and we both knew who would have the final say!

Outside of the planning sessions, Herb also had a penchant (perhaps inadvertently) for not always being completely forthright, especially when we started working together. Herb's perspective was that, as CEO, I was running the company and that he had no particular obligation to express his views, unless he wanted to, on how any particular thing was to be done.

This wasn't always so good. I once hired someone, an earlier CACI military client, then retired, whose experience I thought seemed to fit a senior position we had open at the time. I told Herb that I wanted to make him an offer. Looking back, Herb's response was a mediocre reference, faint praise at best. Since Herb's reaction didn't raise any red flags, I ended up hiring the fellow. After a year and a half though, it was clear that it wasn't working out. The person ran his projects and his business alright, but some client relationships were being affected, and it had become difficult to work with him. The problems couldn't continue. I told Herb that I wanted to fire the man. To my astonishment, Herb wasn't even surprised. However, I was very surprised! It turned out Herb had been personally acquainted with the person before he joined CACI and felt he had a way of annoying people, especially by talking about the wrong things at the wrong times. Why hadn't Herb told me this sooner? Herb thought since I was in charge, I knew what I was doing. Herb had thought maybe I saw something special in the man that he didn't. I was initially upset that Herb hadn't given me his unique insight, or at least, been a more important part of the hiring calculus. I asked him to not to be so reluctant in the future. We had much better communication after that.

LISTENING

Of course, regardless of how articulate a person is, communication is ineffective if no one is listening. The rise in the number of modes of communications has enabled more self-expression. On the downside, it has made listening a lost skill. In conversation, do you listen or do you wait to speak? Today, interrupting and talking over others has eclipsed paying attention. Conversation is a lost art.

It's vital to develop conversational skills – and it can't be by always doing the talking. The process starts with developing an idea, stating it, listening to the response, and then responding yourself. Listening, as a skill, can also be improved. *Active listening* is more than paying attention. It includes body language and gestures to let the other person know you are

214

engaged. It also means giving feedback that shows you were listening, including making note of the facts and references the other person has made. Finally, it's deferring judgment. It's not just reserving counter-opinions, but also refraining from interrupting or making gestures that disrupt the speaker. Many times, the speaker's message is misconstrued or incomplete simply because the listener rushed to judgment.[141]

Developing solid conversational skills may not only be useful, it may help you stand out as well! I didn't realize that communication is truly a skill until about midway through my career. Herb and I used to talk about how so many managers, surprisingly, didn't develop effective communication skills. Then in the mid 1980s, Herb brought a consultant to CACI who held about four or five sessions with us. He indicated that the lack of listening skills

"I listened more than I talked."

Al Neuharth,
Founder, *USAToday*

had become a disability – people simply didn't know how to listen or were unable to listen or even hear! What happens is that people become one-way communicators – all broadcast, no reception. The inability to listen severely limits learning. In turn, bad listening skills impede growth and success potential.

Luckily, listening is a skill that can be improved. After these sessions, I met with my direct reports, discussed the importance of listening in communication and asked them to pass on these lessons. I made it a point to follow up, too.

Overall, the effectiveness of interpersonal communication depends on how well you speak up for yourself and how well you listen to others.

---

[141] Many people today opt for nonverbal communications by sending emails and text messages. Although convenient, these methods are not always conducive for effective communication. These tools fail to capture the nuances, intonations and spontaneous expressions of verbal dialogue. It's no wonder there are so many misunderstandings online.

ORGANIZATIONAL COMMUNICATIONS

To succeed as a leader or manager, you have to be a good communicator. And it's even better if you can become a *great* communicator.

In fact, the "Great Communicator" is what our 40th President, Ronald Reagan was called. Trained as an actor, Reagan understood that communication was most effective in simple and visual ways. For example, he often referred to the United States as "the Shining City on the Hill." He also understood how body language and facial expressions should accompany his messages. Reagan's approach "was always simple, clear, direct and caring. The result of the combination of his vision, his positivity and communication style was his ability to connect with seemingly everyone from the common man to veteran politicians – a powerful skill in politics and business."[142]

As difficult as one-on-one communication can be, organizational communication is even more challenging. The larger scale and scope often presents the opportunity to get your message across to more people in more places. On the other hand, there's a greater chance the message will get muddled, distorted, or even lost along the way.

RULES TO REMEMBER

Here are my four rules in communicating with larger audiences.

My first rule is to **keep it simple**. Think of all the things you hear and read in one day; emails, text messages, phone calls, radio, TV, meetings (individual and group), personal chats, newspapers, reports, music, etc. At the end of the day, you usually only remember the simplest messages, not the complicated theories and long-winded diatribes.

---

[142] Laura Laaman, "Ronald Reagan's timeless lessons of communication," *New Mexico Business Weekly,* June 18, 2004, http://www.bizjournals.com/albuquerque /stories/2004/06/21/smallb4.html.

Then there was the birth of the *sound bite*. Some might say that it's the sound bites that survive. Ronald Regan also became well-known for his short, yet effective messages, such as his famous remark, "trust but verify."[143] TV commercials once started out as one minute long. Over time they shrank to 30 seconds partly because viewers wouldn't pay attention for much longer. Long reports are made more readable with an Executive Summary. Bulleted points in presentations stand out more than full text. Why? Simple is memorable. Perhaps we should say *rememorable?*

The second rule is to **be specific**. I'm frequently asked to be the keynote speaker at industry conferences. The topic is often about the future of the government contracting industry. For example, I spoke at the National Contract Management Association's annual conference in November 2008. Three months later, in February 2009, I spoke at GovCon's small business annual conference. Even though both speeches addressed the same question, the two presentations were dramatically different. Sure, I borrow a few points from old speeches and update them for an upcoming talk. But I never give the same speech twice, since every speaking opportunity and every audience is different. Each presentation has to be tailored for the event and audience, and include timely references. My speeches always start with the same question: *what would I want to hear if I were in the audience?* If you fail to mold your message to your audience, the audience won't be listening for long. And who wants to talk to a room of bobbing sleepy heads?

---

[143] The world of politics has always been full of sound bites. The memorable ones are short, punchy, and say something important. There's Franklin D. Roosevelt's "The only thing we have to fear is fear itself." Winston Churchill had many memorable lines, such as "Never in the field of human conflict was so much owed by so many to so few." John F. Kennedy is best remembered for two sound bites; "Ask not what your country can do for you, ask what you can do for your country" and the inaccurate, but popular "Ich bin ein Berliner." (*Berliner* means someone from Berlin. The addition of the article "ein" unfortunately changed the meaning to a type of German jelly doughnut.) Then there's Shakespeare's line uttered by Julius Caesar as he looks at the old friend who has just stabbed him: "Et tu, Brute?"

The third rule is **repetition**. You may not have been heard the first time! Or not everyone may have been listening. The sheer volume of information and distractions can prevent you from being heard. Repetition also creates emphasis, indicating importance. Repetition also builds familiarity, which can also help establish credibility. I believe and have often said that *repetition is the key to human communication.*

Take commercials again. To introduce a new product, companies will bombard audiences with advertising. The same print ad will be in several magazines over the same months. A commercial will be repeatedly shown during a TV show. The point is that even if you get sick of the ads, you'll still remember them.

Leaders also know this method is essential to communicating. Repeating a message reinforces and ingrains values, standards, and expectations. Organizations are also always changing. People come and go, so the new folks will not have been around when you sent the message that first time. Remember, there's no such thing as making a speech to a passing parade. You have to repeat the message over and over again so everyone will get it as they go by!

The fourth rule to communicating with larger audiences is to **write it down**. Whether it's a document or recording, a physical record is necessary with larger audiences. Think of commencement speakers at graduation ceremonies. They may give excellent speeches, but most of the audience will never remember what was said. What's more, few will remember by the time they depart the venue.

Physical records – the written word – provide a point of reference. Did you read an article in the paper that you want to share with your colleagues? Send them the link. Did you want to see what your Congressman said about an issue in a debate? Check the transcript. Also, physical records promote accuracy. There is always the possibility of your statements being taken out of context, but a physical record can provide the truthful account. And, physical records ensure permanence. If you say something you regret, sure, this might be a problem. But writing it down ahead of time ought to make you think twice. Also larger audiences are ever-changing. So you can resend your message, if need be, when it is a written record. Physical records allow for consistency and efficiency in communicating over the long haul – and that's a fact!

We have taken these lessons to heart in a creative way at CACI. In the late 1970s, our cofounder published internally *Herb's Homilies*. These were some business lessons in sound bite form that he wanted to pass on. Yet Herb felt that a text document – one paragraph after another, page after page – wouldn't be enough. He wanted to illustrate some of the ideas in his *Homilies*. Herb understood people and knew that a bureaucratic style wouldn't work with the CACI audience; a mix of ex-military and civilians, including former government people. These were people who had always been bombarded with bureaucratic reports and memos. Herb wanted something simple, short and memorable. So he decided on easy-to-read vignettes built around a cartoon. Part of Herb's communications style was to kid on the square; to joke, but (seriously) mean it all just the same. Cartoons, Herb felt, would be amusing, yet get the message across.

Herb had struck up a friendship with the well-known cartoonist Virgil Partch, dubbed by some as the greatest ever single-frame cartoonist.[144] He was a "cool cat" with a laid back style. Herb and Virgil both lived in southern California and enjoyed the lifestyle. Herb thought Virgil's single-panel style would be perfect for his homilies.

At first, Virgil wasn't interested, but Herb talked him into taking the job. Virgil was commissioned to do three dozen cartoons at $100 apiece.[145]

The combination of Herb's lessons and Virgil's drawings were a great success. In fact, these cartoons are still used to communicate CACI's culture and business style. I later updated

---

[144] Virgil Partch was best known for his nationally syndicated comic strip *Big George* and two dozen books. He was one of the best ever single-panel, smooth line cartoon humorists. His captions and cartoon art were always perfect fits. I have some of the original work he did for us.

[145] Yep! $100 apiece. Of course, it was a special deal just for Herb and CACI.

Herb's Homilies and developed two more books into a three-part series of CACI management manuals.[146] We also use these cartoons as the basis for CACI's *Culture Spotlights*, a monthly intranet feature that I've used for several years to discuss the company's values in light of current events and company news.

Effective internal communication is important to your organization, but the impact of external communication is often underestimated. For most organizations, especially commercial outfits, external communications are either marketing or public relations. The approach is primarily about promotion and from a small group. That, however, is deadly thinking.

The most important lesson I learned from my family's "Mom & Pop" business is that *the customer is absolutely the most important part of your business*. Nothing happens until a sale is made. A business is not an office, phone number, website, business cards or letterhead! It is a customer who is willing to purchase (pay for!) your offering. Paychecks come from customers.[147] The dotcom's of the 1990s didn't get this at all. They built their fantastic offices before creating and selling the products that customers thought were fantastic (and would pay for).

It's how you present your product and your company that wins business. That might make you reconsider the importance of sales. This, of course, assumes that you have something to sell that customers will *actually* buy. Unfortunately, even a good

---

[146] Every CACI manager receives a copy of our management manuals. They are on CACI's culture, CACI's way of doing business, and our best practices in recruiting. After Virgil Partch's death in 1984, we had to turn to other notable cartoonists to add to our manuals. Our next artist was Partch's friend John Dempsey (a *Playboy* staple for over 50 years). After John died we have most recently engaged Chip Bok, a syndicated editorial cartoonist. All have done a great job for us. Their work has become incorporated into our culture and one of the means by which we communicate it. They all were friends of ours and were fond of working with us.

[147] At CACI, we used to hand out a booklet called "Learning Where Your Paycheck Comes From" to junior managers. It described how money was made at CACI – working for the customers and earning their payments. It's still the basic message all employees need to understand. Our paychecks come from our clients' satisfaction with our products and services, and not out of some company bank account somewhere!

product can fail without a good sales team. Conversely, even a good sales team can only sustain a mediocre product for so long. Just think about what you can achieve with both a great product and a great sales force! This has always been our goal at CACI.

How you present yourself to a customer is crucial. In the contracting world, proposals are like a company's resume. In response to an RFP, we present our technical solutions, skills, experience, and resources that will fulfill the customer's needs and the contract's requirements. To win big-dollar contracts, you have to put together top notch proposals. You can have the smartest team who has already completed a similar project, but if you can't accurately and convincingly convey all of this in your proposal, at the right price, your company simply won't get the job.

> *"The way we communicate with others and with ourselves ultimately determines the quality of our lives."*
>
> Anthony Robbins

One contract with a client in Florida exemplifies this point. When CACI bid for their contract, we were considered a long shot. It was a new client for us, and the incumbent had been there for years. They had the experience and a working familiarity with the customer. Nevertheless, CACI bid for and won that contract. We made a painstaking effort to create the best proposal we could. The incumbent company simply failed to make their case. We did.

In the early 1990s, CACI's UK operations were becoming increasingly vulnerable at a time of recession and tight markets. In our niche of marketing information systems, how could CACI UK stay competitive? Our products and services there were already strong, and of excellent quality. What else could be done? UK managing director, Greg Bradford, and I brainstormed the situation. The problem wasn't what we were selling. The problem was *how* we were selling. Business development was no longer coming just from the sales team. Increasingly, *everyone* in the organization had a role in the sales process. It was how the receptionist greeted clients; how accounting handled invoices;

how IT staff managed and promoted client relationships; and how our sales team pursued their leads. It was all about focus, intensity, and a sense of urgency.

So Greg and I revitalized the organization as one where everyone sells or supports the sales process. To bring this to life, we created a sales motto that we branded "Our winning Sales Culture." CACI UK would be a sales organization from the mailroom up. Greg went to work to re-make sales the focus of the organization. That change made all the difference. It was the basis for our making it through the hard times. Even more so, it set the style of the organization for the success that came in the following years. At CACI UK, everybody works the sales process. In fact, the original poster for the Winning Sales Culture motto still hangs in the office's reception area!

While organizations are represented by each of their members, you still need to create a specific image or brand for the organization – *how you want the organization to be known*. You have to state your purpose or goals, communicate what value you add, define yourself before someone else does, and control your reputation and the organization's reputation. As the organization grows, you can modify the image or brand as necessary. The larger the business, the harder it will be and the longer it will take for change to take hold. So be persistent, but also be patient.

When I first joined CACI in 1972, my unofficial tagline for my area was *advanced logistics systems*, because that's what we were doing for our sophisticated government clients. Over time, CACI grew in size and service offerings. One of our early official taglines that fit at the time was *Advanced Technology Solutions*. Several years later when the IT world exploded, it became *Software. Systems. Simulation.*

As the market evolved, CACI evolved too. That meant re-examining our brand and streamlining our image. We were also serving hundreds of clients on hundreds of contracts and the scope of our offerings had expanded considerably. We also were serving more clients in the government's national security and intelligence arena.

In 2003, I decided that CACI needed to get more definition in our branding. CACI could no longer be considered just a technology company. While technology was our strength, our services had expanded beyond that image. Security and intelligence were just two, yet important examples describing what CACI was doing. So we engaged the services of a marketing consulting group and after several months of dialogue and a $25,000 tab, we finally had something we really liked: *Ever Vigilant.*

Ever Vigilant conveyed that CACI would remain committed to our clients' success and be diligent in meeting their needs in an ever-changing world. The tagline switched the focus to serving our customers rather than CACI's set of services or technologies. This was a major branding and image change. It also showed that CACI was not technology driven, but market driven. It was also unique to CACI and our industry and *Ever Vigilant* tells a complete story about CACI. Talk about an image!

The *Ever Vigilant* tagline is now our motto – a central element of our corporate identity and culture. For our clients, it's an expectation of what CACI will do for them. For the people who represent CACI daily, it's a statement about how we want to perform. It also addresses the threats in this dangerous world. We were fortunate to create such an appropriate tagline, and we plan to keep it for a very long time.

I'm always amazed when a person, team or organization doesn't take advantage of speaking for themselves. What someone else can say about you will never be as accurate or as genuine as what you have to say for yourself. So, there's no point in staying silent. Failing to speak up for yourself also creates questions or doubts about your intentions, competence, or character. If you don't take up for yourself, or defend yourself when you must, no one else will. Telling the world what you're all about and what you believe will always be a challenge and can be difficult to get right. Getting it right can also be very expensive, so be prepared to pay the price. Because *talk is never cheap.*

CHAPTER 13

STEP UP OR STEP ASIDE

"It's hard to lead a cavalry charge if you think you look funny on a horse."

Adlai Stevenson

Who's in charge here? Is your first instinct to think *not me*? Is that because you don't believe you're in a leadership position or don't want to be in a leadership position? If you're not willing to take responsibility for what's going on and what will go on in the future, then read no further.

What is leadership? Admiral Arleigh A. Burke (U.S. Navy admiral and former Chief of Naval Operations) defined leadership as "understanding people and involving them to help you do a job. It takes all of the good characteristics, like integrity, dedication of purpose, selflessness, knowledge, skill, implacability, as well as determination not to accept failure."

Leadership is not a title or position. Far too many executives have been terrible leaders. Have you ever worked in an office or on a project where the person everybody looks to is not the person with the highest title? That's because *leadership* and *management* are not the same thing.

Managers typically work by consensus even though, in my experience, always doing things by consensus leads to mediocrity or failure – accepting the lowest common denominator. Leaders are driven by the mission at hand and by their personality and energy. They have knowledge and skills, answers and direction. They set the goals, identify the tasks, and drive forward to make things happen. Leaders convince others of the importance of the mission. They also refuse to fail.

People look for leadership, not just management. A manager *tells* you what you're supposed to do. A leader *inspires* you to do it. No one says *take me to your manager*. It's *take me to your leader*. People want to *follow their leader*.

Leadership is driven by purpose. There is a goal to achieve, a cause to fulfill, a problem to solve, or an opportunity to seize. Good leaders aim to do the right thing. They respect and trust the people they lead, empowering them to achieve their best. Certainly, there are ego-driven leaders who achieve results, but their narcissism undermines them over time. People don't want to be around them, much less work for them. Strong, yet humble leaders who focus on developing those they lead, while accomplishing the mission, are typically successful more often and for much longer.

> *"Leadership is intangible, and therefore no weapon ever designed can replace it."*
>
> Omar Bradley

From mentoring a colleague to launching a major initiative, leadership opportunities abound. So, ask yourself, *why do I want to lead? Why do I want to be a leader?* Do you enjoy the power and perks that come with a leadership position? Do you see leadership as a duty, obligation, or burden? Are you motivated for the right reasons?

While leadership is a chance to make your mark, the opportunity comes with even greater responsibility. You have a responsibility to the organization and to your team to accomplish your task, using resources wisely, making good decisions, and identifying new opportunities. You are also responsible for maximizing your team's abilities, motivating them to be resourceful and innovative, and recognizing their achievements. Leaders also must be problem-solvers. They are responsible for managing risks and are accountable when mistakes are made. If you're not willing to accept this responsibility, then you better think again about taking charge. It may not be your calling! Leadership is an opportunity – even a privilege – that you must sincerely embrace and want to take on.

Some contend that leaders are born, not made. I believe that the mechanics of leadership can be learned, and skills improved, but character can't be compromised. U.S. Army

General Norman Schwarzkopf said, "Leadership is a potent combination of strategy and character. But if you must be without one, be without the strategy."[148] Stormin' Norman was spot on. Character is the most important component of leadership. It starts with *why* you want to be a leader and *how* you take on the responsibilities.

FOUR INTANGIBLES OF LEADERSHIP

My experience suggests that leadership is all about *character*. By working with several inspirational and effective leaders, I've identified four intangibles of leadership that distinguish the best leaders—and all four intangibles are based on character.

INTEGRITY

The first attribute is *integrity*. Leaders should be trustworthy and dependable. As Peter Drucker once noted, "Management is doing things right; leadership is doing the right things." What's the difference?

During CACI's Abu Ghraib crisis of 2004, one of my responsibilities was to keep the CACI Board of Directors informed about what was happening. In particular, I remember the response to one of my emails from one of our Directors, General Larry Welch, a former Chief of Staff of the U.S. Air Force and a Vietnam veteran combat pilot. I liked that Larry was always straight to the point and I valued his counsel. His email simply stated, "*Jack, just do the right thing.*" Those words captured the principle behind every decision we made during those trying

> "The quality of a leader is reflected in the standards they set for themselves."
>
> Ray Kroc

---

[148] James Charlton, *The Military Quotation Book* (New York: Thomas Dunne Books, 2002). Schwarzkopf served as Commander of U.S. Central Command in the late 1980s and was commander of the Coalition Forces in the Gulf War of 1991. He retired from active service in August 1991 and died in December 2012.

times.

Larry's advice meant, of course, that we would not hide anything, and that we would fully inform our employees, clients, and shareholders. We would tell them what we knew, what we faced and where we stood. And we certainly would not act precipitously just because the media or anyone else thought we should.

Integrity not only shows where you stand, but also where you expect everyone else to stand. The best leaders don't try to install integrity – they instill it, inspire it, exemplify it, model it. Integrity means *moral leadership* – doing the right thing no matter what and inspiring everyone else to do the same.

COURAGE AND CONVICTION

The second interlocking leadership intangible is *courage and conviction.* Courage is *not* allowing your actions and decisions to be controlled by fear, doubt or uncertainty. Conviction is the belief in what you're doing – and the strength to get it done. It's also the willingness to take risks. This does *not* mean that you don't have a fear of failure. What it does mean is that you aren't easily frightened away.

In early 2004, a Canadian IT outsourcing firm had been trying to buy a troubled American company. However, they could not buy the company's line of business that worked on classified national security contracts. Their Canadian CEO believed that there had to be an American company out there that would be interested in the national security piece, and that a three-way deal could work. When the first American partner of the Canadian company backed out, the Canadian CEO still believed that another American company was probably out there. And we were. CACI was ready!

Serge Godin, then CEO of CGI, called and asked me if CACI would be interested in acquiring the Defense and Intelligence Group of American Management Systems.[149] I

---

[149] CGI is an information technology management company based in Montreal, Canada. Founded in 1976, CGI employed about 69,000 people in over 40 countries in

replied "yes." It was a fascinating proposition. This line of business, focusing on the intelligence community, was one we had been expanding and wanted to continue to expand. As CACI's largest acquisition to date, it would be a $415 million cash deal, and add over 1,600 employees and 10 major business operating sites. It was a significant opportunity, but there were many questions. Could we raise the money? Did we have the resources to integrate so many people, offices, and contracts? Would the business hold on? Was there enough momentum and continuity for success? Would their customers stick with us? Would the employees stay?

As we did our early due diligence, my senior staff all recommended "no." Some felt it was too risky to pull off. Others were uncomfortable with the size of the deal and the price of the acquisition. There were also some serious doubts about raising the money and how our shareholders would react. I knew that to become a Tier-1, billion-dollar company, we had to seize this "make-a-difference" opportunity. I also knew we had the talent and M&A experience to make the deal work.

Former British Prime Minister James Callaghan once said, "A leader must have the courage to act against an expert's advice." I'm sure CGI's Serge Godin was also advised that this complex, three-way, public company, multi-national deal was unworkable! However, Serge and I believed that the rewards would outweigh the risks. We were both entrepreneurs and determined to make it happen! I also knew that our CACI team would rise to the occasion to make it work. Serge and I were right. As leaders, we both had the courage and conviction to see it through. CACI and CGI partnered to acquire AMS in a deal that closed in May 2004. The deal has been a resounding success for all parties.

2013. Traded on both the New York and Toronto Stock Exchanges, CGI revenues in 2012 were $4.8 billion (Canadian).

COMMITMENT

The third leadership intangible is *commitment* – being persistent and determined. Pat Riley, who won eight NBA championships (five as a head coach, and one each as a player, assistant coach, and team executive) once said, "There are only two options regarding commitment, you're either in or you're out. There's no such thing as life in-between." Coach Riley is right. Championships are never won by teams who practice occasionally or give 50 percent. The same goes for all goals. Success in anything really important is never achieved without commitment – unrelenting commitment.

In my experience, commitment is made up of two things. First, determination is the emotional energy that a leader possesses to establish goals and get moving toward them. Second, persistence is staying power. It's easy to get energized and sprint into action. Maintaining momentum and reaching big goals, however, is not easy! Achieving major goals can be a long-term effort, but great leaders get it done!

The business world is no different. Success and value are not created overnight. Nor are they guaranteed to last. It took CACI nearly five decades to become a highly respected, top-tier company. My best example of commitment, however, is about Herb Karr, CACI's co-founder. One of his best leadership traits was commitment. In 1987, Herb pushed back against raider-styled shareholders who rudely disrupted our annual meetings trying to force a takeover sale of CACI. I'll never forget his telling me that he would liquidate the company and shut down our contracts before giving in to the "barbarians at the gate." He meant it too! When he died in 1990, those same "barbarians" came after me, but I had learned to fight back. After several years of it, I won the control fight. That's why there is a successful CACI today!

So, leadership starts with integrity, is revealed through courage and conviction, and gets actualized through commitment.

VISION

My fourth intangible of leadership is *vision*. Irish author Jonathan Swift defined vision as "the art of seeing what is invisible to others." The challenge for leaders is to get their team to share that same vision and make it happen!

Vision starts with the attitude that anything is possible. Have you ever heard of a pessimistic political candidate? Or an uninspired inventor? The best leaders operate in the realm of *what's possible*, not just *what's probable*.

What would you think of a man who visualized a helicopter, tank, calculator, double hull boat, and plate tectonics? What if I told you this man was an uneducated painter who lived 500 years ago? Leonardo daVinci may have been the most talented person who ever lived. Clearly, he didn't limit his imagination.

In 1966, characters on a science fiction TV show spoke to one another using hand-held devices. Star Trek not only predicted cell phones, but also influenced and popularized other modern technologies, like Tablet PCs, PDAs and MRIs.

A big part of vision is *intuition*. Leaders not only have a vision of what they want to achieve, they also have ideas about how to achieve it. Did one of your college papers change your life? How about inspiring you to create a new industry?

FedEx founder Fred Smith could answer "yes" to both questions. While at Yale in 1962, Smith wrote an economics paper outlining overnight delivery service in the computer age. He saw the growth of IBM and supercomputers, recognizing that automation would change distribution. He argued that passenger routing systems used by airfreight shippers were inadequate. Smith proposed that shippers needed a system designed for airfreight that could meet demands. He then set the paper aside.

After graduating, Fred Smith spent four years in the U.S. Marines Corps, including service in Vietnam. During his service, Smith saw many supplies arriving late or ending up in the wrong places. When he left the Marines in 1971, computers had begun to take hold in business. So, Smith returned to his college paper idea. Inspired by the bank clearinghouse network, Smith created the hub-and-spoke model for shipping. That same year, the 29-year old Smith incorporated and raised nearly $90 million in venture capital. It took four years before the company showed a profit, but FedEx is now a household word that means priority shipping.

Vision also enables initiative. Having a clear vision of what you want to achieve and a clear idea of how to get it done is a strong motivator. A leader's vision is what connects employees, goals and values together to achieve their best results. As GE's former CEO Jack Welch once said, "Good business leaders create a vision, articulate the vision, passionately own the vision, and relentlessly drive it to completion."

Leadership starts with *integrity*, is revealed through *courage and conviction*, gets actualized through *commitment*, and is driven by *vision*. I describe these attributes as *intangibles* not because they're elusive, but rather, because they're essential. Since they all derive from character, we already possess the means to demonstrate these four attributes. Still, it's up to each of us to cultivate them – to become the best leaders!

You can learn to be an effective leader, but the desire has to come from within. Do you know if you have leadership potential? Do you already seek a leadership role? In either case, the opportunity will arise for you to *step up or step aside*.

APPRAISE: Resolve

The road to success is rarely traveled without a few bumps and necessary course corrections. Fear, mistakes, even failure, can alter the path we're on. However, disruptions and setbacks can even help refine what you want and how to achieve it.

Challenges are also tests of character. It's the difference between rising to the occasion or laying down when things get tough. It's also the fortitude to see things through. These are the realities of striving for and achieving success. They're also what make success a reality. By trying new things and learning from our experiences, we show what we're capable of and how we can resolve to achieve more. Be forewarned: once your goal is met, you'll be expected to do more.

Are you up to the challenge?

CHAPTER 14

SUCCESS ACCEPTS
THE RISK OF FAILURE

"I failed my way to success."
Thomas Edison

There once was a poor old worker who would come home every day from his job, sit in his chair and say, "Dear God, please let me win the lottery, so I can finally get some rest." An angel who always heard the old worker's prayer wondered why God wouldn't grant this one wish. One day, the angel decided to confront God about it. "Lord, this poor soul has worked hard all his life. All he asks is to win the lottery. Why won't you answer his prayer?" God looked at the angel and said, "I would let him win the lottery – if only he would buy a ticket!"

Sounds simple enough, doesn't it? You have to play to win. Taking chances in life isn't always as easy as buying a lottery ticket. However, nothing worthwhile, of significance, ever happens without taking some kind of chance.

Taking chances isn't easy because it takes us out of our comfort zone. Taking a risk can be scary because we're afraid of losing what we already have. Or it requires us to try new things and sometimes think in uncomfortable new ways. Often it means added responsibility. Some people may not know where to begin or how they can gather the resources they need. Sometimes it's simply a lack of conviction or self-confidence.

So what's the benefit of *not* taking some risk for a better situation? At best, you maintain the status quo. On the other hand, situations can deteriorate. It's also true that some people are content with what they have – and that's fine. Yet, while you may not do anything, the circumstances around you are constantly changing. Or an opportunity may disappear, because it's no longer available or because someone else took advantage of it. Your idleness will cost you – and leave you behind.

By the way, I respect people who, ready or not, tell me, "Jack, I want that position. I'm ready for it."

In 1984, when Herb Karr asked me if I would be interested in taking the job of President and CEO of CACI, I didn't pause for a second in saying, "Yes, I'd like the job. When do I start?" I was surprised on the one hand, because it was truly unexpected. On the other hand, I was ready for the job. Though the risk of failure was real, I was confident in my capabilities; and the opportunity for success far outweighed any fear of failure.

If you stand aside, or take a pass on a deal, you may also wind up kicking yourself over it. In 2005, Apple initially took its first cell phone product – the iPhone – and a multi-year exclusivity deal to Verizon Wireless. Apple's first foray into the music player market, the iPod, had become an instant success and industry standard several years earlier. However, Verizon Wireless, balking at Apple's rich financial terms and other demands, decided to pass. A rejected Apple went to AT&T. Within six months of the iPhone launch, about 40 percent of iPhone buyers became new AT&T subscribers. With over 21 million iPhones sold worldwide by the end of 2009, Verizon Wireless found itself waiting for the exclusivity agreement to end – and a second chance – in 2010.[150]

Most risks in life are not so pivotal. The real risk is often the one to our egos. The actual risk of failure is often fearing what it says about us. We're afraid to make a mistake. We fear that one mistake will lead to another. Or that one mistake will end an opportunity. Or that mistakes will create an impression of incompetence. Or that our mistake will be permanent. While understandable, such fears only undermine our confidence and even contribute to negative outcomes.

Only one thing is certain. When it comes to the fear of making a mistake, the only person who doesn't make any

---

[150] Verizon Wireless finally got the iPhone in the spring of 2011. Sprint added the iPhone in the fall of 2011.

mistakes is the person who does nothing! It is rare when simply trusting everything to luck yields successful outcomes.

Peter Drucker once said, "People who don't take risks generally make about two big mistakes a year. People who do take risks generally make about two big mistakes a year." By trying to avoid failure, you are actually avoiding success.

> "I make plenty of mistakes and I'll make plenty more mistakes, too. That's part of the game. You've just got to make sure that the right things overcome the wrong things."
>
> Warren Buffett

The fear of success is also very real. An important part of the scientific method is that the results of an experiment must be verified by replicating them to demonstrate they are consistent. Can you repeat your success or was it a one-time deal? Was it luck? Success is not an end, but a milestone on the road to even greater accomplishments. Success creates more opportunity, added responsibility, and higher expectations. A pat on the back for a job well done is typically followed by a chance for another, frequently bigger, job. For many, though, success is a path that's just too daunting to take.

Be alert – the possibility of failure is real. You can't expect to get it right the first time, every time. To err is human. You may get knocked down, and risk may incur the loss of time, money, and energy. But *failure is fatal only if you can't learn from it.* One of the most ironic sources for this lesson is Attila the Hun, who said, "Learn from defeat! If you fail to sharpen your leadership prowess after confronting unconquered obstacles, your experiences were for naught, and you, as well as your subordinates, will become nothing more than a helpless victim."[151]

I find that **you can't achieve success without embracing your failures.** Steps backward often turn into major leaps forward. Mistakes tell us what we need to do differently, better, or not again.

---

[151] Wess Roberts, *Leadership Secrets of Attila the Hun* (London: Bantam Books, 1989).

CHARACTER: The Ultimate Success Factor

One mistake that we made at CACI came from a seemingly routine project. In 1999, CACI won a contract with the state of South Carolina to develop a large scale, computer-based licensing and registration system for their Department of Motor Vehicles (DMV). Our project was a firm, fixed-price contract for about $25 million. The work, however, was split between the CACI team and South Carolina state employees. CACI would work on systems integration, metrics, and statewide installation. The state would be in charge of populating the databases and quality control.

The project had a rocky start. The CACI team made some equipment mistakes, while decision delays on the client side also hampered progress. Early problems were addressed, but were followed by other issues. For example, integration and testing was taking longer than expected.

One day, the senior project manager on the client side asked his CACI contact, "Could Dr. London come down to Columbia? The Governor wants to see him." It was a first for me. I had met with many clients at their request, but I had never been summoned by a governor before. As I was briefed on the project's status, the Governor of South Carolina, Jim Hodges, was already thinking ahead to a re-election campaign. The state's long-standing troubles with its DMV systems were a bone of contention for the governor in the previous election, and he had promised to solve them.

When I arrived in Columbia, South Carolina's capital, I met with the CACI team there in further preparations for the gubernatorial meeting. When the day came to meet with Governor Hodges, our CACI project manager and I went to the capital building.[152] The Governor came in with a cadre of aides, IT people, and a number of lawyers. He quickly expressed his displeasure with the project's status and progress. He wanted to

---

[152] The South Carolina State House is a grand Greek revival-style building that had just undergone renovation. I admired the marble floors and walls, ornate woodwork, and oil paintings on every wall. The conference room in which the meeting was held was equally impressive. After we arrived, I took my place at the huge conference table. It was quite a learning experience and one that, for many reasons, I will never forget.

fulfill a previous campaign promise for DMV improvement. If delayed, the project could be a big problem for him in the upcoming election. I explained to the Governor the corrective measures that had already been put in place and reviewed the revised project plans. I reminded Governor Hodges that to finish the project, CACI would need the state's continued effort and support. Quality issues with the data supplied by the state had been a considerable part of the project's delay.

I am proud to say that CACI went on to deliver a modern, customer-centric motor vehicle system with digitized driver's licenses, and vehicle title and registrations to the state of South Carolina in August 2002. While it had been delivered late for the reasons stated, the real cost was to CACI. Although some adjustments to the contract were made, the project ended up costing about $6 million more than the original contract price of $25 million. CACI had done several successful projects in state DMV and motor carrier operations before, but this had been the first effort on this larger scale in the statewide DMV, full systems arena. We initially felt the budget and reputation risks were minimal. What we learned was that large scale, fixed-price contracts in that market arena could be potentially disastrous. With these customers, there were simply too many changing variables and political pressures that increased risks to CACI – including technology upgrades, state-level politics, and state-level employee turnover. Nonetheless, we institutionalized the lessons learned from this project. The most important one was to avoid ever again bidding these kinds of jobs on a firm fixed-price basis again.[153]

---

[153] After the initial system delivery, CACI executed a follow-on contract for twenty months of operations and maintenance support, including management of twenty third-party vendors plus professional services from companies such as IBM. During this period, CACI also interfaced the application with computerized vehicle registration (an electronic dealer interface) and implemented an electronic data warehouse. This part of the project generated several million dollars in revenue for us and received high scores in customer feedback surveys. We had made good on our commitment and, I am proud to say, departed with a happy client that had a fully operational system.

Taking risks does not mean gambling. The terms have different meanings, and yet they are often used interchangeably. One implies trying something different or out of your comfort zone that may not succeed. The other is something done at casinos. The big difference is the element of chance. Risk-taking is analytical. You often know many of the variables and can estimate, sometimes even calculate potential outcomes. Nothing is certain, but the outcome isn't completely out of your hands. Gambling, on the other hand, is playing games of chance. Even if the odds are known or calculable, you have little or no control over the variables or the outcomes. In gambling, the stakes are usually short-term. They rarely last. Think of it this way. The game of chance in which you have the greatest chance of winning is a coin toss. Here, at best, you only have a 50 percent chance of winning. You may not even get to pick which side of the coin you want. So, when you have poor odds and little or no control over the situation, success is highly unlikely!

"Law XXXII – Fools rush in where incumbents fear to bid."

Norman Augustine

As a business CEO, I don't believe in high-stakes gambling. Betting the entire company on one event or transaction is stupid. Business is never an all or nothing proposition. At least it doesn't have to be. It's rarely black or white. There are many, many shades of gray. There are always alternatives to be examined or opportunities to be explored. Perhaps they haven't been thought of, but they always exist. Over the years, a few folks at CACI have made suggestions that equate to outright gambling. We even had a director on our board who, at one time, wanted to sell the company for an insignificant premium. Then there was a wild and crazy line of business that an overzealous junior manager wanted to try out. Why would I jeopardize our employees' jobs, clients' projects, and shareholders' investments on nothing more than a giveaway or a foolish bet? I wouldn't and I didn't. Folks with such faulty judgment don't last long at CACI either. Eventually both of them were out the door.

On the other hand, you have to be willing to put your skin in the game. When you are fully behind something, sometimes you have to take bigger risks to prove its worth. For example, in 1990, CACI was in the early stages of transitioning from a smaller business to a large corporation. I had been running the company for six years and was determined to build CACI into a major enterprise. When in April 1990 Herb Karr died unexpectedly, however, some dissident and hostile shareholders thought it was time to sell the company to the highest bidder in a takeover situation. These shareholders were only interested in making a few extra bucks for themselves in the short term – regardless of what was in the best interest of other shareholders or the company's future. Because my goals have always included enhancing and growing shareholder value, this was something that I could not allow to happen.

By the fall of 1991, the dissident shareholders were staging an old-fashioned, knock-down, drag out proxy contest to gain a controlling position on the board of directors. They thought – no surprise – that if they controlled the board, they could get CACI sold and make a quick buck. I had to prove my credibility in advocating the future growth of CACI. So, I used all of my own cash to exercise a tranche of my vested stock options.

This put voting stock in my hands and allowed me to stand up against the dissident shareholders. My pitch was that I had put my money where my mouth was. At the time CACI was performing well. So when I bought my stock and announced my holdings, Wall Street took notice. While there was no change to our stock price (it was already performing well), my actions were noted by major stockholders and they gave me their solid support. The proxy contest came to a head at the annual meeting that November and, although it was a nail biter, we had plenty of votes to take the day.

The calculated risk was more than worth it. Since 1990, CACI has stayed in business as an independent operator and grown from $150 million in annual sales to $3.8 billion in annual sales (2012). Return to shareholders during all of this has been dramatic.

The independent growth plan was the right choice. I had put my money where my mouth was – my skin in the game. And that made all the difference! Having a genuine personal investment in the process and outcome has always made a big difference in how I have looked at CACI.[154]

The trick is calculating risks and deciding which risks are worth taking. Big thinking usually means accepting high risks of failure. As we say around CACI, *if you aim low, you'll hit low*. Small thinkers will succeed every time. The level of risk we're willing to accept varies with each situation. Every time and every circumstance is different. The greatest challenges are obviously the situations where we have the most to lose and the most to gain.

My decision to leave the Navy was such an experience. Not being selected for assignments in Vietnam planted questions in my mind about my future with the Navy. Over the course of a couple of years, I gave the idea of leaving the Navy much serious thought and discussion with my family. So eight years short of retirement benefits, with six months worth of savings, no job lined up, and with many family responsibilities, including my wife and two pre-schoolers, a mortgage and car payments – all during a recession – I left the Navy. Looking back forty years later, I can now say that it sent me on a path that worked out better than I would have ever expected.

The decision to take a major risk is often made with some cost-benefit analysis, even using my favorite, a simple pros versus cons list. While you're looking at the downside consequences of a decision, spend some time deciding what the

---

[154] I worry about how the importance of the "risk-reward" relationship is diminishing in our society. In my view, there is far too great a sense of entitlement. In kids' sports, children are given awards just for participation, not just for winning. Adults often feel they are owed recognitions and rewards just for showing up at work rather than working competitively to earn them. At CACI we believe that we have to work for what we want. And we have to earn it. That often means taking risks. Risk-taking and competition can yield innovation and progress, just as it can lead to failure and loss. Competition is a value-adding experience. It is competition and innovation, in my opinion, that have made the U.S. great and prosperous. In my view, expecting big results with minimal effort is the wrong attitude.

off ramps or *escape tunnels* might be. What alternatives do you have if things get off track? How can you back out or minimize the damage if you need to? Do you have a safety net in place?

I also look at *the maximum downside risk* – the *worst* thing that could happen – and the *likelihood* it will occur. Before I decided to leave the U.S. Navy, I did a careful assessment of all of the factors and made a firm commitment to myself to finish my Navy career serving in the U.S. Navy Reserve. It was a great experience and I worked hard at doing a good job of it.

Any maximum downside analysis has to assess the likelihood of things going haywire. If the chances of things getting fouled up seem high, you'd better study the worst-case scenario very thoroughly. Look before you leap. It can be a long way to the bottom. Amazingly, many people jump into a course of action without even thinking about the implications of a worst case outcome.

When King Ferdinand and Queen Isabella of Spain were trying to decide whether to finance Christopher Columbus in 1492, they concluded that they didn't have much to lose if he failed. And if he was right about the distance to China across the Atlantic, they had everything to gain. Their worst case scenario was that they would lose their money and never see Columbus again. This was significant, but was considered of less significance in comparison to a new, direct Spanish route to the Orient with its abundant treasures of silks and spices. Even for 15th-century cost-benefit analysis, this seems like an easy decision. Besides, Columbus was committed to his voyage and to completing his mission!

Ferdinand and Isabella's risk certainly paid off.[155] It was an age of exploration and adventure, and the trend lines soon became clear. The world was round and larger than people

---

[155] I have been to their tomb in Granada, Spain, as well as that of Christopher Columbus in Seville. The Spanish revere them and I also think they were quite remarkable people. They knew how to take risks and make decisions. Talk about leaders and entrepreneurs – these people really knew what it was all about!

thought, with many places to discover. Columbus was willing to take an enormous risk to attain a goal of fortune and acclaim.[156]

We see risk-taking in all facets of life today. In professional sports, teams develop by drafting new players and trading veterans. Rookies are assessed during their college careers and at various camps, while veteran players can be judged on their professional performances. Despite this, the teams can't be sure how the players will turn out or if they will work well together. Draft picks can go bust. Veterans may underperform. Players may get hurt and be unable to play for months. On the other hand, undrafted players may become stars, while average pros may excel on new teams. No matter how much potential a player may or may not have, there is a chance that it will not work out or that the real star was overlooked.

In this analysis, there's no way to account for every possibility or variable. These variables are called *unknowns* for a good reason. The willingness to take risks, however, must include the ability to deal with unknowns. These surprises can work in your favor.

For example, in 1985, the Coca-Cola Company took what they called "arguably the biggest risk in consumer goods history."[157] In order to boost sales in a sluggish soda market, Coca-Cola introduced a reformulated version of its popular soft drink, called New Coke. Initial market research and sales showed favorable acceptance of New Coke, but the company had underestimated the public's attachment to old Coke. The massive impact of the vocal minority who resented the change was immediate. Loyal drinkers hoarded cases of the old Coke. The company was inundated with calls and letters. Protests were held, even songs were written in honor of the older formula. Just 79 days later, the company reintroduced Coca-Cola Classic. Many

---

[156] On several occasions, I have visited the fascinating plaza in central Madrid dedicated to the adventures of Columbus, setting out on a large stone map plots of the three voyages he made to the New World. His remarkable accomplishments have had a far-reaching and long-lasting global impact. They transformed the world and its future from that time forward.

[157] Coca Cola corporate website, http://www.thecoca- colacompany.com/heritage /cokelore _ newcoke.html.

observers called it one of the biggest marketing blunders in history. Yet Coca Cola saw a silver lining. In their eyes, New Coke was a success because it revitalized the brand and reattached the public to Coke. In fact, Coke drinkers today are invited to share their stories about the introduction of New Coke on Coca Cola's website. Coca-Cola's risk may have been a bust at first, but it eventually worked out quite well for the company.

Coca-Cola took a calculated risk because they knew that longevity in the business world requires innovative change. Changing their trademark product may not have been the way to go, but they felt they couldn't rely on the same beverage that started the company in 1886. Beginning in the 1940s, Coca-Cola introduced several new drinks – Fanta, Sprite, Tab, Fresca, and Diet Coke – over the next four decades. In 1960, Coca-Cola Company added juices, a new line of business with the acquisition of the Minute Maid Company. Today, Coca-Cola can claim to be "the world's most ubiquitous brand, with more than 1.7 billion beverage servings sold each day."[158]

In the changing world of technology, you have to foresee change to stay ahead in business. As former Lockheed Martin CEO, Norman Augustine pointed out, "While accepting risk is an element of life, choosing it is an essential element of corporate success." At CACI, we knew that adapting to change and creating change were the only ways for us to get anywhere.

In the early 1990s, it was clear that tools like email and the Internet, as well as the various technologies around them would be fundamental to the IT world. Specifically, the future I saw was in networks and telecommunications, although I wasn't so bold as to see them merging to the extent they have. By 1992, CACI had been selected to be the Federal Computer Conference Net integrator. The writing was on the wall that a company would have to be a networking/telecom leader to stay competitive in the IT services industry.

CACI launched an active M&A program in 1992. Over the next several years, we moved into the networks and telecommunications market space through acquisitions, and

---

[158] Coca Cola corporate website, http://heritage.coca-cola.com/.

became increasingly involved in network security and information assurance. Soon CACI identified contractor support opportunities emerging in the government's intelligence communities. To take advantage of these opportunities, we turned our M&A focus to companies with intelligence and government security contracts. That strategic decision over the years has worked wonders for the company.

Our first opportunity to move into these new markets came in 1998 when an investment banking industry colleague called me. I had known the man for several years around our industry and his firm had followed CACI as investment opportunities for their clients. He told me that he had an acquisition opportunity. He knew we were actively hunting for companies in this field. The company, Questech, had a solid contract base with some intelligence agencies. They had about $90 million in sales and an excellent professional staff. It sounded right up our alley, so my colleague set up a meeting. A day later I met Vince Salvatori, CEO of Questech, at an upscale Italian restaurant in Tysons Corner, Virginia. Vince and I hit it off from the start. Over the course of that afternoon, we put the basics of the deal together.

That acquisition was CACI's first major move into the intelligence arena.[159] CACI took a risk by entering new fields beyond our traditional systems and software development work. The risk paid off in spades. The deal strengthened CACI's information security capabilities and enabled us to move into the areas of signal and information processing and analysis, electronic and information warfare, and command and control systems. As part of the deal, Vince Salvatori joined CACI's Board of Directors, where he served with distinction for several years. Another Questech executive, Bill Fairl, would become CACI's President of U.S. Operations in 2007. I always point to Bill's remarkable career when I tell people in acquired companies how

---

[159] CACI had won a number of smaller intelligence contracts over the years, but nothing like those that Questech had. We had also been interested in this field for some time.

their careers can move ahead at CACI.[160] The deal also gave us the skills, knowledge and confidence to try larger acquisitions, like the $415 million acquisition of the Defense and Intelligence Group of American Management Systems in 2004.

Growth is about taking risks. From the confidence and skills gained in your successes to the lessons learned from your mistakes, you can't get anywhere in business or in life without taking some risks. So whether it's changing your career, starting a new business, exploring new worlds, or simply buying a lottery ticket, *you have to take the risk of failure in order to succeed.*

---

[160] Bill Fairl retired from CACI in September 2012.

CHAPTER 15

ALL THE TRAUMA IS IN YOUR HEAD

"We have nothing to fear but fear itself."
Franklin Delano Roosevelt

When trying to figure out a problem, have you ever been told not to *over think* it? When self-doubt begins to overcome you, have you ever been told not to psyche yourself out? Have you ever been part of an organization that was unable to grow because they couldn't decide what to do (*analysis paralysis*)? I may call it the *trauma in your head* here, but the concept is familiar. To our detriment, we often allow our fears, concerns, and questions to control our decision-making. Many times, we learn later that all of our doubts were unfounded, and that we were capable of far more than we thought.

    I learned this lesson in a very unusual way – under water. As graduation approaches at the Naval Academy, each Midshipman selects a specialty to start their Naval career. I had developed an interest in aviation in high school. One of my high school football coaches also happened to teach the flying course, so in my senior year of high school I thought I would give it a try. I did some 12 hours of flying time with the coach, and it was exhilarating! That experience stuck in my mind during my time at the Academy. In the late 1950s, the military had the newest planes and latest technologies. It was clear that Naval aviation had a big future.

    I met all the qualifications for the aviation program and was selected to go to flight school in Pensacola, Florida after graduation in 1959. As it turns out, you don't get to fly right away at flight school. You spend several months in ground school, learning terminology, types of airplanes and plane components, aeronautical engineering, instrumentation – and about crashes!

One training exercise is called the *Dilbert Dunker* drill. It simulates an airplane crashing into the water by dropping a mock cockpit down a 25 foot ramp into a large, deep pool. Before the Dunker, you are trained on how to brace for the impact, free yourself from shoulder and seat harnesses, and swim to the surface. The point of the exercise was more than simply escaping from a submerged airplane. It was to see if you could also handle a mild crisis and a touch of trauma. As you sit atop that ramp, looking down and waiting for the cage to drop, all sorts of thoughts can race through your head. *Will I get whacked? What if something goes wrong? What if I can't release the restraints? I'm nervous. Can I do this?* It's natural to be nervous, but you can't let it get to you. You have to learn to control the emotional part. Letting your emotions take control is how mistakes get made. Sitting atop that ramp, I reminded myself that I wasn't the first person to do the Dunker, and if others could do it, so could I. Before I could finish that thought, my cage was released and down I went! I stayed calm and let my training take over. Sure enough, I got out, swam up, and gave the thumbs up to let my supervisors know all was well. All of the trauma – fear, doubts, questions – had, in fact, been in my head.

Other people's fears can also be an obstacle. During flight school, I would call home to catch up with my family. My father would always ask me question after question about my training: *What if your radio fails? What if your engine quits? What if your plane catches fire? What if one of the wings falls off? What if your parachute fails to open?* I tried to reassure him by telling him that there were emergency procedures, back-up plans, and systems for all of these scenarios. No matter what answer I gave him, he kept building up the potential problems to catastrophic proportions. Finally, one day I told him that if all those things happened at the same time, there would be no survivors! He gasped with frustration. I appreciated his concern as a parent, but there was no answer that I could give that would make him feel better – or at least stop asking those worst-case scenario questions. (Of course, he was a great father, and it was all because he cared and wanted me to be safe.)

You can't always alleviate other people's fears. In some cases, you can answer a few questions and the issue is resolved. At other times, no answer can make the other person happy. So, don't add unnecessary pressure. And don't let other people's worries sabotage you. For example, suppose you want to go back to school. You've done your research, found a program, created a financial plan, and have been accepted. Of course you'll have questions: *Will this degree add value to my career? Can I afford not to work? Can I get back into an academic routine?* Furthermore, you may have friends, family, or colleagues who will ask you questions: *Why do you want to do that? You'll be so much older than everyone else. That degree is a waste of time.* Others may envy your initiative and find it easy to criticize you to make themselves feel better about not being as ambitious. You can't let other people's thoughts, concerns or criticisms undermine your confidence and ability.

When the year 2000 arrived, the much-hyped Y2K bug that was supposed to wipe out anything connected to modern technology never happened. Organizations worldwide spent millions to prevent anticipated problems with their IT systems. In the U.S., the Year 2000 Information and Readiness Disclosure Act was passed and coordinated by the President's Council on Year 2000 Conversion.[161] In the end, few problems were reported on January 1, 2000 and the days after. The anticipated trauma never materialized.

On April 18, 2011, similar anxiety emerged when credit rating agency Standard & Poor's (S&P) issued a negative outlook on the U.S.'s sovereign-debt rating for the first time in its 151 year history. The U.S. was running a budget deficit of more than 11 percent of gross domestic product (GDP) and net government debt was rising to 80 percent or more of GDP. Without progress towards a balanced budget, it would "render U.S. fiscal profile meaningfully weaker than that of peer AAA sovereigns" and S&P warned that it could lower the U.S.' AAA rating down to AA as a

---

[161] Orlando DeBruce and Jennifer Jones, "White House shifts Y2K focus to states," *CNN,* February 23, 1999, http://articles.cnn.com/1999-02-23/tech/9902_23 _shift.y2k.idg_1_federal-systems-quarterly-report-state-systems?_s=PM:TECH.

result.[162] By June, Moody's issued its own warning; in July S&P put U.S. debt on a 90-day credit watch.

On August 2, 2011, Congress voted to raise the debt ceiling of the federal government by means of the Budget Control Act of 2011. On Friday, August 5th, S&P downgraded the U.S. to AA. The downgrade was immediately criticized by officials at the U.S. Treasury Department, by both political parties, as well as by many prominent business people and economists. Observers also feared that the downgrade might raise interest rates required to finance U.S. debt and, hence, interest costs.

The following Monday, August 8th, global stock markets declined, with a 5 to 7 percent drop in U.S. stock indices. However, the price of Treasury bonds and Gold futures rose. "The downgrade just put investors on an already-heightened state of alert," said Rob Lutts, chief investment officer of Cabot Money Management. "People are exiting any equities they have, and selling off any assets that have any risk exposure."[163]

By the end of 2011, however, there was little fallout. "If the world viewed America's debt as riskier now because S&P's opinion changed, one would imagine rates would rise. Beyond the U.S., the Big Three credit raters issued a raft of downgrades and downgrade threats this year. Markets have overall yawned, likely because they rightly view the raters as, at best, merely confirming what's already widely known."[164]

In reality, situations usually don't turn out as badly as we think they will. Many people tend to overreact. They conjure up demons and dragons that never emerge. And by doing so, they unnerve themselves. We face many challenges in life, but too often we let our fear and doubts control us instead of our self-confidence and ability.

---

[162] Standard & Poor's, " Research Update: United States of America 'AAA/A-1+' Rating Affirmed; Outlook Revised To Negative," April 18, 2011, http://www.standardandpoors.com/ratings/articles/en/us/?assetID=1245302886884.

[163] Ken Sweet, "Dow plunges after S&P downgrade," CNNMoney, August 8, 2011, http://money.cnn.com/2011/08/08/markets/markets_newyork/index.htm?iref=BN1&hpt=hp_t1.

[164] Lara Hoffmans, "Top 10 Stories from 2011," Forbes, December 30, 2011, http://www.forbes.com/sites/larahoffmans/2011/12/30/fisher-investments-top-10/.

OVERCOMING FEAR

How can you stop giving in to the trauma in your head?

EXPERIENCE

First, let your emotions happen. What happens when somebody makes you angry? Or a situation annoys you? Or you're frustrated by a task or assignment, especially one that you didn't want? In my career, often my first reaction to problems and situations was not indicative of how I handled it. For example, if we unexpectedly did not win a *recompete* contract, my initial reaction might have been to get very upset (even lose my cool). After calming down, I would want to find out the facts, then I would act upon them. Who won the contract? How was their bid better than ours? What could we have done differently? Sometimes, it's best to let your first reaction happen because it's a chance to vent and get beyond emotions that could cloud your thinking. It's only an emotional response and not how you will actually proceed.

Another reason to let your emotions happen is that sometimes *your gut is telling you something*. Remember, your gut feeling is your experience and instinct, not just some random, momentary reaction. If an opportunity is too good to be true, it probably is. If you can't see the value or market for a product or service no matter how well it's pitched to you, you're probably right to be cautious. You'd better not buy it.

If you're not having a gut reaction to a situation, you can *defer to experience*. You can think back on similar challenges and use those solutions to guide you. When a good client has a unique or unusual request, do you disappoint the client? Not if you want to keep their business. You find or make the way.

CACI had a project for the Library of Congress to preserve a collection of Veterans' History Project interviews on the Library's computer hard drives that had to be accessible to all who visit the Veterans History Project website. Getting the thousands of DVDs loaded to a hard drive would be a tedious task – until the CACI support team came up with an innovative solution. Through a team member's familiarity with robotic DVD duplicators, which usually write files in the other direction – from a hard drive to DVDs – the CACI team discovered a way to reverse the process by reprogramming the duplicators to "rip" (or import) the Library's DVD files to the desired hard drive format. Another teammate then wrote a series of batch scripts that leveraged open source software to consolidate each DVD into a single MPEG2 file, which compresses high-quality video streams using as little bandwidth as possible.

CACI's creative solution increased productivity and reduced labor requirements, providing a 40 percent cost savings over rates charged by established media conversion firms. Not only was the Library of Congress project director thrilled with the new scalable solution, but the CACI team also expanded the company's opportunities.

Your experience will often tell you how to avoid, change, or solve a problem. I remember the first time someone quit on me. It was early in my career, and I was in charge of a project developing a simulation model for high-value spare part usage for the U.S. Navy's Trident submarines.[165] The project was only a one-and-a-half man, year-long task, but it was work to be done with specific skills. So imagine my alarm when my key employee decided to leave for another job. We were over halfway through the effort at the time. I didn't have time or money to train someone up. I had lots of anxiety, but not much time to do anything about it. Not only was it possible that I would not find anyone qualified to do the job, I also worried that I may not get my project done on time. Job vacancies at the time were filled by placing an ad in the classifieds section of the *Washington Post,* receiving resumes, and interviewing candidates – and I didn't have time for newspaper ads and regular mail. However, the telephone worked just fine. I didn't

---

[165] Trident submarines are the *Ohio* class nuclear-powered submarines deployed by the U.S. Navy. They were designed specifically for extended war-deterrence patrols. In 2013, the Navy had a total of 18 *Ohio*-class submarines each armed with 24 Trident II submarine-launched ballistic missiles.

have time for the candidates to come to me, but I could go straight to them.

I listed everyone in my people network who had related experience or who had large people networks of their own, and I started calling each person for referrals. I made dozens of calls. Soon, I found a part-time consultant with simulation modeling experience from the academic technical community who quickly came on board as a part-timer and enabled me to get our model done on time. My hiring solution was one that I would not have thought of had I not been in such a bind. Here we see that necessity truly is the mother of invention.

While it's good to have those breakthrough moments when the occasional emergency occurs, why wait until a serious situation arises for that to happen? What if you could harness that capability all of the time?

If the trauma is in your head, so is the solution. The first step is *self-control*. The trick is deciding in your head how you'll behave: how to act and react. Recognize the difference between a mountain and molehill. Creating and dealing with a mountain takes a lot more time, effort, and money, than a measly molehill. If you always choose exaggeration and panic, you'll always get exaggeration and panic. However, if you choose to not give in to panic, then you've already reduced the trauma into something manageable.

> *"We have to start teaching ourselves not to be afraid."*
>
> William Faulkner

Years ago, when I had to face some adversarial directors in board meetings, I found that some battles were small while others were substantial. These battles were invariably about schemes to sell the company cheap or to force nonsense mergers solely out of personal greed or animus in the boardroom.[166] I didn't want to fight them, but I had to. So I made an effort to maintain professionalism and decorum, and to argue my points

---

[166] One strange case for a merger came about because one of our directors had significant holdings in each of the companies and would, upon a merger, become by far the major stockholder in the surviving company.

factually and persuasively. Not only is it a matter of personal dignity, but others will pick up on it and those who don't will stand out. Since CACI has grown successfully, it shows which choice proved best.

Another way to change how you handle yourself is to *think of every challenge as an opportunity* to try something you've never done before. Work with new people and products. Learn new tools, skills, and processes. And know how to deal with similar situations if they emerge again. Getting through these situations gives you confidence and motivation. If you can squash your molehill or conquer your mountain, what else could you do? That's also how *success breeds success*!

FOCUS

The next building blocks in overcoming our fear are focus and concentration. Sadly most people simply don't know how to focus. Think about the professional athlete – the basketball player attempting a free throw, a golfer lining up a putt, a sprinter visualizing a race. These are examples of focus in sports. Professional athletes spend years learning, practicing, and improving their abilities. Yet focus also means the commitment that got the athlete to that competitive moment. Championships and medals are seldom won by people who give less than 100 percent or treat their sport like a casual hobby. Likewise, success in business or any other worthwhile activity isn't achieved without investing serious effort.

Now imagine responsibilities and goals with added consequences. For example, I learned about the importance and capability to focus while flying airplanes. When you're responsible for an aircraft and the lives aboard it, you quickly realize that concentration (and anticipation) means success. My capacity to focus and concentrate has leveraged my gray matter!

Likewise, you must choose to give it your best. Identify the steps needed to meet your challenge, and then take those steps. Avoid distractions. Distractions and diversions only lead to mistakes, reduce quality and productivity, and cause delays. Other interests and responsibilities may require you to change your focus temporarily. It's easy to get distracted by TV, Internet, and hobbies. Moreover, distractions often come from other people. Co-workers' comments or criticisms may cause you to feel inadequate, annoyed or distracted. Or like my father's worries about my flying, you may spend a lot of time trying to alleviate other people's concerns. Also, your doubts may resurface from time to time. Your concentration and focus can only be broken if you let it. Only you can choose to get back on task. However, you're not expected to be 100 percent focused 100 percent of the time. No one can do that day in and day out. This is not about perfection. It is about how well you can do something versus doing it poorly or not doing it at all.

> *"You can conquer almost any fear if you will only make up your mind to do so. For remember, fear doesn't exist anywhere except in your mind."*
>
> Dale Carnegie

The goal is to do the job efficiently, effectively, and productively. It's about doing the best we can do.

PREPARE

The final step is preparation. If a problem has been causing you concern, you will probably have enough time to prepare for it. Preparation allows you to identify the necessary steps, obtain relevant information and resources, contact key people, and discover obstacles to overcome in achieving your goals. For example, when I decided I wanted to go to the Naval Academy, I increased my studies, took a course for the college boards, researched financial aid options, and contacted my congressman and senators' offices about obtaining their sponsorship. When CACI wants to acquire a company, we do our due diligence, meet with key executives and employees on both sides, and plan for the transition. Preparation helps alleviate your concerns or fears by eliminating the unknowns and anticipating the knowns.

The Blue Angels are a prime example of what real preparation is all about. The U.S. Navy's flight demonstration squadron has been known as the premiere aerobatic team for over 60 years. For these pilots, detailed preparation is everything. Performing with the Blue Angels is a highly competitive honor, yet a serious responsibility. Navy pilots chosen to become Blue Angels come out of fleet carrier squadrons and are seasoned, highly-skilled aviators. Simply put, they are the best. The teamwork required for the high speed, low-altitude flying in the tight Blue Angel formation takes hundreds of hours to develop. Each pilot must complete 120 training flights during winter training in order to safely perform a public demonstration. The team then practices flight maneuvers in chairs, going through every step from walking to and from the planes, as well as to whom they say hello along the way. The Blue Angels walk through it over and over again before even taking it to the air. After each aerial practice and performance, the team debriefs all of the details immediately after the demonstration.

Training starts in January, and practice continues through the show season which ends in November. During the season, a typical week starts with practice on Tuesday and Wednesday mornings, then out to maneuvers at the show venue on Thursdays, followed by a practice air show on Friday. The main air shows are typically conducted on Saturdays and Sundays, with the team returning home on Sunday evenings. Mondays are the only routine day off.

Why such an intense schedule? While thrilling, the Blue Angels aerobatics are also dangerous. One wrong move can be very costly.[167] With 40 shows and 8 million spectators each season, the motivation to put on a first rate show is very strong.

They have a tradition to uphold. This team of navy pilots is the best of the best, and they represent all of the naval aviators, past and present, who have worn those gold wings and have flown all around the world, in war and peace, for over 100 years.

For any serious and costly endeavor, the more you work on preparation and details, the better you will get at overcoming

---

[167] As of 2013, there have been 26 deaths in training and performance accidents in the Blue Angels' history from the time they began performing in 1946.

the trauma in your head. Practice doesn't guarantee success, but it greatly increases your chances.

Then there are the situations that are truly scary, life-or-death situations. You can take all of these same steps to help deal with the fear, but sometimes all of the preparation in the world isn't enough. At these times, you take a deep breath, perhaps say a little prayer, and find out what you're made of.

I heard a story from a rather unexpected source that epitomizes this lesson. Michael Caine is a famous actor known for classic films like *Zulu, Dirty Rotten Scoundrels,* and *The Cider House Rules* for which he won an Academy Award. However, an 18-year old Caine was called up for national service in the British Army in 1951 and was deployed to South Korea, as part of the Royal Fusiliers. During a patrol in a valley of rice paddies, Caine's platoon realized they were being followed by Chinese soldiers. His commander came up with the risky idea of running towards the Chinese line, around the enemy soldiers, then back towards their own line. The ploy worked as the Chinese searched for Caine's platoon in the wrong place. Caine recalls, "That night we went back to our bunkers and celebrated with a beer. We were just happy to be alive ... I faced a moment when I knew I was going to die and I didn't run, I wasn't a coward, and it affected me deeply. I was at peace with myself, and that's guided my life – not just in terms of whether someone's going to kill me, but in everything."[168]

In these rare and unpredictable situations, focus on what you can do rather than panic. As the saying goes, "What doesn't kill you makes you stronger!"

So the next time you face a challenge, problem or adversity, assess the situation for what it really is, and trust yourself to do the right thing. This is what character-based success is all about. Don't give in to the doubts and fears because *all the trauma is in your head.*

---

[168] "Michael Caine – Caine Almost Died in Korean War," *ContactMusic.com,* November 3, 2009, http://www.contactmusic.com/news/caine-almost-died-in-korean-war_1121104.

CHAPTER 16

SAYING WHEN

"Genius sometimes consists of knowing when to stop."
Charles de Gaulle

Tragic endings in literature are compelling. Deeply flawed characters draw both sympathy and ire. Shakespeare's famous tragedies, like *Hamlet* and *Romeo and Juliet,* are examples of masterful stories of missteps, miscalculations, and misdeeds.

In reality, tragedies are not so entertaining. Until March 2008, Bear Stearns had been a respected global investment bank and securities brokerage firm. Overexposure to mortgage-backed assets (at the core of the subprime mortgage crisis) led to its collapse and sale to JP Morgan Chase months later. The once multi-billion dollar company was sold for the bargain price of $236 million. Employees, who owned 30 percent of the company's stock, lost millions in savings, and over 14,700 employees lost their jobs.

We all like to think that we make the best decisions we can at the time, but sometimes even the best laid plans go awry. Circumstances change. The unpredictable happens. Decisions are sometimes made under duress or doubt. Or, as in the case of Bear Stearns, people become subject to the decisions and mistakes of other people. Nevertheless, something can usually be done to make a situation better when things are going wrong.

There are basically two times that you need to know *when to say when.* The first is *knowing how much to give.* The second is *knowing when to stop.* In both situations, you reach a point where you have to re-evaluate what you're doing and why.

Knowing how much to give refers to input. There's the saying that you get out of something what you put into it. This is true to a certain extent. Input, however, is usually viewed from a

261

bureaucratic perspective; more effort, more people, more money. The proper question, however, should be: will the inputs really yield the needed results?

I came across this question often in operations research. In the early 1970s, Frederick Brooks was an IBM software engineer who observed that adding more workers to a project that was falling behind schedule caused it to run even further behind. The conclusion became known as Brooks' Law.[169] Its essence has been called the "mythical man month."

The theory, though, is applicable beyond software projects. A common mistake is to add more resources in an attempt to achieve a goal or solve a problem. More resources can complicate what you're trying to achieve. In these cases, throwing more at a problem only gives you a worse problem.[170]

How much more effectively do things go when everyone's input isn't required? Over the years, I've seen some excellent reports produced by teams, usually small in number, a handful of experts and serious contributors. Then I have also seen reports that are ruined by the *too many chefs in the kitchen* syndrome. Another problem scenario is where a few people write a report only to have to rewrite and change it after many others have reviewed it and wanted to see their suggestions incorporated. This is the *chop cycle* approach gone berserk. The final document typically is a worse product. You'll recognize these reports easily – they look like they were written by a committee because they were!

Then there's the classic: throwing more money at a problem. We see this done by individuals as well as at the highest levels of government. For example, there are schools that

---

[169] Brooks' law specifically states that "adding manpower to a late software project makes it later." He attributed the delay to time lost to on-boarding new programmers and communications overhead. In 1975, Brooks wrote a book on this theory called *The Mythical Man Month: Essays on Software Engineering.* I am a great fan of Brooks and at CACI we used to talk about the "mythical man month" all the time in managing our software development and simulation model building projects.

[170] Many believe that the U.S. government is too often plagued by this problem – as an institution that somehow doesn't seem to appreciate the Brooks' Law (the mythical man month) phenomenon.

increase per student spending yet don't improve test scores or raise graduation rates. There were many doubts about federal money being used to prop up failing companies and banks in the financial crises over 2008 and 2009. The problem is not the spending itself. The problem is spending more instead of focusing on how the money is spent.

Overkill is also a problem of priorities. In the book *Parkinson's Law,* I read a reference to what the author called the *Law of Triviality*: "time spent on any item of the agenda will be in inverse proportion to the sum involved." Parkinson's argument was that organizations give disproportionate importance and attention to trivial issues. I've seen this happen many times in my career, in the military and in business. We see the same problem with individuals too. They can be the perfectionists who hyper-focus on the details or they are people who exaggerate the importance of their small piece of the pie. The result is getting everybody distracted by lesser issues, at the expense of the larger challenges – failing to see the big picture!

There are also two corollaries about focusing on the wrong things. The first is trying to solve *non-problems.* You often hear people say *if this and that happen, what will we do?* Well, typically *this and that* haven't happened – and probably won't happen. Yes, the economy may tank. An account or employees could be lost. And an asteroid could be streaking toward the Earth. So which one do you want to prepare for first? Some situations will require contingency planning, but they are few and far between. The number of possible contingencies is simply infinite.[171]

The second corollary is *trying to do everything.* There are virtually an infinite number of possible things you could be doing. You only have time to do a few of them, so choose wisely. Knowing what to do and what not to do greatly influences how effective you are. Most of the time, there are only a limited

---

[171] When you foresee a possible difficulty, ask yourself this question: Would you have time to solve the problem *after* it arose? We find that most of the time the answer will be "yes." If the problem doesn't arise, you can concentrate all of your time on exploiting your best opportunities and exploring for even better ones.

number of things that you can do to generate the results you want anyway. As a shrewd observer once said, "Few things matter very much; most things don't matter at all." By trying to do everything, you risk spreading your resources too thin and gaining nothing. Doing too much (or too much of the wrong thing) is one sign that you may need to *say when*.

Then there's the situation where we have given enough. *The law of diminishing returns states that the continued application of effort or skill declines in effectiveness after a certain level or result has been achieved.* For example, a team can keep working on a proposal, but after a while it won't make it any better. Or it's the point where an athlete who has trained for competition can't do anything more to prepare. Basically, you can keep doing more, but you won't get any more out of it or from it.

Finally, there's insanity, which Albert Einstein defined as *doing the same thing over and over again and expecting different results.* It's those people who don't put in the extra effort, ask or apply for promotions, continue their education, or move to a better company, who then wonder why their career isn't going anywhere. Or it's the company that doesn't respond to market changes and doesn't see why they're not competitive.

Why is this futility so hard to recognize? Sometimes it's because what we've been doing has worked so well for so long that its assumed productivity is taken for granted. In other cases, it's a failure to understand how or what has changed. And sometimes, it's just laziness or even the fear of doing something new. The result, however, will always be the same.

Sometimes, it's not a question of how much you give – it's how much others will *take* from you. Think of the family member who is always left to organize everything. Or the co-worker who picks up the slack for the person who doesn't seem to ever get their work done. It could even be a friend who always needs attention or help. There are just as many generous people and team players as there are people who will take advantage of them. It's crucial to know when you're contributing and when you're being exploited!

The purpose of our effort is to achieve results. A common problem, however, is that we keep adding and doing more without assessing what we're getting out of it. Often it's counterproductive. If you're going to put something into it, make sure you know what you're really getting out of it.

Saying *when* is also knowing *when to stop*. This is not the same as *giving up* – a result of weakness or laziness or not wanting to give the effort, time or resources required, or lacking faith in yourself and your goals. Knowing when to stop is the realization that you're not going to get what you want to achieve, regardless of anything more you might do.

"It's better to have a horrible ending than horrors without end." I first heard this phrase in the 1970s. Richard Hayes, a CACI colleague, used it in a presentation he gave on project management. It stuck with me because it was so logical – simply stop problems before they get any worse. There was also no judgment involved. Nothing is said about who was at fault; there is no implication of blame. Herb Karr liked it for how it applied to those employees who didn't work out – which could be described as *situational incompatibility*. In cases where skills or personalities were mismatches, it would be better to let them go somewhere else where they would be happier or more productive. Sometimes these people were brilliant, masters of the software craft who just didn't fit on our team or our projects. We called these people *brilliant misfits* (misfits for our company), and they had to go.

The lesson about horrible endings is applicable far beyond incompatible employees. We are by nature both optimistic, yet skeptical. When things go wrong, we hope that they will work themselves out. At the same time, we are tentative. When we are afraid to speak up or step up, fearing our actions will make things worse, problems persist, even grow, with no end in sight. It's like a toothache. At first, the pain is annoying, but tolerable. The ache could go away on its own, but what if it doesn't? Going to the dentist and possibly having a procedure may seem intimidating or inconvenient. But waiting too long could result in a bigger problem, like a root canal. Circumstances leading to business mistakes or failures can result in even more pervasive pain and become far worse if you don't pay attention to them. How long do you endure the pain before you do something about it?

There has to be a point when we say 'enough'. How do you know when that is?

First, assess the problem. Not every error snowballs into a problem or crisis. When is a cough just a cough and when is it the flu? How do you recognize the difference? While there are no definitive tell-tale signs, there are observations that can be made. When there's a hiccup, ask yourself if this is an isolated incident or individual event. Or is it the latest in a trend of things that may continue to go wrong? A connection may not be immediately apparent, but may emerge with further review. On the other hand, forcing a link between the pieces isn't helpful either. For example, if an employee makes an important error in writing code for software, is it an honest mistake or a lack of know-how? If it's the former, the error can be fixed as soon as it is identified. Even if it's the latter, an employee can receive training to refresh their skills. Then there's another possibility – a problem with the software itself. Don't react to a situation until you understand what the problem really is.

In addition to observing the incidents, look at their results and impacts. Take the company that uses certain formulas to develop quotas for their sales teams, yet the teams are still unable to meet their goals. If it's one team member failing, it's probably an isolated problem. Perhaps they have the wrong skill set. If it's a more widespread problem, then you have to take a closer look. *Were current economic and industry conditions taken into consideration when quotas were set? Have the teams always been struggling? Is there high turnover in the sales division? Were the formulas the cause of the problems? Is the product not holding up to the competition or market needs?* You have to assess why things didn't work. And you had better get to it right now!

Another way to differentiate between a single issue and a bigger problem is looking at complacency. Take the job seeker, for example. If 100 resumes were sent out without a response, what are the odds that sending out 100 more will get an interview? More often, it's a case of hoping a problem will take care of itself.

Many companies, it seems, ignore signs of trouble because they hope it will go away on its own. To me, this is a formula for disaster. The *head in the sand* management response – ignoring reality – is fatal. In my experience, the strategy of *wishful thinking* rarely works.

The bursting of the dot.com bubble is a prime example. In the 1990s, scores of new technology companies popped up. They had clever names, cool offices, and hip employees. They all boasted new tools and services that would revolutionize business, even people's lives. Where are they now? They're gone because they refused to accept the fact that they had a big problem: No customers! Many dot.com companies were based on a single strategy: build it and they will come. The problem was that no one came. If they did, they didn't stay for long and didn't buy anything anyway.

CACI tried its hand in the dot.com world in the 1990s. We mistakenly tried to please shareholders who thought CACI might be missing out on a gold mine. I wasn't sure what this new industry offered under all the glitz and attention of those times. Yet many smart executives, detailed reports, and expert advice agreed that this was the way to go. So we dedicated several million dollars and staff, some hired specifically for this market, to developing Business-to-Business (B2B) software. My instincts were right though. Despite the glitzy websites and offices, most dot.com's offered no real products or worthwhile services. Luckily, CACI was smart enough to pull out early. We had spent several million dollars doing things we had no business doing. At least we caught our mistake and worked past it.[172] And our

> *"A stumble may prevent a fall."*
>
> English Proverb

---

[172] I couldn't help but think that Herb Karr (who died in 1990) would have never been sucked into the dot.com business in the first place. He would have cut to the chase. What are they offering? Why would someone pay for it? And for how long? I'm certain Herb would have answered "not much" and "not for long."

core business, our real business, continued to grow!

Every person and organization has problems. However, repeated difficulties indicate a trend. The choice is yours – a horrible ending or horrors without end?

BREAKING THROUGH

If you know what the problem is, you usually know what has to be done to solve it. Sometimes it's as easy as going to the dentist to examine a toothache. Sometimes, it's more challenging and will affect many people, like restructuring a poorly performing division in a company. Yet taking the step from acknowledgement to action is the hardest part. So how do you take it? Call it a reality check, swallowing your pride, or facing your fears. You have to break through mental road blocks.

> *"Most people spend more time and energy going around problems than in trying to solve them."*
>
> Dale Carnegie

First, **don't make excuses**. It's easy to blame the economy, another person, traffic, computer problems, competitors, the weather, customers, bad information, no information, or "the dog that ate my homework." Making excuses exacerbates your problem – they are the factors that you already knew of – and did nothing about! Excuses prevent action. Don't make them.

Second, **don't waste more time defending a mistake**. It doesn't matter if it's yours or someone else's. Everyone makes mistakes. You may even have to deal with the person(s) who made the mistake. The priority, however, is to find a solution. Be *mission-focused*. Dwelling on the error to find blame is counterproductive. If you know what went wrong, acknowledge it, fix it and move on.

Third, **don't take it or make it personal**. Pull your ego out of the equation. Save the conspiracy theories for the movies and the back-bench politicians. Preserving reputation and credibility are important, but it rarely comes down to one person. Recognize your role in the situation and the solution. The problem may concern you, but it's never all about you. (If it is, your troubles have just begun!)

Finally, **have faith**. There is a future after the crisis. Believe that there is something better out there, but don't expect to get happy immediately. Things may get worse before they get better. Hope becomes reality if you plan ahead. Set new standards and goals, improve processes and procedures, or identify bold changes. The horrors won't end if you don't take steps to end them!

This isn't a case of *easier said than done*. I speak from experience. Years before the dot.com debacle, I had to end some horrors – before the horrors ended CACI. In the late 1970s and early '80s, CACI expanded operations into Europe. The company's senior leaders opened offices in London, Amsterdam, and Munich, just to name a few! CACI's work at this time also took us to the Middle East. The company had a major contract with the U.S. Navy to provide IT and support services in the development of a Saudi Arabian navy.[173]

By 1984, however, things had changed. CACI's long-running contract for the Saudi Arabian Navy was winding down. The European offices weren't performing and the costs were out of control. Something had to be done. In 1981, Herb fired Bill Fain, who had been President for 10 years or so.[174] Herb then took over the job for the next three years, but it was clear that he didn't want to remain that involved in CACI's day-to-day operations. In fact, he was quite uncomfortable, sometimes miserable, in that role. So, in June of 1984, Herb asked me to take on the job of President and CEO.

---

[173] The Royal Saudi Navy – also known as the Royal Saudi Naval Forces (RSNF) – was founded in 1960, but significantly expanded with U.S. assistance after 1972 to match the Iranian Navy. These were the days before the Iranian revolution that threw out Shah Reza Pahlavi in 1979. There was a similar project for the Iranian Navy in the 1970s supported by the U.S. government and U.S. Navy. CACI's contract for the RSNF was actually with the U.S. Navy and set up as a foreign military sales (FMS) contract with the U.S. government.

[174] Fain was never the "CEO," nor was Herb Karr. As it turns out, I was the first executive at CACI to officially have the title and responsibility as the Chief Executive Officer (CEO).

I had my work cut out for me. I spent the next six months working 24/7 getting situated in my new role and preparing for the forthcoming changes. The most pressing change was shutting down most of the underperforming European operations. In January 1985, CACI's chief legal counsel (and one of CACI's earliest employees), Jim Berkson, and I got on a plane and headed over the Atlantic to take care of business.[175]

While the writing had been on the wall for some time, Jim and I needed to take the next steps in person. I had no qualms in doing whatever needed to be done. That included firing people when necessary. There had been an employee in the Hamburg office that was fired after we discovered that he was selling software to "tombstone clients." He had been making up names and processing the paperwork to show sales, getting the upfront sales bonuses. It turned out that he was planning to bail out soon anyway, before the fake sales were discovered. This was clearly not CACI's idea of integrity. Thankfully, the problem was discovered and resolved within a couple of months. The employee also was quickly shown the door!

What was agonizing for me, though, was having to fire the head of European operations, Ron Steorts. He had been the man who hired me at CACI in 1972. He had been my first boss at CACI and later a colleague. I liked and admired Ron, but he didn't seem inclined to make the necessary decisions to cut our excess costs. The truth was, however, that Herb had gotten to the end of his rope with Ron. Unfortunately, sentiments had to be put aside. I was given the task by Herb and Ron was let go.

Jim and I visited several other offices throughout Europe. Most of them had to be closed to stop the financial bleeding. For example, we discovered during a briefing in Munich, Germany that the geographic marketing and demographic software that was doing so well in the U.S. and UK wasn't feasible in Germany.

---

[175] Jim Berkson was for many years CACI's corporate treasurer, secretary and executive vice president and general counsel. Jim was very helpful to me and CACI during the years of our early struggles. He served on CACI's board of directors from the 1960s until his retirement from the board in 1993. Jim passed away in April 2011 at the age of 90. He was always one of my strong supporters and loyal to CACI's future.

As a result of World War II, the German government, at the time, would not allow anyone else to develop or hold a comprehensive database of the country's population in the fashion we needed. They saw dangers on the back of what the Nazis had done earlier having known, for example, the names and locations of the population in the Netherlands. We did, however, decide to keep our Amsterdam office open as their business platform had been doing better, but that only lasted a few more years. We sold or shut down a number of operations that weren't making it. I knew we couldn't sprint ahead if we had to drag all of this dead weight along with us.

Several good things came out of the closings. First, we turned our UK operations around by taking prompt decisive actions. Letting Ron go was not easy and we chose to tell some of the staff about it personally. Greg Bradford, an American, had already been in London for over a year as CACI's top contracts and legal counsel. My intention was for him to take over Ron's position on an acting basis, but Greg beat me to the punch. Before I got to that part of our meeting, Greg said that he wanted the job! I've always found ambition to be a great sign for future success. This time was no exception. When Greg took over, he changed the profile of the UK operations to be profit-driven. He let go those people who didn't match that profile (or otherwise weren't compatible) and he brought on those who did. Having the right people made all the difference. Not only is the UK arm of the company one of the strongest, it has grown successfully and Greg Bradford is still running the show!

Another casualty of the Europe trip was the corporate fleet of airplanes. In total, CACI had five private planes that were used to fly staff to different CACI sites, including many of the now defunct European offices. Jim Berkson and I had even flown around Europe in one. The planes had always bothered me. The cost of maintaining the fleet and paying for pilots seemed inappropriate, especially given the current circumstances. When we got back to Washington, I had to break the news of my decision to Herb. And it was a real bone of contention. Herb was fond of the airplanes, but he eventually accepted that they were not economically viable for the company and provided no added value otherwise. We would keep the one that Herb used to go back and forth from his California homes and offices for a few more years. Selling off the planes didn't affect operations much and the eliminated costs were a meaningful boost to CACI's bottom line.

During this time I also cut my own salary by 10% and asked Herb to do the same. It really angered him, but he did go along with the program and made the 10% cut. I wanted to make this statement to our people about their leaders' commitment to CACI's success. And several others took cuts as well.

The size of the task should never be an excuse to do nothing. At its worst, a toothache may be just as hard to deal with personally as a corporate restructuring. Yet even the biggest and most bitter pills can be swallowed! In my new role as CEO, I learned quickly when to say *enough* and *no*. Managing a turnaround requires fast action and decisive moves.

CACI isn't the only company to learn these hard lessons. Beginning in the 1990s, the rise of the Internet and new media created one of the most dynamic periods in business. Up and coming technology firms were changing how business was conducted. It was the time of the "dot.coms". Many larger, older companies also wanted to transform for the new digital age. What followed was a surge in mergers and acquisitions activity.

In 2000, a new company, AOL Time Warner, was created when AOL purchased Time Warner for $164 billion. The deal was valued at $350 billion, making it the largest merger in American business history. The idea behind the deal was straightforward: merge a leading content company with a primary distributor of online content. Content meets customers.[176] The marriage of new and old media was heralded as the future of communications. But not everyone was so sure. The Federal Trade Commission allowed the deal to go forward, even though their economists warned the deal did not make financial sense. Several executives in the two companies, many

---

[176] Larry Kramer, "Why the AOL-Time Warner Merger Was a Good Idea," *The Daily Beast,* May 4, 2009, http://www.thedailybeast.com/blogs-and-stories/2009-05-04/how-time-warner-blew-it/.

caught off guard, did not support the deal. It didn't make sense to them either.

The deal was made at the highest levels of both companies, between AOL's Chairman Steve Case and Time Warner's CEO Gerald Levin. Many executives in both companies did not find out about the merger until the day the deal was announced. Organizational compatibility was not given the requisite consideration. The two companies each had a distinct and different culture. AOL, the poster child of the early dot.com era, was dynamic, electronic, and entrepreneurial. Time Warner, on the other hand, was old line, staid, established, and cautious. Employee buy-in, especially from Time Warner, was lacking.[177]

Another problem was that Time Warner's brands didn't need AOL to distribute their content online. The various components of AOL Time Warner eventually began to work in their own silos, pulling the company in opposite directions. The merger could have worked had AOL and Time Warner leveraged each other's strengths and assets. Perhaps it was a failing of the leadership or a failing of the basic game plan. Either way, the synergy needed for the leveraging simply never happened. It was a flawed deal from the start!

Other factors exacerbated AOL Time Warner's problems. The dot-com bubble burst. Online advertising slowed down. High-speed Internet access began to replace AOL's dial-up service. Market valuations of similar internet companies dropped significantly. As a result, AOL struggled to meet the financial forecasts on which the deal was based. By 2002, AOL Time Warner reported a record $99 billion loss![178]

---

[177] In CACI's M&A program, the people and culture of the acquisition target corporation is a major, high-priority focus of our due diligence. We have to see a clear and positive merger path for the people coming into CACI. Cultures have to fit!

[178] This included a fourth quarter charge of $45.5 billion related to the depreciation of the America Online unit. Stories claiming AOL improperly inflated advertising revenue prompted investigations by the Securities and Exchange Commission and the Justice Department. The company eventually paid hefty fines and was forced to restate past earnings. Here was a case of missing integrity, in addition to the missing business strategy.

The next seven years saw many challenges. The company dropped AOL from its name and restructured some of its divisions. Key executives, including the architects of the deal, left the company. By 2003, Case had resigned as chairman, while Levin and COO Bob Pittman were shown the door. There were countless job losses and employee retirement accounts were decimated. The rise of Apple, Amazon, and other technologies were also changing the publishing industry and content delivery.

By the end of 2007, Time Warner's new CEO began talking about bringing the ill-fated relationship to an end. In May 2009, Time Warner announced that it would spin off AOL as a separate independent company. By December 2009, it was a done deal. The combined values of the companies would now only be about one-seventh of their valuation on the day of the merger.

The AOL Time Warner merger seemed at first like a marriage made in heaven. However, as painful as the divorce was, forcing the merger to go on any longer would have been horrors without end. It was simply best for them to go their separate ways.[179]

There are no guarantees in life. The unexpected does happen. Risks don't always pay off. As poet Robert Burns wrote: "Even the best laid plans of mice and men go awry." As terrible as problems are, accepting *endless horrors* is a failure of action and leadership. Avoid the tragedy. It's better to have a horrible ending than horrors without end. It's all about *saying when.*

---

[179] The separation forced both companies to regroup. Changing its focus from access to content, AOL has since developed a new brand identity to distance itself from its old internet image. Time Warner continued making changes, selling off media divisions and sports interests, as well as spinning off its cable arm. A huge pile of bad decisions had cost lots of people lots of money. The old Latin adage holds: caveat emptor – buyer beware!

CHAPTER 17

SUCCESS BREEDS SUCCESS

"Winning is a habit. Unfortunately, so is losing."
Vince Lombardi

Since its inception in 1967, there have been 47 Super Bowls played to decide the best among the (now) 32 teams in professional football. Three teams have won a combined 16 Super Bowls, more than one-third of all of them: Pittsburgh Steelers, Dallas Cowboys, and San Francisco 49ers. The team with the most Super Bowl wins, the Pittsburgh Steelers, has won six (nearly 13 percent) of the 47. In comparison, 14 teams have never won a Super Bowl, of which four have never even gone to the big game.

In 2009, six months after the Pittsburgh Steelers won Super Bowl XVIII (their sixth), the city's hockey team, the Pittsburgh Penguins, won their third Stanley Cup championship. The double victories reclaimed Pittsburgh as the City of Champions in 2009, 30 years after the city had originally earned the title when the 1979 Steelers and the Pittsburgh Pirates won the Super Bowl and World Series, respectively.[180]

Winning *is* a habit. Success is a mindset. Once successful, you expect to stay successful, or become successful again. No one wants to go from first to worst.

---

[180] The Steelers also appeared in two additional Super Bowls, XXX and XXXV, which they lost. As for the Pittsburgh Pirates, I have long been a fan. I had been to the old Forbes Field in Pittsburgh in the late 1940s with my parents and younger brother on a family vacation. We came all the way from Oklahoma on a summer road trip. It was a special occasion; a night game where we watched in amazement as the legendary Ralph Kiner knocked one out of the park. After that, I soon became the owner of a Ralph Kiner baseball bat made by the famous Louisville slugger company, Hillerich & Bradsby. (I have also been through their plant in Kentucky.)

CHARACTER: The Ultimate Success Factor

Regardless of how you measure it, success is a challenge. Yet, what hampers most people is how they define *success*. For many people, success is rigidly defined – stated in terms that are too narrow, intangible or short-sighted. Changing how you perceive success is the first step in achieving it over and over again.

TEN FACTS ABOUT SUCCESS

There are several immutable facts about success.

1. Success is not automatic. Achievement is not pre-ordained. The school valedictorian is frequently not the most successful alumnus. The winner of the Heisman Trophy for the best player in college football (in any given year) may not even have a big professional career.[181] No matter how many factors are working in your favor, success is not guaranteed.

2. Success is not always repeatable. In sports, back-to-back championships in consecutive years are the exception, not the norm. In the music industry, the term *one hit wonder* is given to artists with only one hit single. What do Harper Lee *(To Kill A Mockingbird)*, Margaret Mitchell *(Gone With the Wind)*, and J.D. Salinger *(The Catcher in the Rye)* have in common? They are the authors of some of the best known books in American literature. Yet all three never were able to repeat the success of these titles. Remember the Hula Hoop, Pet Rock, Beanie Babies or Cabbage Patch Kid dolls? The companies behind these fad products failed to follow-up with anything else. Companies spend about $260 billion annually on new products, yet more than 65 percent of them fail. Succeeding once is commendable. Succeeding over and over again is extraordinary. It's also the hallmark of the real super star!

---

[181] Of the 75 Heisman Trophy winners to date, only 8 have been inducted into the Pro Football Hall of Fame. There was one from the U.S. Naval Academy who has been very successful. Roger Staubach won the Heisman Trophy in 1963. After a tour in Vietnam, Staubach went on to a remarkable career in professional football, winning two Super Bowls (once MVP) with the Dallas Cowboys and induction into the Pro Football Hall of Fame. Today, he is a successful businessman in the commercial real estate field.

3. Success is not permanent. It's not a self-sustaining state. For example, a singer may have numerous chart-topping hits, but fade from memory within a few years. An actor may star in a long-running hit TV series, but fail to have notable projects afterwards. In sports, an athlete's career may be cut short by an injury. Nothing lasts forever, particularly success.

Success is marked by milestones, typically measured by a point in time. Achieving goals is a metric; such as getting a job, winning a game, or earning an award. The residual effects of success may linger, but the achievement is momentary.

At the turn of the 21st century, CACI set a goal of becoming a Tier 1 company in the government services contracting industry. In our minds, we would accomplish that goal once we hit $1 billion in revenue. To achieve this lofty goal, we developed a plan that included the sizable acquisition of the Defense and Intelligence Group of AMS in May 2004. That deal helped us blow past our goal. In August, our fiscal year 2004 results showed that we hit $1.146 billion. Yes, we celebrated our success – and then quickly set a new goal to become a $3 billion company. In August 2011, CACI announced that revenues for fiscal year 2012 reached $3.8 billion. In business and in life, you can't rest on your laurels. That familiar question pops up again and again: What's next? Success is a series of milestones. You have to keep achieving them.

4. Success is an attitude. It begins with an expectation – a belief that you will give it your best effort and achieve the best results possible. Your attitude about success is not a self-fulfilling prophecy, but if you believe you are going to fail, you probably will! You won't try as hard and neither will anyone around you. On the other hand, if you expect the best from yourself and others, your chances of succeeding will skyrocket!

CACI's former CEO Paul Cofoni encouraged our team to *be the very best*. This motto was intentionally simple, yet effective. During orientation, employees are told they were selected for their position because the company believes they are the best. Furthermore, they learn CACI's vision is to be the best in everything we do. This includes not only client satisfaction, but shareholder returns, innovation, compliance and corporate values – our culture. Management training resources are designed to develop the very best leaders. The message is also reiterated in employee communications. It's an expectation for the entire company to rally around, and it reflects CACI's attitude toward success.

5. Success is a priority. Priorities are those things that are most important to us. We allocate more time, energy, and resources to them. We focus on them. In return, we hopefully see the fruits of our labors. Take CACI's vision of being the best. It may begin as an attitude we want instilled in every employee, but it only becomes real when they take action on it. Consider the case of two analysts who write monthly status reports. One diligently verifies the data, follows up on open items, and even checks grammar and spelling. The second assumes that the data is correct, up-to-date, and spell-checked. The first analyst values success more. Success requires effort. Effort is made when it's important to us. If you want to succeed, make success important to you!

6. Success is a commitment. Success is achieved only through a continuous application of effort, innovation, and ambition. Effort is the actual work. Consider the marathon runner. This isn't a person who was sitting at home one day and suddenly felt the urge to run 26.2 miles. From the first-timer to the elite athlete, these runners train for months. They follow programs designed to gradually increase their ability and distance. They learn how to overcome physical and mental challenges. Without this dedicated training, they won't likely finish the race.[182]

Remember, effort should be proportional to goals. The smaller the goals, the less effort required to achieve them. And the bigger you think, the bigger you have to execute. Big goals

---

[182] I have some marathoners in my family. My daughter, son-in-law, and daughter-in-law have all completed the U.S. Marine Corps Marathon that is run from Arlington National Cemetery to the Iwo Jima Monument. The 26.2 mile course runs through various Washington, DC neighborhoods and passes by many points of interest, including the National Mall and the Pentagon. My daughter and her husband have also run the New York City and Honolulu marathons. My daughter also ran the San Diego marathon.

bring big successes – and big results – when they're achieved. Be a *big thinker*!

Innovation is the ability to make changes for improvement. It also means adapting to change when it's necessary. It may mean confronting your challenges and forecasting the changes that will make things better.

Today, the Finnish multinational company Nokia is a multi-billion dollar manufacturer of mobile devices and other Internet and communications products. Did you know Nokia started as a wood pulp mill, making paper in 1865? Nokia was actually the name of the town where the company's second paper mill was built. Between 1902 and 1922, Nokia became a conglomerate with lines of business in electricity generation, rubber, and communication and electrical cables.

For the next 45 years, Nokia operated in many industries like tires, footwear, plastics, and aluminum. The company established its first electronics department in 1960. It wasn't until 1967 – 102 years after the company first began – that Nokia entered the telecommunications industry. Had they not been innovative, adapted to the changes and captured opportunities in their industries, we may have never even heard of Nokia.

Ambition is the desire to achieve. Success is an evolving process, increasing in complexity and importance. Your achievements put you in a position for more responsibility and opportunity. Promotions, for example, recognize good performance. For on-going success, you need more opportunities and must take on more of them.

One notorious example was Napoleon Bonaparte, whose ambition drove him to do the things he did, whether or not they could be called successes. He was seen as a tyrant to some and a visionary to others. Napoleon, once the self-proclaimed Emperor of France, dominated the political and military landscape of Europe for over 20 years. He was indeed well-known for his ambition as much as his military conquests. He was not content to just govern France. By strategically seizing opportunities, Napoleon conquered most of Europe and even extended French control into the African and Asian continents.[183] Bonaparte is also known for the Napoleonic code, which laid the administrative and judicial foundations for much of Western Europe. Although I'm not a great admirer of Napoleon, I acknowledge that he was completely committed to his goal of ruling Europe. And he achieved it – for a short while. Napoleon learned that nothing lasts forever. Empires rise gradually because it takes time to build strength, assimilate, and unify people. However, empires fall quickly when they become too hard to maintain. Empires that have lasted the longest have done so because their leaders knew that their successes weren't self-sustaining. They knew they had to work at it to keep it all going!

The same lesson applies in personal success and achievement. Success will be elusive if it's perceived as something static – as if once successful, you'll always remain successful. Success will always take time and dedication to achieve.

Understanding the real nature of success is the first part of achieving it. The second part is understanding how success is a cumulative and transferable process where one success can lead to the next.

7. Success is empowering. Positive results give you confidence. Successfully executing a difficult recipe may lead you to try more complicated dishes. Completing a 10K race might get you thinking about running a half- or full-marathon. In business, early successes in winning contracts gave me and the CACI team the encouragement to bid on even larger contracts. The same can be said of CACI in its remarkable long-running string of successful M&A deals.

---

[183] Napoleon even set his sights on the New World when he forced Spain to cede the Louisiana Territory to France in 1800. Napoleon's American ambitions, however, would be cut short. While en route to America to take possession of the territory, Napoleon's army was destroyed in Haiti by a slave revolt and tropical disease. A frustrated Napoleon had no choice but to abandon his ambitions of conquering America. In 1803 he sold the territory to U.S. President Thomas Jefferson to raise money for his looming war with Britain. The deal is known as the Louisiana Purchase and it greatly increased the size of the United States of America.

I can think of no better example of empowerment and success than the American Revolution. Declaring independence from England meant war, but by December 1776 the outlook for America was grim. After several major defeats in New York, the Continental Army, led by General George Washington, was forced to retreat through New Jersey to Pennsylvania. Many residents in Philadelphia and the Second Continental Congress fled to the south to avoid the advancing British. Supplies were low and reinforcements slow to come. Morale within the Continental Army was low. Many soldiers planned to leave once their enlistment expired, while some deserted in advance.

Not easily daunted, Washington had been thinking about making a bold move since arriving in Pennsylvania. The recent publishing of two inspirational pamphlets by Thomas Paine reinforced the American cause among Washington's forces. The arrival of Generals John Sullivan and Horatio Gates' forces and militia at Washington's camp also bolstered the Continental Army's strength.

Washington decided that the Hessian forces (German mercenaries in the British Army) across the icy Delaware River in Trenton, New Jersey would be the perfect target for a surprise attack just after Christmas. The challenging and dangerous attack worked. The Hessians were soundly defeated with many captured, while the few remaining withdrew back into New Jersey with the British forces. Within a week, Washington's army had crossed the Delaware again and defeated British forces under Lord Cornwallis at Princeton.

The dramatic victories at Trenton and Princeton empowered the American Revolution at a critical time. Washington's audacity paid off because his troops gained further respect and confidence in him. In turn, Washington's determination and creativity demonstrated the resilience of his forces. As a result, many soldiers reenlisted and new recruits were attracted to the cause. The victories also re-inspired

Americans to believe that the war was indeed winnable.[184] One successful act makes another possible because you believe you can do it – again!

8. Success is enabling. Achievement reflects that you follow certain steps or possess resources that yield results. Positive results let you know that whatever you're doing is working. It could be a skill set, such as problem solving, languages, or communications. It could be the approach or strategy you use. Success opens the door to new approaches (people, resources, or strategies) that enable us to achieve even more. For example, once I found the right indicators and a process for hiring the right people, I did a much better job in bringing on the best candidates.

CACI's M&A program is another great example of how the tools of our success helped lead us to further accomplishments. After a couple of early M&A failures in the late 1960s and a hiatus until the 1990s, CACI developed a process to identify, acquire, and integrate new companies. Since 1992, we have had 59 acquisitions! With some minor adjustments after each successful acquisition, CACI now has a field tested way of growing the company. We know what we're doing!

Some small accomplishment or personal triumph – something that you do well or have done right – can enable you to achieve more. Identify something that you should be systematically exploiting. When you find something that works, work the blazes out of it!

9. Success is a building block. Achievement is rather pointless if you can only see it as an individual or isolated case. Of course, there are exceptions. For a sustained record of success, the one-offs aren't the issue. Successes must be seen as building blocks. One positive result can yield other positive results. Doing one thing well can help you do other things well. For example, promotions often come with raises, new benefits or perks, and grander titles. But they also come with bigger

---

[184] I have been to the location of Washington's crossing on Christmas Night, to the battlefield, and to the Hessian barracks in Trenton where these remarkable and world-altering events took place.

challenges, additional responsibilities, and higher expectations. Some see these as burdens, but they are opportunities for future success because you have to keep proving to yourself, as well as others, that you can keep achieving. The process of earning and assembling these blocks creates ultimate success – on your own terms and for the long run.

A good example of one success leading to another is how CACI accomplished its goal of building a business to support the intelligence community (and market). Even though we had some Intel work in the early 1990s, it was the strategic acquisition of Questech Inc. in 1998 that got us going. Their Intel contract base was a big jump for us. It provided a platform for continued growth, acquisitions, larger contract bids and the recruiting of more intel experts. Today 40% of our business is in this market. In this case, success truly did breed success.

10. Success is about positioning. For CACI, the Questech acquisition enabled us to enhance our systems engineering capabilities and get us into the intelligence arena in a serious way. However, we actually had learned the positioning lesson years earlier. Within my first year at CACI, I helped obtain a contract and task order for an automated data system (ADS) initial planning document for the Trident submarine logistics program. Under a new Navy directive, a detailed planning document would state the Navy's needs for all of the automated data systems associated with the logistics requirements of the entire submarine program. It was a critical project because defining the needs of the systems and putting the details together was going to be the basis of the Navy's case to Congress for funding the purchase of the equipment and systems.

Two factors played a large role in CACI winning this contract. First, I had just finished my doctorate at George Washington University. My dissertation had been on the economic analysis of large-scale management information systems. The analysis included things like advanced planning and anticipated costs. It was right up the Navy's alley. For the Trident project, I also had a colleague who was a retired Navy submarine logistician and supply corps officer. He had been out of the Navy for several years and had become a seasoned technical analyst. Together, the two of us were well-equipped to do the job. And our first result was highly successful. Trident became the *first* program to submit and get a plan approved under the new Navy directive! And CACI (the two of us) had done the heavy lifting back stage to make it happen.

This early success earned CACI significant recognition. About a year later, CACI's Trident contract was over, but our work had been noticed. The Naval Sea Systems Command had taken and customized our Trident plan, and submitted it through their chain of command to Congress. Their plan was approved. Word spread around town that CACI had been the contract authors of this plan. Suddenly, we were popular consultants with the naval aviation and sea systems communities. Over several years, CACI was awarded ADS planning contracts for the Naval Aviation Logistics Data Analysis System, or NALDA, (shore-based) and the Naval Aviation Logistics and Command Management Information System, or NALCOMIS, (maintenance and supply operations systems on aircraft carriers). Soon after, one of the Navy's ship building programs asked us to do an ADS plan project for some smaller ships. CACI soon became known for not just our ADS plans, but for plans that would get Congressional level approvals. Within 10 years, CACI had developed seven ADS plans.[185] It was our reputation for these successes, one after another, that provided the platform to build the company.

There are two keys in making positioning work. First, keep learning. What you know has gotten you this far. Yet for every challenge, the success factors are different. It may mean adapting methods or learning new skills to create new opportunities.

---

[185] All of these legacy systems that were developed from CACI plans still exist within the Navy today in one form or another. In fact, I was both surprised and proud to see one of these legacy systems still operating in an updated and modernized version aboard the USS *Kitty Hawk* when I visited Yokosuka Naval Base (Japan) in 2003 – nearly thirty years later!

While I was in the Navy, I realized that I needed to sharpen my focus to create new opportunities. At the time, I thought a concentration on anti-submarine warfare (juxtaposed against the era's Soviet nuclear submarine and missile delivery threat) would be critical for some time to come. Vietnam changed that. By not being deployed, I realized that my advancement opportunities would likely dwindle. My interest in aeronautical engineering wasn't new, but expertise in automated logistics systems would be a new dimension that would pique others' interests in me. So, I enrolled in a doctoral program that would position me in this field. Not only did the doctoral program help me find a job when I left the Navy, it helped me win some of my first contracts at CACI.

> *"The secret of success is constancy in purpose."*
>
> Benjamin Franklin

Second, accept the existence of valuable alternatives. Plan B may not only be a backup to Plan A, but it may also be the more fruitful option. For example, Lee Iacocca made his name in the auto industry during a 32-year career at Ford. He started in engineering, but his career flourished after moving to sales and marketing. Iacocca was pivotal to Ford's success. His contributions included the design of several Ford cars and the revival of the Mercury brand in the late 1960s. Iacocca became the president of Ford in 1970. While he would enjoy the first five years of his time in this role, problems with Henry Ford II led to his termination in 1978.

That Ford had posted a $2 billion profit for the same year was not lost on other companies. After being fired from Ford, Iaccoca was approached by Lockheed, Radio Shack, Renault, and several business schools. Chrysler, however, went all out for Iaccoca. Chrysler was on the verge of bankruptcy after losing millions in recalls of two faulty models. In his autobiography, Iacocca said, "If I'd had the slightest idea what lay ahead for me when I joined Chrysler, I wouldn't have gone over there for all the money in the world."[186] It would take a year of meetings, research, and consideration before Iacocca agreed to join the company.

Iacocca went on to rebuild Chrysler, restructuring the company in its entirety. Realizing the company needed major capital to make the changes, Iaccoca convinced Congress to guarantee loans to Chrysler. Under Iacocca, Chrysler introduced several new models, including the minivan, which had been rejected at Ford. In the 1980s, Chrysler rebounded. Iacocca even appeared in television commercials, becoming known for the trademark phrase, "If you can find a better car, buy it." Iacocca's road to success was long and bumpy, but he made it work.[187]

It should be clear by now that success is an evolutionary process. Life is a series of decisions, actions, and events. Success (or failure) is the cumulative effect of all of those things. To continue being successful, you must continuously look for new opportunities – and eventually concentrate your resources on the most promising ones. And to keep moving forward, you need to constantly refresh the list of opportunities or alternatives you choose from. This means searching for new solutions, new people, new methods, and all the other new directions that have driven your success. So don't be afraid to allocate some percentage of your time to pure exploration. CACI's co-founder, Herb Karr, used to say that exploration was a vital part of a CEO's role. He thought that 5 to 10 percent of the CEO's time should be spent looking for the new, undiscovered, or underutilized. And I couldn't agree more. You have to spend some time looking for brand new opportunities – then use the rest of your time to exploit your best opportunities. As Thomas Edison said, "Success is 10 percent inspiration and 90 percent perspiration."

---

[186] Lee Iacocca with William Novak, *Iacocca, An Autobiography* (New York: Bantam Books, 1984).

[187] I met and visited with Lee Iacocca in 1985 at a luncheon when he was in Washington, DC leading a fundraising effort to restore the Statue of Liberty and Ellis Island. His efforts helped raise $250 million in private donations for the project. With the CACI turnaround of 1984-85 high on my mind, our short talk was about turnarounds and how to make them succeed.

Need some inspiration? Most actors struggle as starving artists, but others take a more adventurous course. For example, Ron Howard started off as a child actor, famous for his roles as Opie Taylor in the *Andy Griffith Show* and Richie Cunningham in *Happy Days*. However, Howard found lasting success behind the camera. As a director, Howard's most notable films include *Splash, Apollo 13,* and *A Beautiful Mind,* which earned him a Best Director Oscar. As a producer, Howard's production company has developed numerous successful films and television shows.

Arnold Schwarzenegger went from *Terminator* to *Governator*. Schwarzenegger parlayed his success as a bodybuilder in the 1970s into a lucrative film career in the 1980s, including title roles in the *Terminator* and *Conan the Barbarian* series. Although he married into the Democratic Kennedy family (his former wife is journalist Maria Shriver), Schwarzenegger ran as a Republican for Governor of California and won in 2003. He was re-elected for a second term in 2007.

Ronald Reagan started his acting career in the 1930s and became a recognized name. His interest in politics would be piqued after serving several terms between 1947-1960 as the president of the Screen Actors Guild and as a spokesman for General Electric. By 1966, Reagan had been elected governor of California, winning re-election in 1970. Reagan unsuccessfully challenged incumbent Gerald Ford for the Republican Presidential candidacy in 1976. However, he won the candidacy and Oval Office in 1980 and 1984, becoming the 40th President of the United States.

These moves represent some major career shifts and the courage to grab the brass ring, grab onto opportunities that evolved into even greater successes. My own journey from the military to the business world is another example of this evolutionary process, albeit on a much different scale. However, the lesson should be very clear – take every opportunity to succeed!

CHARACTER-BASED SUCCESS IN ACTION

I've described success here with little value judgment as to the ends or means of finding success. However, I view character-based success as an achievement that creates value of merit. It can be sustained, enduring and respected. The principles behind success can apply equally to good intentions as well as bad intentions. Napoleon, ironically, may have said it best: "Great ambition is the passion of a great character. Those endowed with it may perform very good or very bad acts. All depends on the principles which direct them."

THE BAD AND UGLY

Scottish writer Robert Louis Stevenson once said, "Everyone sooner or later sits down to a banquet of consequences." Great athletes, for example, are known for their success stories, and for their problems. Doping has defrocked over 50 Olympic medalists since 1968, including marquee athletes like Ben Johnson and Marion Jones. Baseball legend Pete Rose is the all-time Major League leader in four statistical categories, winner of three World Series rings, three batting titles, one Most Valuable Player Award, two Gold Gloves, the Rookie of the Year Award, and 17 All-Star Game appearances. Yet Rose was banned from the sport in 1989 after it became known that he had gambled on baseball games while both a player and a manager.

Bad choices can also be damaging to others. In March 2006, three white members of the Duke University lacrosse team were accused of raping an African-American stripper during a team party. Within weeks, Duke University cancelled the rest of the lacrosse season and fired the team's coach. Fellow students and faculty publicly denounced the accused players. Some players had to transfer to other schools.

Yet none of it was true. Local district attorney Mike Nifong was out to make a name for himself with the case. The police violated their policies by allowing Nifong to lead the case and by not properly investigating the claims. Moreover, while the three players had credible alibis, the accuser's story quickly fell apart. By December 2006, Nifong faced ethics charges brought by the North Carolina State Bar. He later lost his law license and was found guilty of criminal contempt. In April 2007, North Carolina Attorney General, Roy Cooper, dropped all charges against the three Duke players, declaring them "the victims of a 'tragic rush to accuse' by a rogue prosecutor."[188]

Unfortunately, bad choices are also made by those who should know much better. Randall "Duke" Cunningham was a 14-year California Congressman and celebrated Vietnam War Navy fighter pilot.[189] Cunningham won his Congressional seat in 1990 promising to be "a congressman we can be proud of" after his opponent was hit with a sexual harassment scandal. However, in 2005, Cunningham pled guilty to accepting at least $2.4 million in bribes, as well as mail fraud, wire fraud and tax evasion. As a member of the House of Representatives Defense Appropriations Subcommittee, Cunningham took favors, gifts and money from unethical defense contractors who wanted his help in obtaining contracts. In 2006, he was sentenced to eight years and four months in prison and ordered to pay $1.8 million in restitution.[190]

Other reprehensible examples come from Corporate America. Leaders at Enron, AIG, WorldCom, Lehman Brothers, and Bear Sterns (among many others) took too many risks and

---

[188] Aaron Beard, "Prosecutors Drop Charges in Duke Case," *San Francisco Chronicle,* April 12, 2007. Of the three accused players, one player graduated from Duke in 2006, but the other two transferred to different schools. The former players are reportedly seeking $30 million over five years for the violation of their rights and seeking new criminal justice reform laws in a federal civil-rights lawsuit against the city of Durham, North Carolina. In February 2013, Duke University settled out of court a lawsuit brought by 38 former lacrosse players who had filed more than 20 claims against the university, including intentional infliction of emotional distress, negligence and civil rights violations.

[189] Cunningham was only one of two Navy flying aces from the Vietnam War to obtain five confirmed aerial victories during that conflict. Cunningham and the other ace are the two last Navy aircrew to have achieved "Ace" status.

[190] Tony Perry, "The Penalty for Cunningham is Severe," *Los Angeles Times,* March 4, 2006, http://articles.latimes.com/2006/mar/04/local/me-duke4.

too much for granted. I doubt their shareholders, creditors and associates would have approved of their poor choices.

However, one of the most notorious cases in the business world had been building over time. Bernie Madoff, a Wall Street stalwart and three-time non-executive chairman of the NASDAQ stock market was arrested in December 2008 for operating arguably the largest Ponzi scheme in history.[191] Begun in the early 1990s – when he was NASDAQ chairman – Madoff's Ponzi scheme defrauded thousands of investors of some $18 billion. Madoff pled guilty to 11 federal crimes and is now serving the maximum sentence of 150 years in prison for his crimes, while many of his former investors struggle to rebuild their savings and their lives.[192]

I have never believed that the ends justify the means, because unethical and dishonest means never yield genuine or lasting results – or real success. By defining success as a positive, value-adding process and goal, it becomes both harder and easier to achieve it. It's harder because success is something long-term, requiring sustained motivation and consistent effort. Luckily, it's easier because you can make it an evolving, growing and learning process. This way, you're not setting yourself up for failure by defining success too narrowly. This is the way I've looked at success over my 40-plus years in business – and it's how I'll keep looking at it.

THE GOOD

Thankfully, for every bad and ugly example of success, there are many more examples where good intentions and actions have triumphed.

Take Jane Goodall, the foremost expert on chimpanzees. For over 50 years, Goodall has been a scientist, educator and

---

[191] A Ponzi scheme is an investment fraud where alleged returns to existing investors are actually funds contributed by new investors.

[192] Madoff's 46-year old son, Mark, committed suicide in December 2010. The younger Madoff was being investigated for tax fraud, although officials reportedly did not have enough evidence to charge him criminally.

advocate for animal research and habitat protection. While still in her twenties and without a university education, Goodall was credited with making groundbreaking discoveries about chimpanzees, such as their communication methods, social structures, and use of tools. Her early success was a result of two years of patient observation and eventual interaction with chimpanzees in the lakeside forests of Tanzania. Her in-depth study of chimpanzees and conservation work has continued for decades.

In 1977, she co-founded the Jane Goodall Institute, an international wildlife and environment conservation organization with nineteen offices around the world. Its global environmental and humanitarian youth program, Roots & Shoots, was established in 1991 and now boasts over 10,000 groups in over 100 countries. Goodall has also authored 14 scientific books, 10 children's books on animal welfare, and has been featured in 17 films and many television programs. Among her numerous recognitions are the J. Paul Getty Wildlife Conservation Prize in 1984, being named a Messenger of Peace by the United Nations in 2002, and formally made a Dame of the British Empire by Queen Elizabeth II of England in 2003. Today, Goodall is still active in her late 70s, giving university lectures, meeting with government officials, and fundraising for the Institute.

For Goodall, success has been defined by the pursuit of her passion for animal welfare and the outcome of her efforts, not monetary gain or celebrity. In fact, her professional acclaim became an important platform to continue her research and advocacy. Jane Goodall serves as a prime example of character-based success.

An example of character-based success on an organizational level is Doctors Without Borders (aka Medecins Sans Frontieres or MSF). For centuries, doctors have taken a version of the Hippocratic Oath swearing to practice medicine ethically. For the thousands of doctors and staff members who work for MSF, they also forego the comfort of a lucrative practice to work in some of the most volatile and impoverished parts of the world for a mere $1,400 a month. MSF is an international medical humanitarian organization that provides aid to people in nearly 60 countries that have been affected by armed conflict, epidemics, lack of health care, or natural disasters. In 2009, MSF medical teams gave more than 7.5 million outpatient consultations; delivered 110,000 babies; treated 1.1 million people for malaria; treated 200,000 malnourished children; provided 165,000 people living with HIV/AIDS with antiretroviral therapy; vaccinated 7.9 million people against meningitis; and conducted 50,000 surgeries.[193]

MSF was founded in Paris in 1971 by a group of young French journalists and doctors frustrated by the Red Cross' neutrality and confidentiality restrictions in Africa. MSF is independent, not aligned with any political, religious or economic powers in order to maintain their freedom of speech and action. They have been critical of countries, like Ethiopia, for diverting aid, and made an unprecedented call for military intervention in Rwanda during the 1994 genocide. They've also publicly criticized multinational pharmaceutical companies for not providing affordable drugs to areas MSF serves.

MSF is funded through some 3.8 million individual and private donors and run largely by 27,000 volunteer personnel worldwide. In 1999, MSF won the Nobel Peace Prize in recognition of its "pioneering humanitarian work on several continents."[194] Yet the only reward MSF's volunteers and staff typically earn is the personal fulfillment that such public service provides. Operating in the most volatile parts of the world, MSF staff faces dangerous situations. The head of the Dagestan mission was kidnapped and held hostage from 2002 to 2004. MSF withdrew from Afghanistan in 2004 after five volunteers were killed in an ambush by unidentified militia. In 2007 and 2008, three more volunteers were killed in Africa. While many medical professionals find success in private practice or research,

---

[193] Doctor without Borders, "How We Work," http://www.doctorswithoutborders.org /aboutus/activities.cfin?ref=main-menu.
[194] "The Nobel Peace Prize 1999," Nobelprize.org, http://nobelprize.org/nobel_prizes/ peace /laureates/1999/.

MSF's success is defined by helping the otherwise helpless worldwide.

Organizational examples of character based success aren't limited to non-profit organizations. There are many companies that fit the bill. Take United Parcel Service (UPS), for example. UPS was founded in 1907 as a messenger company in Seattle, Washington by an enterprising 19-year-old, James E. "Jim" Casey who saw a need for private messenger and delivery services. Today, UPS is the world's largest package delivery company and a leading provider of transportation and logistics services in more than 220 countries and territories worldwide. This multi-billion dollar company employs nearly 400,000 staff around the world. So how can a company in such a high-pressure, time-sensitive industry be an example of character-based success?

UPS commercials were once well-known for asking "What can brown do for you?" referring to the color of the company's fleet and employee uniforms.[195] The most common answer might be delivering packages, yet that would only be part of it. From the beginning, UPS has focused on making *the right thing to do* a hallmark of UPS culture.[196] From using environmentally-friendly electric cars in the 1930s to spending $300 million a year on employee training programs today, UPS has been committed to ensuring that they are doing as much as they can for their stakeholders.

UPS maintains comprehensive codes of business conduct, implemented through a robust compliance program, with tools and initiatives that both train employees and measure their effectiveness. The code is also translated into 12 languages and is modified for the local laws and customs of UPS international operations.

---

[195] UPS's newest commercials proclaim "We Love Logistics."
[196] The UPS Code of Business Conduct: Leading with Integrity, http://www.press room.ups.com/Fact+Sheets/The+UPS+Code+of+Business+Conduct%3A+Leading+w ith+Integrity.

UPS has even taken the unique steps to integrate their business and corporate responsibility strategies; categorizing their efforts into marketplace, environment, workplace and community. For example, in 2011 the *Circle of Honor* program rewarded over 5,843 safe drivers who did not have any accidents in 25 or more years of service. Since 1968, the *Community Internship Program* has immersed senior executives in community affairs to improve problem-solving skills and gain a better understanding of challenges in their employees' lives. During the month-long program at one of the program's four sites, UPS managers work with non-profit agencies tackling a variety of socio-economic issues, such as homelessness, illiteracy, and substance abuse. The UPS Foundation, established in 1951, supports more than 4,300 non-profits each year, contributing $93.5 million in global philanthropic initiatives in 2011.

Their efforts have not gone unnoticed. Among UPS' recognitions are placement on the Ethisphere Institute's list of the world's most ethical companies since 2007, ranking number six on the Reputation Institute's list of Most Reputable Companies, listing as one of *Corporate Responsibility Magazine's* 100 Best Corporate Citizens, the Dow Jones Sustainability Index for seven consecutive years, and making *Fortune's* list of the World's Most Admired Companies. All this while becoming a $53 billion company!

In 1957, long before corporate value statements became popular, UPS founder Jim Casey said: "We have become known to all who deal with us as people of integrity, and that priceless asset is more valuable than anything else we possess."[197] And the company has stuck to that statement!

Over the years I have tried to build CACI into a role model for character-based success in action. Early on we identified the values with which we wanted to operate and grow our business, and they have served us well for over fifty years. We created our Standards of Ethics and Business Conduct to guide our employees. And our employee awards program includes the Ethos Award for integrity and honesty. We also developed a Code

---

[197] Ibid.

of Business Ethics and Conduct for our Board of Directors to ensure that it conducts business with honesty and integrity.

Our commitment to doing the right thing has received some attention! In 2008, the Ethisphere Institute ranked CACI third in an ethics survey of the Top 100 Government Contractors. CACI ranked first in two categories: Ethics Training and Communications, and Ethics Internal Control Systems. In 2008 and 2009, CACI was included in *Fortune* magazine's list of Most Admired Companies. And in 2009, we were named the Most Admired Company in Virginia!

For several years running, CACI has been recognized as a leading employer of veterans by Military Times EDGE, G.I. Jobs Magazine, and CivilianJobs.com. Since 2012, the White House has recognized CACI for its support of *Joining Forces*, a national initiative to give service members and their families' education, wellness, and job opportunities. We have also been recognized for our corporate learning programs, while our employees regularly receive recognition by our customers and industry organizations for their contributions. In the ultra-competitive government contracting industry, CACI has owed its longevity to always doing the right thing.

Benjamin Franklin once said that "the secret of success is constancy to purpose." For some folks, their purpose is achieving a goal at any cost. However, denying your conscience is not a price that you should pay. The Goodall, MSF, and UPS examples clearly show that character doesn't have to be compromised; rather it is essential in achieving long-term success. Achievement is a building block. One faulty block can cause the whole structure to fail, while one solid block on top of another will create an enduring legacy. That's how *success breeds success*.

BUILD: Momentum

It's as simple as the laws of physics: A body in motion stays in motion, a body at rest stays at rest. While Newton's first law of motion helps explain the complexities of nature, it also simplifies the complexities of personal success. If you do nothing, you'll gain nothing and go nowhere. However, if you're doing something, you'll be moving in some direction. So how do you stay in motion? It's momentum – the power residing in a moving object. As a constantly moving object, what powers you? How do you build momentum – the momentum for ongoing and lasting success?

Momentum is built through character. Character provides the moral compass that keeps you moving in the right direction. You are the only constant factor in your life. We all chart our own path, confronting our own challenges, and pursuing our own goals. Not everyone is on the same path, but **the most critical success factor for everyone is character**. Unfortunately, not everyone knows this or knows it's *the* one thing that we have complete control over.

And not everyone is headed in the right direction or travelling at the same pace. Suppose you notice an accountant at your office working diligently on a project, coming in early, leaving late, and giving extra attention to every financial detail. This sounds like a strong work ethic. But what if that accountant was actually embezzling money from the company and spending the extra time and effort covering their tracks? That's a different story.

There is simply no substitute for integrity, both in the goals we want to achieve and the means by which we try to achieve them. Success is not an endpoint, although it can be marked by various milestones. If success were an endpoint, you would stop moving once you reached it. You would stop your momentum. But why would you want to do that?

That's why I focus on **character-driven success** – acting with integrity, performing to the best of your ability, appreciating your accomplishments and the people who help you. Success momentum is personal, ethical, and ongoing (repeatable).

Character-driven success is repeatable for three reasons.

First, it is an iterative process. The steps you take to achieve a desired result can be used to achieve a subsequent goal. The process to become a teacher, for example, will start with the desire to help children learn. The next steps will be obtaining the appropriate degree and learning from other teachers. Then there's on-the-job experience where a teacher will face challenges such as helping struggling students or dealing with students with behavior problems. What if you discover during your teaching career that you'd like to take on a bigger role, such as becoming a school principal? The good news is that you don't have to start from scratch. The same process that helped you become a successful teacher will help you become a successful principal; envisioning the goal, education, networking, and challenging experiences. Whether it's your career or some other goal, the results from one iteration can be used as the starting point for the next iteration.

Second, there's always more to learn. Throughout life, we figure out what works and doesn't work in achieving goals. We also learn that setbacks and course changes are normal – even necessary. We also have to adjust to changing circumstances and actors. If we're smart (and lucky), we take advantage of opportunities to try different things that may end up changing what we want to do. For example, the job of an IT project manager is to manage a team, a schedule, and a budget to implement a software product or system for a client. While the description of their role may stay the same from the first project to their fifth, project managers won't work the same way by the fifth project. Over time, they will learn how to manage and inspire different personality types on their teams. They will learn how to perform certain tasks more efficiently or adjust the schedule accordingly. And they will learn how to do more with less. In addition, the values and perspectives behind character-driven success will also have helped this project manager grow with the position's increasing challenges.

Third, character-driven success is transferable and scalable. The principles discussed here are the same whether you're trying to master a skill, get a Master's degree or become a Master Chef. Having a bad attitude, for example, will hurt you in each scenario. You can't learn how to play a musical instrument well if you don't practice. You won't earn your degree if you don't give sufficient effort to your assignments. And you certainly won't rise through the ranks in the U.S. Navy if you don't respect and obey the lawful orders of your senior officers!

On a positive note, the principles, such as learning from role models, are applicable in each case. There are many fascinating role models. The renowned American folk artist Anna Mary Robertson Moses is known as "Grandma Moses" because she didn't start her painting career until her seventies after abandoning a career in embroidery because of arthritis. So maybe it's not too late after all to try something new. Before success hit the legendary rock group Queen, guitarist Brian May had already earned a bachelor's degree in physics and mathematics from Imperial College London. May abandoned his Ph.D. program to pursue his music career, but returned 30 years later to finish his doctorate in 2007. Education is never a waste! Master Chef Marco Pierre White overcame dyslexia to become the world's youngest chef to have ever been awarded 3 Michelin stars. Undiagnosed until his son was found to have the same problem, Pierre White taught himself how to read and spell. After retiring from the restaurant business, Pierre White's success continued in British television and he is also famous for training fellow celebrity chef Gordon Ramsay.

If ever there was a prime example of character-based success, it would be that of Virginian George Washington. Washington understood the importance of character, both as a personal moral compass and as the source of his momentum. It was because of this understanding that he grew in stature throughout his life and created such a remarkable and lasting legacy of success.

George Washington was raised in a prosperous middle class family in Virginia, but his father's early death meant Washington had to assume responsibilities as the head of his family. Washington later inherited the position of district adjutant and became a major in the Virginia militia upon his brother's death – all by the age of twenty in 1752.

Washington later served in the French and Indian War (1754-1763), being noted by his superior officers for his bravery. His service with the British army provided an education in military, political, and leadership skills. During this time Washington began to develop his command presence and leadership style, which focused on discipline and training. After the war, Washington became a successful landowner, political figure, and family man.

In 1775, the Second Continental Congress chose Washington to be commander-in-chief of the Continental Army. Perhaps he is best known for his bold military tactic to cross the Delaware River and surprise enemy forces at Trenton on the morning after Christmas Day, December 26, 1776. But Washington was also praised for how he managed his generals, promoted cohesion and increased morale among the soldiers, as well as for how he coordinated with state officials and Congress to obtain supplies and other needs.

Washington was well-positioned to take control of the young country when victory was secured from England in 1783, but resigned his command because of his deep commitment to the democratic ideals for which he fought. His military success and his collegial management of the Constitutional Convention of 1787 made Washington the natural choice to become the first President of the United States in 1789.

The office of President was created with Washington in mind, giving him the opportunity to define the office. Washington focused on unifying the nation and establishing a national government. Congress also voted to pay Washington a $25,000 annual salary. Washington was already well-off and initially declined the sizable salary, preferring to be recognized as a public servant, but later realized that the refusal could set a precedent that the office was only attainable by the wealthy.

Washington soon realized that everything he did set a precedent. He decided that the office of the President would be formal, but not regal. He rebuked efforts for his role to be called 'king' (or any other majestic titles), settling on "Mr. President". Washington reluctantly served a second term and refused to run for a third.[198] Other precedents and innovations begun by President Washington include appointing a cabinet and delivering an inaugural address.

George Washington had many challenges and responsibilities in life, but was steadfast in his character, maintaining an unwavering moral compass. He took counsel from his core values and faith, never deviating from them. Throughout his military career, Washington learned by trial and observation, as well as failure and success. As a national leader, he resisted the opportunity to seize power, instead fulfilling the role of President and becoming an enduring role model. George Washington was not perfect or saintly by any means, but he truly understood the importance of character and why it was the basis of his (and our nation's) success. Today, we call George Washington the father of our country. I am confident that for George Washington, it all began with his understanding that **character is the ultimate success factor**.

Over the years, I have been asked questions about personal growth and professional development. At this point in my life, my response is always framed around the concept of character. Time and time again, I've seen that **character is the power that keeps each one of us moving in the right direction**. It is the keystone of true success. Still, it's up to each one of us as individuals to understand, to build and to make the most out of the momentum in our lives.

Nearly forty years ago, my family gave me a framed photo of Vince Lombardi with one of his quotations. It has hung on my office wall ever since:

"It is becoming increasingly difficult to be tolerant of a society that has sympathy only for misfits, only for the maladjusted, only for the criminal, only for the loser. Have

---

[198] This precedent stood until the third and fourth election of Franklin D. Roosevelt. The two-term limit later became the law of the land in the 22nd Amendment ratified in 1951.

sympathy for them. Help them. But I think it's also time for all of us to stand up and cheer for the doer, the achiever, the one who recognizes a problem and does something about it, one who looks for something extra to do for his country – the winner, the leader."

I believe Lombardi was right; success is the result of doing and achieving – and stepping up to the challenge because your character demands it.

In this book, I have avoided using terms such as *secrets, formula,* or the *steps to success.* The truth is there is no magic formula. You are the key to your success. You are the only one that defines yourself, your character and your success. It's up to you! It's your choice.

The only real failure is the failure not to do the right thing. As you go forward, remember the message in this book this way:

> *A solid character is the keystone in creating the blueprint for your future – the structure that guides your actions – the resolve to overcome challenges and reach your goals – to build the momentum that takes you through a life of success.*

In the end, character-based success is up to you. Make it *your* way of life!

ACKNOWLEDGEMENTS

This project has been a collaboration with Z. Selin Hur, my associate at CACI. Ms. Hur has served with me since 2004 and has been a valued contributor in support of our strategic and cultural communications, as well as our CACI thought leadership efforts. Her work with me has been innovative and resourceful. Selin participated fully from the start in creating and developing the book's themes and conceptual design. She provided structure and organization, researching and integrating key examples to highlight and underscore the important concepts of the book. Selin also contributed to the photo section of the book and helped to drive the production of the book, working with our publisher. I have enjoyed working on the book with her and thank her for her support and valuable contributions.

I have special thanks, too, for my wife and loyal partner, Dr. Jennifer Burkhart London. She contributed to the book in many ways from her unique perspective as a business psychologist – understanding people and especially understanding what motivates people. Jennifer reinforced the idea of a book based on the importance of character – doing the right thing. She was instrumental in creating and evaluating the message of this book and in working with me in assessing the behavioral and psychological viewpoints and opinions presented. Her efforts were both essential and timely in the completion of the book. She was a principal reviewer of early drafts and made many suggestions for improvement. Her editorial expertise and her critical eye for ideas and written dialogue were invaluable to the final manuscript.

I also extend my appreciation to Stan Poczatek, our superb graphic designer at CACI who created the book jacket. I asked Stan for excellence and, as always, he excelled. My gratitude also goes to Dennis Lowery at Adducent, Inc. He was an enthusiastic and discerning partner who made our book idea into an actual book. And thanks to Taylor Kiland for introducing him to us.

Finally, I would like to thank those colleagues who graciously took the time to review our manuscript at various phases. They include CACI UK's Chief Executive and Managing Director, Greg Bradford, who has been part of the CACI story for over 30 years. Another longtime CACI colleague, Executive Vice President of Business Communications, Jody Brown also provided insightful feedback and publication consultation.

If this book is a reflection on a lifetime of experiences, then I would also have to acknowledge my remarkable parents and the many family members, friends, colleagues, mentors and acquaintances who have shaped my beliefs, values and direction. Many of them have been written about in this book.

BIBLIOGRAPHY

2010 Marquet Report on Embezzlement, http://www.marque tinternational.com/pdf/the_2011_marquet_report_on_embezzl ement.pdf

Alan Axelrod, *Profiles in Audacity, Great Decisions and How They Were Made* (New York: Sterling Publishing, 2006).

Roy F. Baumeister, Kathleen D. Vohs, and Dianne M. Tice, "The Strength Model of Self-Control," *Current Directions in Psychological Science,* Vol. 16, No.6, 2007, pgs.351-355.

Aaron Beard, "Prosecutors Drop Charges in Duke Case," *San Francisco Chronicle,* April 12, 2007.

Abe Brown, "RIM's PlayBook Failed Because of Marketing Indecision," *Inc*.com, October 3, 2011, http://technology.inc. com/2011/10/03/rims-playbook-failed-because-of-marketing-indecision/.

"Michael Caine – Caine Almost Died in Korean War," *ContactMusic.com,* November 3, 2009, http://www.contact music.com/news/caine-almost-died-in-korean-war_1121104.

James Charlton, *The Military Quotation Book* (New York: Thomas Dunne Books, 2002).

Coca Cola Heritage, http://www.thecoca-colacompany. com/heritage/cokelore _ newcoke.html.

Orlando DeBruce and Jennifer Jones, "White House shifts Y2K focus to states," *CNN,* February 23, 1999, http://articles.cnn. com/1999-02-23/tech/9902_23_shift.y2k.idg_1_federal-systems-quarterly-report-state-systems?_s=PM:TECH.

Doctors Without Borders, http://www.doctorswithoutborders .org/aboutus/activities.cfin?ref=main-menu.

Seth Eisenberg, "Condoleezza Rice's Journey and Advice for Our Own," *FatherhoodChannel.com,* October 17, 2010, http://fatherhoodchannel.com/20 1 Oil 0/17 /condoleezza-rices-inspiring-journey-and-advice-for-our-own-0 17/.

Bill Gates, "Salman Khan, Educator – The 2012 Time 100," *Time,* April 18, 2012, http://www.time.com/time/specials/packages /article/0,28804,2111975_2111976_2111942,00.html.

Sanjay Gupta, "Khan Academy: The Future of Education?" *60 Minutes,* March 11, 2012http://www.cbsnews.com/8301-18560_162-57394905/khan-academy-the-future-of-education/?tag=currentVideoInfo;videoMetaInfo.

Lara Hoffmans, "Top 10 Stories from 2011," *Forbes,* December 30, 2011, http://www.forbes.com/sites/larahoffmans/2011 /12/30/fisher-investments-top-10/.

Lee Iacocca with William Novak, *Iacocca, An Autobiography* (New York: Bantam Books, 1984).

"In Battle of the Tech Titans, Steve Jobs Most Admired Entrepreneur for Teens, Leaving Facebook's Mark Zuckerberg in the Dust; Junior Achievement Survey Shows Few Teens Esteem Facebook Founder Despite Widespread Use of Social Media," October 6, 2010, http://www.pmewswire.com/news-releases/in-battle-of-thetech-titans-steve-jobs-most-admired-entrepreneur-for-teens-leaving-facebooks-mark-zuckerberg-in-the-dust-104402028.html.

"Josephson Institute of Ethics Releases Study on High School Character and Adult Conduct, Character Study Reveals Predictors of Lying and Cheating," October 29, 2009, http://josephsoninstitute.org/surveys/index.html.

Bibliography

John F. Kennedy Library Foundation, http://www.jflclibrary.org /Education+and+Public+Programs/Profile+in+Courage+Award /Profiles+in+Courage.htm.

David A. Kaplan, "Gates' Favorite Teacher," *CNNMoney*, August 23, 2010, http://money.cnn.com/2010/08/23/technology/ sal_khan_academy.fortune/index.htm.

Khan Academy, www.khanacademy.org.

Denise Koch, "WJZ Talks to Chicken Man Jim Perdue," May 14, 2008, http://wjz.com/specialreports/chicken.jim.perdue. 272293 6 .html.

Larry Kramer, "Why the AOL-Time Warner Merger Was a Good Idea," *The Daily Beast,* May 4, 2009, http://www.thedailybeast .com/blogs -and-stories/2009-05-04/how-time-warner-blew-it/.

Laura Laaman, "Ronald Reagan's timeless lessons of communication," *New Mexico Business Weekly,* June 18, 2004, http://www.bizjournals.com/albuquerque/stories/2004/06/21/ smallb4.html.

David Lieberman, "Blockbuster files for Chapter 11 bankruptcy, will reorganize," *USA Today,* September 23, 2010, http://www. usatoday.com/money/media/20 1 0-09-23-blockbuster23 ST _ N.htm.

Niccolo Machiavelli, *The Prince* (Chicago: University of Chicago Press, 1998).

Nielsen, "The State of the Media: The Social Media Report Q3 2011," September 13, 2011, http://blog.nielsen.com/nielsenwire /social/.

"The Nobel Peace Prize 1999," Nobelprize.org, http://nobelprize. org/nobel_prizes/peace/laureates/1999/.

Kris Osborn, "Gates urges ramping up MRAP acquisition," *Army Times*, May 9, 2007, http://www.armytimes.com/news/2007/05/defense_mrap_070509/.

C. Northcote Parkinson, *Parkinson's Law and Other Studies in Administration* (Cambridge: Riverside Press, 1957).

Laurence J. Peter and Raymond Hull, *The Peter Principle, Why Things Always Go Wrong* (New York: HarperCollins, 2009).

Thomas J. Peters and Robert H. Waterman, Jr., *In Search of Excellence, Lessons from America's Best-Run Companies* (New York: Harper & Row, 1982).

Perdue History, http://www.perdue.com/company/history/generations.html.

Tony Perry, "The Penalty is Severe for Cunningham," *Los Angeles Times,* March 4, 2006, http://articles.latimes.com/2006/mar/04/local/me-duke4.

Ben Sherwood, "Lessons in Survival, The science that explains why elite military forces bounce back faster than the rest of us," *Newsweek,* February 14, 2009, http://www.newsweek.com/2009/02/ 13/lessons-in-survival.html.

Aaron Smith, "Why Americans Use Social Media," *Pew Internet,* November 15, 2011, http://pewinternet.org/Reports/2011/Why-Americans-Use-Social-Media/Main-report.aspx.

Standard & Poor's, "Research Update: United States of America 'AAA/A-1+' Rating Affirmed;

Outlook Revised To Negative," April 18, 2011, http://www.
standardandpoors.com/ratings/articles/en/us?assetID=1245302
886884.

Ken Sweet, "Dow plunges after S&P downgrade," *CNNMoney,*
August 8, 2011, http://money.cnn.com/2011/08/08/
markets/markets_newyork/index.htm?iref=BN1&hpt=hp_t1.

Susan Tardnico, "Is Social Media Sabotaging Real
Communication," *Forbes*, April 30, 2012, http://www.
forbes.com/sites/susantardanico/2012/04/30/is-social-media-
destroying-real-communication/.

James Temple, "Salman Khan, math Master of the Internet," *San
Francisco Chronicle*, December 14, 2009,
http://www.sfgate.com/cgi-bin/article.cgi?f=/c/a/2009/12/13/
BUKV1B11Q1.DTL#ixzz1tYToCCki.

Sun Tzu, *The Art of War* (New York: Cosimo, 2010).

The UPS Code of Business Conduct: Leading with Integrity,
http://www.pressroom.ups.com/Fact+Sheets/The+UPS+Code+
of+Business+Conduct%3A+Leading+with+Integrity.

U.S. Food and Drug Administration, "Recalls, Market
Withdrawals, & Safety Alerts," http://www.fda.gov/Safety
/Recalls/ArchiveRecalls/2012/default.htm.

U.S. Naval Academy, www.usna.edu.

Jack Welch, *Winning* (New York: Harper Collins, 2005).

ABOUT THE AUTHORS

J. Phillip "Jack" London is Executive Chairman and Chairman of the Board of CACI (NYSE), a $3.8 billion information technology and professional services company that celebrated its 50th year in business in 2012. He served as CACI's President and Chief Executive Officer for 23 years between 1984 and 2007. Under Dr. London's direct leadership CACI grew from a small professional services consulting firm to become a pacesetter in IT and communications solutions across markets throughout North America and Western Europe.

Dr. London joined the firm of CACI International Inc in 1972 and was promoted to Vice President in 1976. In 1981, he was elected to the Board of Directors and became President and Chief Executive Officer on July 1, 1984. In April 1990, he was elected Chairman of the Board. In his position Dr. London oversees corporate strategic initiatives, advances client missions, cultivates key client relationships and monitors major financial transactions, including CACI's legacy mergers and acquisitions (M&A) program that he began in 1992. He has an established role as a public figure representing CACI to customers and the federal information technology (IT) industry. Dr. London's efforts also focus on the evolution and transformation of defense, intelligence, information technology and network communications.

J. Phillip London graduated from the U.S. Naval Academy in 1959. Designated a Naval Aviator in 1961, he served on the aircraft carrier USS *Randolph* (CVS-15), with anti-submarine warfare (ASW) units arrayed against Soviet nuclear missile submarine forces. He served during the US-USSR Cuban Missile Crisis of 1962. Earlier, he was with the USS *Randolph* in the Caribbean Sea on February 20, 1962 during the at-sea recovery of NASA *Mercury* astronaut John Glenn.

Dr. London attended the U.S. Naval Postgraduate School in Monterey, California and graduated in June 1967 with a Master of Science in Operations Research. Afterwards, he was assigned to the U.S. Naval Academy where he taught Naval

Operations Analysis and Naval Strategy. In 1969, he was assigned as Aide and Administrative Assistant to the Vice Chief of the Naval Material Command, Washington, DC during the height of the Vietnam War, where he supported the command in its war material and munitions programs. During this time, he received a Doctor of Business Administration degree, conferred "with distinction," in 1970 from the George Washington University.

In 1971, Dr. London was transferred to the Naval Reserve with an Honorable Discharge from active duty. He served in the U.S. Naval Reserve until 1983 when he retired from duty with the rank of Captain. His last assignment was as Commanding Officer of a Naval Aeronautical Engineering Unit of the Naval Air Systems Command, Washington, DC.

Dr. London's industry recognitions include being named CEO of the Year by the George Washington University and Entrepreneur of the Year by Ernst & Young. Each year since 2002, the Human Resources Leadership Awards of Greater Washington has presented its annual Ethics in Business Award in Dr. London's name. In 2003 he received the distinguished John W. Dixon Award from the Association of the United States Army for outstanding industry leadership to the warfighter. He was the 2007 recipient of the Navy League of the United States' prestigious Fleet Admiral Chester W. Nimitz Award for outstanding leadership and commitment to the naval support industry. Dr. London was inducted into the Washington Business Hall of Fame in 2010 and the Halls of Fame for the Arlington, Virginia Chamber of Commerce and U.S. Naval Postgraduate School in Monterey, CA in 2011. Dr. London was the 10th Anniversary Hall of Fame Inductee at the 2012 Greater Washington Government Contracting Awards presented by the Fairfax County Chamber of Commerce, Professional Services Council and *Washington Technology*. Captain London was selected to be the 2013 recipient of the Reserve Officers Association's Nathan Hale Award for patriotic service. Also in 2013, Dr. London was awarded the Ellis Island Medal of Honor for heritage preservation by the National Ethnic Coalition of Organizations gala on Ellis Island in New York.

Dr. London serves on the Board of Directors of the U.S. Naval Institute, the U.S. Navy Memorial Foundation, the Naval Historical Foundation, and CAUSE (Comfort for America's Uniformed Services), the "wounded warriors" support organization. He has served as a member of the Executive Committee and the Board of Directors of the Armed Forces Communications and Electronics Association, and the Northern Virginia Technology Council. He has served on numerous other boards and foundations. Dr. London has also been a member of the National Military Intelligence Association, the Intelligence and National Security Alliance, the Navy League, the Naval Order of the U.S.A., the American Legion, and the Association of the U.S. Army (AUSA). He is a 32° Scottish Rite Mason (K.C.C.H.).

Captain London is a member of the Massachusetts Society of the Cincinnati (founded in 1783), representing his relative Captain Samuel Nicholson of the Continental Navy (1776-1783) during the American Revolution, and the first captain of the USS *Constitution* ("Old Ironsides") in 1798.

Dr. London is the author of *Our Good Name; A Company's Fight to Defend Its Honor and Get the Truth Told About Abu Ghraib* (2008), a book detailing the story of how CACI was falsely accused of wrongdoing in the Abu Ghraib prison abuses of 2003 and the company's successful crisis management response to the scandal.

Dr. London currently resides with his wife Dr. Jennifer Burkhart London and their sons in McLean, VA.

Z. Selin Hur is a Strategic Programs, Principal at CACI International Inc in Arlington, VA. She works with the company's Executive Chairman to provide thought leadership in national security and information technology, and supports the company's strategic growth initiatives. Ms. Hur also contributes to CACI's leadership development and corporate culture programs. In these roles, she prepares numerous articles and speeches on defense, technology, and organizational development. Ms. Hur was part of the crisis management team when CACI was falsely implicated in the Iraq prison abuse scandal. She was also a major contributor to *Our Good Name; A Company's Fight to Defend Its Honor and Get the Truth Told About Abu Ghraib* (2008), a book detailing CACI's successful crisis management approach to the scandal.

Prior to joining CACI, Ms. Hur was a management consultant providing advisory services in strategic planning, communications, and business development to consulting and information technology firms worldwide. At EDS, she was an information technology project manager for government and financial sector clients, including the National Association of Securities Dealers, Korea First Bank, and the Navy Marine Corps Intranet program. Ms. Hur also worked in the World Bank's Private Sector Development group where she developed corporate governance best practices and public policy assessments for private sector-led growth in developing countries. She was also part of the team that established the Global Corporate Governance Foundation, a joint initiative of the World Bank and Organization for Economic Co-operation and Development. Ms. Hur has also developed country market entry strategies for Fortune 500 companies. Fluent in Turkish, Ms. Hur is also conversant in German, French and Spanish.

Ms. Hur received a Master of Business Administration degree from the Katz Graduate School of Business and a Master of Public and International Affairs degree from the Graduate School of Public and International Affairs at the University of Pittsburgh in 1997. She received a Bachelors of Arts degree in International Affairs and Economics from the American University in 1994. Ms. Hur serves on the American University

Alumni Board and volunteers for the University of Pittsburgh's PART (Pitt Alumni Recruiting Team). She has also volunteered on behalf of various philanthropic organizations.

Ms. Hur currently resides in Arlington, VA.

Jennifer Burkhart London, Ph.D. is a professional consultant and licensed psychologist who specializes in the application of psychological principles to business and management. She has a diversified background in marketing and business development. Her assignments have included market plan development, business development, strategic planning, community relations and media relations management. Her clients have ranged from small privately held businesses to Fortune 100 corporations.

Dr. London received a doctoral degree in Psychology from the Ohio State University and completed her training in marketing at the University of Pittsburgh. She has authored numerous professional publications, including journal and newspaper articles, and book chapters regarding technical and business subjects. She has also conducted editorial reviews of professional journal articles and taught graduate level psychology courses.

Working with the mid-Atlantic offices of Deloitte & Touche and PricewaterhouseCoopers, she was responsible for building regional firm visibility, developing best practice strategies, spearheading the firms' product and service initiatives, and working with Partners to quickly move initiatives to new and existing clients. She led the process of market evaluation and development of strategic market plans for positioning the firms to increase market share and business development opportunities.

Dr. London has also conducted mergers and acquisitions search work for private clients and corporations. For CACI, her efforts resulted in the acquisition of six companies.

Dr. London's invaluable analytic input, behavioral insights and recommendations on corporate messaging and image enhancement were fundamental to CACI's push back during the Abu Ghraib crisis. In this effort, she was a member of the crisis management team and helped craft the conceptual framework for CACI's highly-effective hypercrisis management strategy. She also provided important review and feedback as a major contributor in the development of *Our Good Name; A Company's Fight to Defend Its Honor and Get the Truth Told*

About Abu Ghraib (2008) and was instrumental in the final editorial review.

Dr. London's professional activities have included the New York Academy of Sciences, American Psychological Association, Psi Chi National Honor Society in Psychology and Who's Who Worldwide. She has served on committees of the Greater Washington Board of Trade, Northern Virginia Technology Council, and the Association for Corporate Growth. In addition she has chaired and participated in numerous charitable and philanthropic organizations.

Dr. London currently resides in McLean Virginia with Dr. J.P. London and their sons.

INDEX

C

D

Darwin, Charles, 102, 132
daVinci, Leonardo, 231
decisions/decision-making, 181
Deen, Paula, 117
Dell, Michael, 53
Dilbert Dunker, 250
DiPiazza, Sam, 32
distinction, 129
Doctors Without Borders (Medicins sans Frontier), 291-293
dot.com, 174, 267, 269. *See also* CACI
Douglass, Frederick, 50
Drucker, Peter, 196, 227, 237
Duke University lacrosse team, 288-289; and Mike Nifong, 289

E

Earhart, Amelia, 62-63; and Bernt Balchen, 63; and Amy Phipps Guest, 62
Edison, Thomas, 113-114, 169, 286
Einstein, Albert, 50, 53, 77, 114-115, 192, 264
Ellis Island, 113
endings, 261
ethics, *See* integrity

F

Facebook, 70, 110-111, 208; and Mark Zuckerberg, 110
failure, *See* risk
Fairchild Semiconductor, 119-120
fear, 249
FedEx, 117, 231-232. *See also* Fred Smith
Flood, Curt, and free agency, 184-185
Ford Motor Company, 111, 139n103, 186, 187, 285-286; and Henry Ford, 77, 186. *See also* Lee Iacocca
forecasting, 94-98

"I am the master of my fate;
I am the captain of my soul."

William Ernest Henley

"Relativity applies to physics, not ethics."

Albert Einstein

"Winning
is a habit.
Unfortunately,
so is losing"

Vince Lombardi

"Attitude is a little
thing that makes a
big difference."

Winston Churchill

"DO WHAT YOU CAN, WITH WHAT YOU HAVE,
WHERE YOU ARE."

THEODORE ROOSEVELT

"Leadership is a potent combination
of strategy and character.
But if you must be without one,
be without the strategy."

Norman Schwarzkopf